SENNA
THE TRUTH

FRANCO NUGNES

SENNA
THE TRUTH

Published in the UK by Pitch Publishing, 2025

Pitch Publishing
9 Donnington Park, , 85 Birdham Road, , Chichester,
West Sussex, PO20 7AJ
www.pitchpublishing.co.uk
info@pitchpublishing.co.uk

© 2025 Franco Nugnes

A CIP catalogue record is available for this book
from the British Library.

Editorial director Italian version: Roberto Mugavero
Editorial co-ordination Italian version: Martina Mugavero
Series editor Italian version: Emiliano Tozzi
Editor Italian version: Elisa Azzimondi
Cover design: Italian version Alessandro Battara
Graphics: Edizioni Minerva Graphic Office

Translated into English by Michele Serafini (of Agenzia Letteraria MM)

This work was translated with the contribution of the Centre for Books and
Reading of the Italian Ministry of Culture

Images courtesy of: © Lat Images/Getty Images, © Franco Nugnes, © Giorgio Ascanelli, © Autosprint Archive, © Carlo Cavicchi, © Pietro Corradini, © Andrea Ficarelli, © Isotta Fraschini Archive, © Giovanni Gordini, © Gian Carlo Minardi, © Angelo Orsi, © Piero Paglioriti, © Alberto Sabbatini, © Domenico Salcito, © Giorgio Stirano, © Luca Taffettani, © Zoi Archive.

The publisher remains at the disposal of any claimants who could not be traced

Senna. Le verità
di Franco Nugnes
Copyright © 2024. First edition published by Edizioni Minerva, Bologna (Italy)
This edition is published in agreement with Minerva Soluzioni Editoriali s.r.l., Italy

Artistic and literary property reserved for all countries.
Any reproduction, even partial, is prohibited.

ISBN: 978 1 83680 201 3

First Italian edition April 2024

Printed and bound in India by Replika Press Pvt. Ltd.

Printed and bound on FSC® certified paper in line with
our continuing commitment to ethical business practices,
sustainability and the environment.

SENNA
THE TRUTH

CONTENTS

PREFACE   9

AUTHOR'S NOTE   21

CHAPTER 1   23
Why does the myth of Senna endure after 30 years?

CHAPTER 2   29
Andrea Ficarelli: Ayrton's discoverer

CHAPTER 3   47
Angelo Orsi: Ayrton's true confidant

CHAPTER 4   69
Manager Ramirez caught up in the disputes between Senna and Prost

CHAPTER 5   85
Ascanelli and that silent lap in the Honda NSX at Suzuka

CHAPTER 6   99
Fiorio: Here's how I convinced Senna to come to Ferrari

CHAPTER 7   111
Comas: saved by Senna, but helpless in the face of Ayrton's tragedy

CHAPTER 8   119
The coveted Lamborghini V12 and the secret test in Indycar

CHAPTER 9   127
Minardi and the million dollar piece of advice

CHAPTER 10   137
Williams: from beginning to end, the drama of a circular story

CHAPTER 11   145
Williams FW16: there was snow on the Silverstone debut

CHAPTER 12   153
Two pole positions and two retirements: a disastrous start

CHAPTER 13   165
Ratzenberger the day before, an alarm unheard

CHAPTER 14   177
Two flags in the cockpit for a tribute that never happened

CHAPTER 15   181
The safety car driver: the last person to see Senna alive

CHAPTER 16   189
The doctor recounts the rescue: there was no hope

CHAPTER 17   199
The hovering medical helicopter was breaking normal procedures

CHAPTER 18   207
Why did the 'killer uniball' strike like a blade?

CHAPTER 19   219
Tarquini's intuition kick-starts the investigation into the steering column

CHAPTER 20   227
Design errors emerge and Newey suffers

CHAPTER 21 235
Stefanini: the pillar of an investigation which started with a car accident

CHAPTER 22 247
Gambucci: the race director of the Imola circuit

CHAPTER 23 259
Bendinelli: the secret deal with Frank Williams, discussed in Munich

CHAPTER 24 269
The mystery of the control unit

CHAPTER 25 275
Telemetry explained to *Rombo* magazine by a Ferrari engineer!

CHAPTER 26 287
Piola: creator of the big steering wheel that didn't fit in the Williams

CHAPTER 27 297
This is why Patrese refused to get into Senna's FW16

CHAPTER 28 307
That in-car camera footage that appeared when it seemed it did not exist

CHAPTER 29 313
The RAI TV director who did not turn the tragedy into a show

CHAPTER 30 321
Passerini: stubborn magistrate breaks his silence after 30 years

CHAPTER 31 335
Those who analysed the steering column never had any doubts about the breakage

CHAPTER 32 345
The director of *Autosprint* did not bow to pressure

CHAPTER 33 357
Williams's defence: Stirano, Didcot's Italian

CHAPTER 34 373
Senna's 'first' Formula 1 car was Reutemann's Ferrari

CHAPTER 35 385
Montezemolo: Ayrton wanted to leave Williams to come to Maranello

CHAPTER 36 393
After the helmet and the FW16-02 were demolished, no signs of the tragedy remain

APPENDIX 396
The protagonists in Magic's story

ACKNOWLEDGEMENTS
400

Dedicated to the other half of me

PREFACE

WE REALLY needed this book. And only Franco Nugnes could have written it, both because he was and still is a thoroughbred journalist and because no one like him followed day by day, I would even venture to say hour by hour, what happened from the moment of the great Ayrton's death to the court ruling that established the cause that had made the Williams, driven by the Brazilian ace, go off the track.

Now that the decades have piled up, just a few remember the great David versus Goliath battle that *Autosprint* – at the time a top-selling and, above all, highly authoritative weekly magazine – engaged against the entire Formula 1 circus to get to the truth.

I was the editor-in-chief of *Autosprint* and I entrusted the author of these invaluable pages, my utmost trustworthy friend Franco Nugnes, with the task of not letting go, of investigating in collaboration with the *Polizia Stradale* (the Italian traffic police) and the public prosecutor to get to the truth. Those were convulsive days at first, and then tiring, because the Formula 1 system wanted to keep everything hidden. It was summer, but an increasingly thick fog hung over the investigation. Those who knew things denied them, while those who ignored facts conformed to the common thinking, which was to keep everything quiet. Or forget about it, because what would be the point anyway?

At *Autosprint* we were left alone, but no one could imagine how tenacious we were. We wanted to know, not to condemn, but still to defend the dignity of a champion on whose account too many had ventured naive, sometimes fanciful, very often false hypotheses and reasons for his going off the track. We didn't have Williams in our sights, let alone its otherwise excellent technicians, but we were sure that on Senna's single-seater that damn steering column had broken down. We screamed it loud, week after week and for months and months. At one point, we even saw the investigation threaten to get bogged down, but our 'agent in Havana' (Franco Nugnes) was stubborn and tenacious to the point that he was not just a 'truffle dog' any longer, but a valuable collaborator with the men of justice. It was a very long job, even though, little by little, the light was getting brighter and the solution more and more unassailable.

Finally, it took me years to convince Franco Nugnes to retrieve all his notes – a precious and exclusive material – and reconstruct the facts as they had happened. It was not easy. For those who had experienced those moments up close, reliving them was painful. But it had to be done, because the times of the chronicle were long gone and it was necessary to fix history.

In the end, Franco gave in, he listened to me and dived into the subject again, regaining his old-fashioned flair, and out came this volume that I consider a genuine, extraordinary document, that will remain in time and make history.

Even the most sceptical – no longer that many today, but the majority at the time – will find here answers leaving no appeal. The text, which is as comprehensive as ever, flows like a novel, but contains documents that were unknown back then, sometimes even shocking, and many parallel stories that are truly worth reading. There is not a single chapter that is not a discovery, even for insiders who thought they knew everything. There are great champions and, behind the curtain, no less important characters, all with their contributions and the emotions they experienced.

A well-rounded Ayrton is revealed through unimaginable testimonies kept hidden until today, collected when the passing of time has allowed them to resurface. Many books have come out on Senna, some very interesting, others very well written, too many unable to go beyond chronicle or beatification. We are confronted here with an academic text: those who choose not to dive into these pages will never know what they have missed.

Carlo Cavicchi

SENNA
THE TRUTH

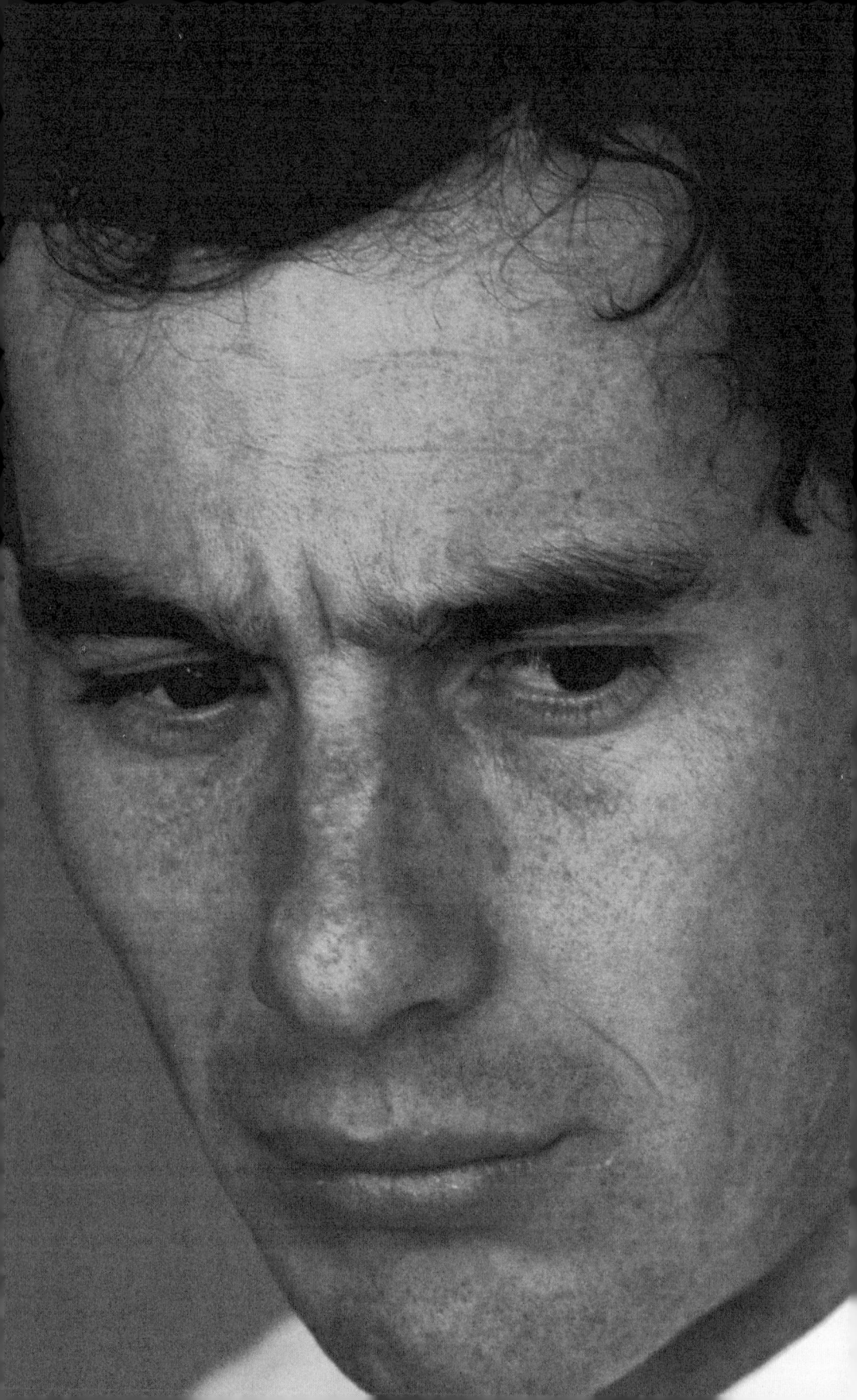

'HELLO, CAN you hear me?'

The voice was hoarse and the tone low, resigned: 'Who are you? I can't understand. The line sounds disturbed …'

'This is me speaking softly, I don't want to be heard. I have to tell you something very delicate and [with] just a little time available, because I have to give an answer.'

On the other end of the line was Massimo Gambucci, freshly appointed director of the Enzo and Dino Ferrari Circuit, who had been handed the keys to the Imola circuit on 2 May 1994 by Giorgio Poggi, the director at Sagis (the track's management company) who had left office the night before. The tragic weekend of the San Marino GP had nothing to do with it; it was a change in the top management that had been planned for some time.

Gambucci had been promoted precisely at the most difficult moment in the history of the racetrack, which, on the afternoon of Monday, 2 May, was placed under seizure by the judicial authorities. There was a surreal quiet in the facility. The engines were silent. F1 seemed over after the tragedies of Roland Ratzenberger during Saturday's qualifying and Ayrton Senna during Sunday's race. The racing world was stunned: in two days, the latest arrival in the 'Circus' and the most acclaimed champion had both died.

'Listen Franco,' Massimo resumed in a more decisive tone, 'the racetrack is under seizure and a police inspector has been assigned to make the initial investigation. He is from the *Stradale* [the traffic police] and has started the investigations at the track as if he were to ascertain a normal accident on the urban network. If this is the beginning of the investigation we are off to a bad start.'

'The news of the sequestration has already been relayed by the agencies,' I replied, 'and the track, I guess, has become off limits to us journalists.'

'That's not why I called you,' Gambucci urged. 'I have the feeling that the policeman doesn't know anything about Formula 1 and he informed me in advance that, tomorrow, we should rebuild Senna's Williams, putting every piece near the wreck in the closest possible position to where it was originally mounted. Do you feel up to giving me a hand? I'm authorised to get a track-steward to help me and I'd choose you for your experience with F1: maybe you could see something we might miss.'

I remained silent, almost stunned by the astounding proposal. 'Don't talk about it with anyone,' Gambucci insisted. 'Perhaps by looking at the FW16 we might be able to give some useful pointers to the investigators.'

'I thank you for the appreciation, of course I accept. I will be at your disposal.'

'Don't you dare say that you are a journalist,' Massimo concluded, 'and speak as little as possible: remember that you will be there only as a track-steward.'

At the click of the phone call, although I was still sitting in front of my desk in the newsroom, the whole world began to swirl around me. That night I slept: I saw and replayed Ayrton's accident in my mind and, like everyone else, I couldn't absorb the fact that the Brazilian ace was actually no longer with us. I kept wondering what had killed the three-time world champion …

Televisions kept searching for news: updates, live broadcasts multiplied on all networks, with experts giving their impressions: fault of the track for the dangerous bumps at *Tamburello*. No way! Driver error (we had to hear that too)! Or, mechanical failure. Everyone had their say, and instead of trying to clear the air, a self-feeding media fuss was raised, while the F1 world clammed up to defend the Circus, which had never been so much under attack on a planetary level.

The next day, on the short car journey from the Conti Editore offices in San Lazzaro di Savena to Imola, I did not even realise I was driving the 34 kilometres between the two locations: it was as if I was in a haze. What terrible things would my eyes witness? What would I be able to understand? Had Massimo chosen the right person for such a delicate job?

So many unanswered questions, yet surely this could also be my big chance to follow the investigation from the inside. And maybe I might make a small contribution to the search for truth.

At the racetrack gate my name was noted and they let me in without any fuss. I arrived directly in the pit area, where it was rumoured that both Senna's Williams and Ratzenberger's Simtek were stored. Nothing of the sort: the cars, with all their debris, had been collected in a garage under the Agip grandstand, at *Variante Bassa*. It was the base where the Sagis stewards met.

Once I got there, Gambucci, after greeting me, handed me a race-marshal's coat: it was one size too big, but it didn't matter. I had a new identity: track-steward. I must admit that I felt particularly uncomfortable in that role, which was not my own.

In the meantime, Stefano Stefanini, the *Stradale* inspector, arrived. He unsealed the shutter-stock and, after the usual pleasantries, opened the creaking roller shutter: on the right-hand side were empty tables and chairs with a worn-out air, and on the other side, separated, were the two single-seaters. Wrecks with rubbish bags behind them that contained all the smallest fragments collected from the track.

Outside, spring weather; inside, an indescribable chill caused by the air of death, which had begun to make me sweat. What was left of the Williams showed that the impact against the *Tamburello* wall had been violent.

'You must help me,' said the policeman, 'to put everything back in place, in the hope of finding some clues that will then allow the appointed experts to identify the possible causes of the two tragedies.'

I moved to the rear of the Williams and, glancing at Ayrton's car, a gruesome detail did not escape my notice: on the right side of the bonnet, where the Rothmans sponsor's inscription stood out, was a tiny grey lump. I was not prepared for that sight. My heart suddenly jumped into my throat and my pulse became pounding. Immediately a gag of vomit rose in my throat, followed by the urge to run far away. I didn't want to memorise that image: it was a small fragment of Senna's brain. What on earth could have hit the genius, who went by the nickname of 'Magic', so hard to cause such devastation?

I did not expect that horrendous sight, and at that moment all reasoning went haywire. I had to regain normal breathing and try to compose myself. I felt a sort of refusal to accept what was in front of me.

Stefanini, more accustomed to tragic and bloody scenarios, was instead in highly professional mode: he was looking for the right front wheel that had torn off in the impact against the *Tamburello* wall. Years later – over time we have also become friends – Stefano confessed to me how difficult it was for him that day. Each of us played a professional role, but the apparent coldness did not correspond to the poignant emotions we kept hidden inside.

I noticed the tyre and pointed it out to the policeman as he moved aside to pick it up and fix it on the right side of the chassis. The suspension arms had torn off after the collision. In a rather mechanical manner we re-allocated what was left of the front wing and parts of the bodywork, while in the cockpit, on the seat, there was a piece of steering column attached to the steering wheel, which was held to the chassis by a serpentine electric cable.

Gabriele Tarquini, a former F1 driver and leader at the time of the British Touring Car Championship (BTCC) with the Alfa Romeo 155, had noticed with great observational skills that very same piece of column outside the car in the pictures we had published in *Autosprint*. That is why this guy from Abruzzo had confessed to us his disturbing doubt as to what might have happened at *Tamburello*. He had made the hypothesis that the steering column might have broken.

'Man, Tarquini was right!' I thought after seeing the broken column up close. His theory immediately seemed plausible to me.

The next Tuesday we came out with the following headline on the cover of *Autosprint*: 'The Suspect'. It was the first hint towards a truth.

Publicly, I could not state that I had seen the steering column, just as I could never admit, to this day, that after the first visit to the box, where 'caretaker' Massimo Gambucci kept watch for months at night, I ventured on other nocturnal incursions, during which, little by little, many obscure points became clear in my mind.

We knew that a police patrol would come to check the seals on the shutter every two hours, but the policemen could not imagine that the pegs which anchored the shutter were easily slipping out of the asphalt into which they had been driven. Obviously, I was not officially authorised to enter the garage: I was to all intents and purposes a stowaway, an 'accomplice' of Massimo, who was prepared to risk an indictment in the hope that this would shed light on the too many mysteries of the Senna case. And so, like amateur thieves, in the darkness of the garage we searched for those clues that then allowed us to reconstruct a complex puzzle in a design that gradually became clearer and clearer, despite repeated attempts at deception and the conspiracy of silence of a system that had very little desire to shed full light on what had happened.

A LEGEND.
THE GREATEST PILOT EVER

AUTHOR'S NOTE

IT WAS a sad day, but it turned into a great opportunity. I had to change my skin: take off the shoes of a motorsports journalist to become an investigator. Easy to say, complicated to do. It is one thing to go looking for the winning solutions hidden in a single-seater, and another to dig into a wall that seemed unwilling to talk about the strange death of the world's best driver; to dig into a tragedy that unfolded worldwide during the 1994 San Marino GP. F1 seemed to have turned away, choosing silence, while public opinion, the fans, wanted to know: what had happened to Ayrton Senna?

I searched for answers, I searched for truth. It was not an easy journey. As a person, I am respectful of the rules, but in the Senna investigation I realised that, in particular situations, one must have the courage to cross the thin line of legality to follow a clue, a thread, a hope of objectivity in a path full of 'black holes'.

They were intense and difficult months: professionally exciting, since alongside my colleagues at *Autosprint* we opened a gash in the silence; but there were also many emotionally shattering moments, since we had full awareness that, in order to get to some certainties about Ayrton, it was necessary to trample on some rules.

So many sleepless nights, but never a doubt, a second thought.

Hence my search for the truth, or rather the truths, about an event that changed the way I see life …

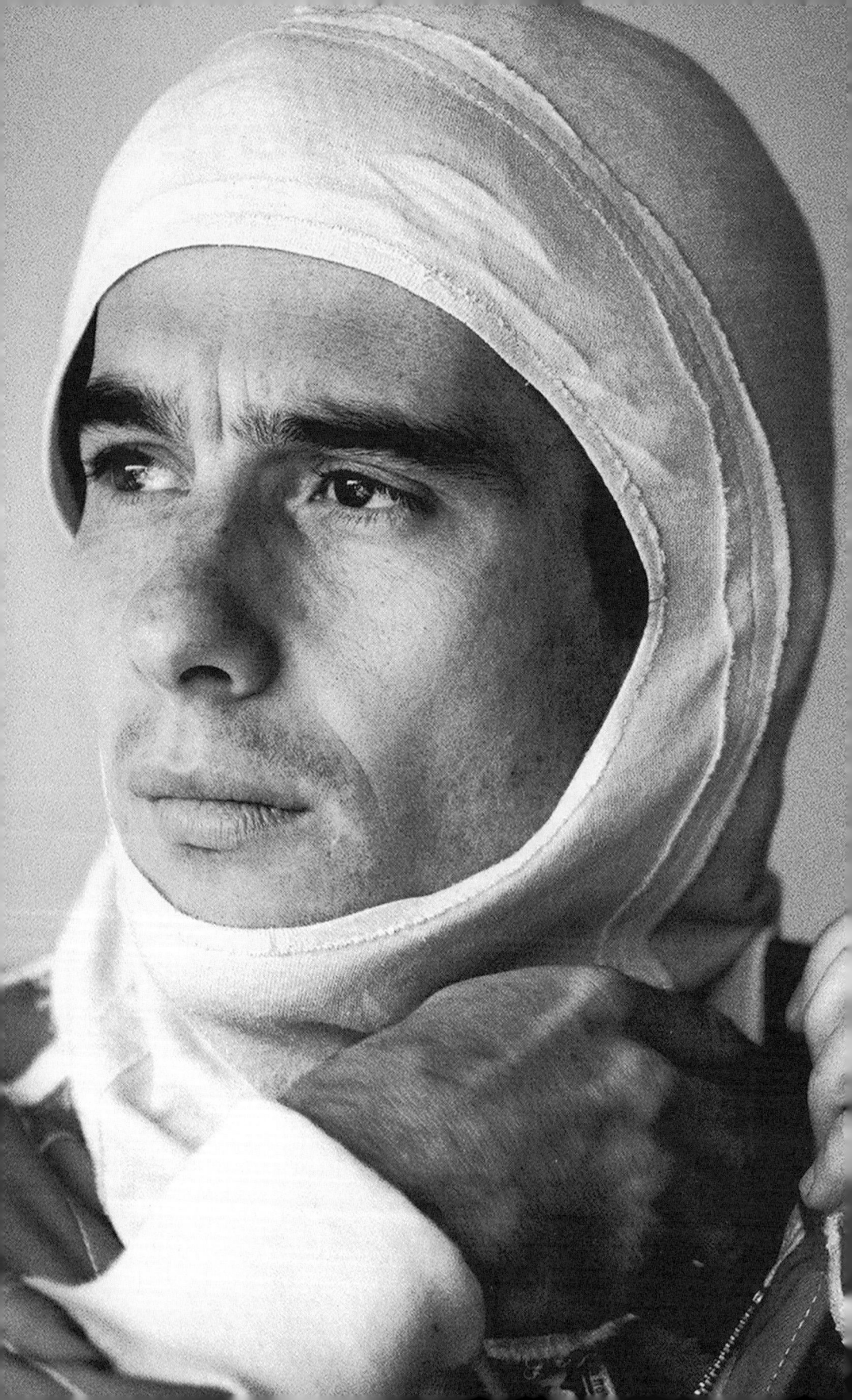

CHAPTER 1

WHY DOES THE MYTH OF SENNA ENDURE AFTER 30 YEARS?

WHO IS Ayrton Senna? A myth. The greatest driver ever. These are the answers that can be gathered when asking about the Brazilian, and not only among racing fans, as he was a character who appealed to a planetary audience much wider than just the one of motorsport. He had a large female fanbase; women liked him a lot: a boy from a good family, polite, with affectionate manners and a gentle gaze which let a vein of impending sadness shine through, even when he smiled. As if he were always missing something, or spasmodically searching for what he had not managed to find out yet: perfection. It was not *saudade*, the typical melancholy of Brazilians far from home. Not at all, because Ayrton from São Paulo had become a citizen of the world. His veiled gaze, his sketched smile were expressions of a profound interiority, which had also led him to forms of transcendence. Far beyond religiosity, he had even found a way to talk to God.

In short, he was not just a motor racing champion. Senna was much more: some had predicted that, after his F1 successes, he might become president of Brazil, or a UN ambassador, because whatever he decided to undertake, he would do it to the best of his ability. Starting with the charity work he did for the children of the *favelas*, without seeking any form of publicity.

Such an unusual guy could only be divisive. With him or against him. He always surrounded himself with people he had to trust blindly. He demanded a lot of himself and he also demanded the same of those around him. His motto was 'Driven to perfection'. He had it printed on the T-shirt he wore under his fireproof overalls. Driven to perfection. A slogan that had become his way of life. A mantra. When he was just four years old, daddy Milton had built him a kart to race around the home farm, not imagining that he had instilled the racing bug in his child. Ayrton, on the other hand, had made it his reason for living.

He had come to Italy, kind of 'adopted' by Angelo Parrilla. If it rained, the young Italian talents would park their vehicles in the paddock and make merry in groups, waiting for the sun to shine again. Not the Brazilian: he would wear out the track trying to perfect his driving style, improving his sensitivity in the wet, driven by a maniacal motivation. He looked cocky and might have appeared the opposite of a nice guy. In reality he was reserved. Shy. He had to overcome this weakness by forging a strong character within himself, with a self-discipline devoted to controlling his impulses, to raising his self-confidence both physically and emotionally. No wonder, then, the three world titles, the 41 victories and 65 pole positions in 161 GPs. Numbers do not do justice to Senna's true greatness. Statistics do not render the value of Magic, because in Ayrton's time there was less racing and calendars did not have 24 races per season, but only 16.

There was no need to write a book on the exploits of the Brazilian. Many beautiful and exhaustive ones have already been published. I must explain then why, 30 years after his death, urged on by the constant prodding of Carlo Cavicchi, my incomparable 'maestro' of journalism, I accepted Roberto Mugavero's proposal. Because even though Ayrton Senna passed away on 1 May 1994, he never really died. The silent pilgrimage of those who go to pay homage to the statue that commemorates him in the *Acque Minerali* park, in the heart of the Enzo and Dino Ferrari Racetrack, happens daily, just like the flock of Brazilians, and others, who visit the Morumbi cemetery in São Paulo, where he is buried. Three decades have not diluted the memory of this extraordinary champion: on the contrary, they have strengthened his legend. This phenomenon should be studied on a sociological level, because the myth has passed down from fathers to sons. Youngsters, who have never seen Ayrton race, know him. They know everything because his memory is alive on social media: videos, photos, anecdotes are published daily in all languages. And a champion such as Lewis Hamilton, the record-breaking driver in modern F1, has

Ayrton Senna with Juan Manuel Fangio, his youthful idol: the Brazilian's goal was to win five world titles like the Argentine.

been inspired by Senna, who was the idol of his youth. Ayrton, therefore, is a present figure.

For 30 years I have kept the trial documents locked in a box, with the shocking photographs of the helmet that I never wanted to publish, and all such original documents like the telemetry, or the VHS tape from the in-car camera, that at a certain point in the investigation was anonymously delivered to me from Great Britain, while for months its existence had been denied.

A lot of emotion was also enclosed in that box. While in the issues of *Autosprint* the journalistic enquiry had unfolded, which in part had contributed to the search for truths (the failure of the steering column, the uniball that had turned into a sharp blade and had pierced Senna's head), in the box dwelled the pain, the anger about the absurd, in some ways stupid end of Magic. By the time I cut the string that tied the lid and opened the box, the effect of passing time had already settled the feelings and softened the memories.

Then, the idea of writing this book took shape: I decided to hear again from all my sources of information from that time, and the protagonists who had in some way crossed their paths with Senna's death. And out came anecdotes, memories and even some backstory. The passing of time has also changed the perspective under which the facts have been re-read. Patrick Head and Adrian Newey [the technical director and designer at Williams] remain with the minority view that the steering column did not break. They faced a difficult dilemma. They had understood what changes needed to be made to the car, but they did not have time to make and test those changes. With his pole position in the San Marino GP, Ayrton wanted to start his run-up to a fourth World Championship and did not intend to wait any longer, after the two previous retirements.

Magic's greatness emerges from a kaleidoscope of very human stories. Each one brought out a side of an utterly special man, and not only because he could drive a race car like a champion.

It's only fair that both Senna's helmet and the wreck of his Williams were demolished: there is no need for those symbols to eternalise his story.

SUCH AN UNUSUAL TYPE COULD ONLY BE DIVISIVE. WITH HIM OR AGAINST HIM.

CHAPTER 2

ANDREA FICARELLI: AYRTON'S DISCOVERER

'THE MAIN reason for living is discovery.'

James Dean, the American actor, was a nonconformist, a rebel. He did not want to play by the rules, just like Andrea Ficarelli, a young journalist from Reggio Emilia, who had made a name for himself in karting by winning an Italian title in 1977. He used to edit the karting column in the weekly *Autosprint* and had founded a monthly magazine dedicated to a discipline that only a few wrote about. Ficarelli gave over the magazine's first cover to an unknown driver, a certain Ayrton Senna, neglecting the home-grown talents and stirring up strong controversy for that anti-nationalistic attitude. He was not swayed by the fact that the heart of world karting was in Italy. His journalistic nonconformity allowed him to realise that the Brazilian was a diamond in the rough, and he wanted to help him highlight his value. For this reason, Andrea Ficarelli can rightfully be considered Ayrton's discoverer in Europe and some thought he was also his first manager. In reality, more than a promoter of Ayrton, Andrea had sensed the uncommon abilities and qualities of a peer who would also become his friend ...

'I met him on his sporting debut in Europe: it was at Le Mans in the 1978 World Karting Championship. I had several journalistic collaborations at the time, but I was just at the beginning of my career, since I was only 20 years old. I knew nothing about Ayrton, like everyone else at the time. He had finished third in qualifying and had come close to winning the race: if there had not been a collision with the American, Allen, he could have won. He was a surprise to everyone. And you could see from the way he raced that he was special, an ace. I always like to say that the real gap between Senna and the others was seen especially in karting: when the tyres weren't glued to the ground like they are now his superiority could be spotted on sight. At the time, nobody thought that he would be destined for motor racing: that transition was not as automatic as it is today, because many drivers simply remained professionals in karting: Fullerton for example, who would also become Ayrton's team-mate later. The karting specialists therefore saw him as a potential professional and thought he would remain in that category forever.'

In Carlo Cavicchi's book Senna Vero [The Real Senna], *Angelo Parrilla said: 'During the first year Senna spent a lot of money, a real record amount for those times.' Money funded by his father. Let's say $10,000. 'The second year just half of that sum, because I cared more [about] having him as a driver. The third year nothing, I made him race and he kept the money he won to race in Formula Ford.'*

'For karting at that time,' explains Ficarelli, 'we are talking about a significant budget.'

Dad Milton was an entrepreneur and owned many farms in Brazil. He had decided to support his son's passion for karting, but was against the idea of him racing in a car.

I remember asking Parrilla if he envisaged Ayrton's transition to motor racing. Such a question would make people laugh nowadays, because it's natural to think that a young talent from karting will land in single-seaters. I remember Angelo answering: 'No, it will never happen.' The answer seemed definitive and he added: 'If he tried, his father would break his legs. And if Milton doesn't do it, then I will!' Of course it was just a joke, but it identified what Ayrton's career might have been: karting driver. Full stop.

When did you find out who Ayrton really was?
A few months after that first World Championship. I had gone to Milan and found him at the Dap headquarters in Viale Lucania, where I spent at least a couple of hours with him, chatting. It was the first occasion on which we established a friendship, and that was easy to maintain on later

The Dap kart with which Ayrton won at the beginning of his career.

The Brazilian in his first year of F1 with Andrea Ficarelli, the first journalist who believed in him.

Senna with his wife Lilian Vasconcelos, whom he wed in 1981: the marriage lasted a few months.

occasions. I went to England, when he finally decided to switch to four wheels. The first home he found in Britain was in Eaton, not far from Snetterton and close to Van Diemen's headquarters, where his Formula Ford car was maintained. He used to live simply and modestly. And to drive around he used a four-door Alfasud, borrowed from Mauricio Gugelmin, his flatmate.

Previously there had been a brief English experience with his wife, Lilian de Vasconcelos Souza.
The marriage lasted little more than eight months: the young blonde had grown up at Ayrton's side and so, when he decided to race in Formula Ford in Great Britain, he wanted to take his first girlfriend with him. Not wanting to waste time, he married her. For Lilian, English life soon proved hard, very hard, with her husband always on the track. At the beginning she would follow him there, but then, not speaking the language, she chose to stay home. Once she was asked whether it was true that she saw the mechanics more often than her husband, to which she jokingly replied: 'If anything, it's him who has it off with the mechanics, because he spends all his time with them.' Obviously it was a joke, but it was easily exploited by those who wanted to label him as homosexual, as Nelson Piquet did. Ayrton never wanted to talk about his wife with me. I had a feeling that, had I asked him a question about her, he would have given me an answer, but I never pushed him to elaborate on that subject. I remember that he lived with someone in Eaton: his wife was no longer there, because he had left her in São Paulo, and he had decided to race in Britain, even without the consent of his father, who was no longer willing to help him financially.

Ayrton had left his wife at the São Paulo airport and the two did not see each other again ...
By mentality, if he closed with someone he closed permanently, leaving no windows open. He was that kind of guy.

Lilian de Vasconcelos Souza, an interior decorator who married three times and has a son, admitted in a recent interview with Brazil's *Globo* that she married Ayrton too early and that Senna had only one vocation at that time: racing.

But who was Senna? Young by age, yet a boy who became a man very early ...
Ayrton was aware of his talent, and within himself he did not lack the self-confidence to consider himself the best driver at the time, but he always tried not to bring out this awareness in an arrogant manner. He was also a little insecure, especially at the beginning of his career, and for this reason often tense and nervous, and even if it seems excessive to say so, he really needed concentration to find himself.

The term 'nervous' is recurrent in the words of several of Ayrton's friends ...
When he described himself in his own Italian, he said he was trying to 'get his head together'. He did not want mental interference in what he was doing. Let me give an example to explain the concept: in karting, between heats of a race, Ayrton would clean every corner of his vehicle with a rag. He was almost maniacal even though it was extra-lucid. He sought a mental squareness and wanted his kart to be perfectly in order. When the mechanics told him: 'Leave it Ayrton, this is a job for us to do,' he promptly replied: 'I want to do it because it helps me relax.' He had only the race in his head and nothing else: all his attention was focused on the result. Had he gone for a walk in the paddock with the others, he would not have been able to create the abstraction he was looking for.

He was a guy who did not socialise much with the other drivers ...
He had a strong tendency to isolate himself, even when he was among others. He did not do it to pose as a superstar, but out of a personal need. It was not conceit, he chose to be alone to overcome what might have seemed a weakness. Being focused on a goal was always the strong point of his person and his career.

Why dedicate to him the first cover of Karting, *the magazine you launched and edited?*
His arrival was something disruptive, but above all at the time there was a sort of monopoly of IAME [Italian American Motor Engineering, a kart manufacturer from Bergamo] and its president, Bruno Grana, didn't like the fact that I had exalted a Brazilian while there were many promising Italian drivers. I decided to support Ayrton because I saw a champion in him: I was aware that, with my choice, I was going against a system, and I certainly noticed that there was a clear attempt to minimise the value of this guy in the karting world. The Senna phenomenon broke

Senna in 1983 with the West Surrey Ralt RT3-Toyota, with which he won the British F3 championship, collecting 15 poles and 12 victories.

out much later, when everyone realised who he really was, but initially there was a lot of reticence in considering him as he deserved. And this was true even when he debuted in F1; many Italian journalists did not give him the credit he deserved, while the paddock insiders immediately sniffed out his potential. McLaren's Ron Dennis offered him a contract before he even raced in F3, but Ron was only willing to hire him for the championship in the cadet series, without any guarantee of bringing him to F1 in 1984. For this reason he turned the offer down. This is further proof of how aware he was of his abilities.

Even at the beginning of his career, despite being very young, he set himself a deadline to become F1 world champion ...
In the 1983 F3 season, which he did with West Surrey Racing, he ran 21 races, scoring 15 pole positions and 12 victories, to which must be added the pole start and the Macao success. Three F1 teams offered him the opportunity to test their single-seaters: Toleman, Brabham and Williams. He did his first laps with Williams, but a GP landing [contract] seemed possible with Toleman or Brabham. In reality Calisto Tanzi, owner of Parmalat and Brabham's sponsor, did not want him, because his idea was to bet on an Italian driver, after a run-off between Pierluigi Martini and Teo Fabi. Ayrton sought me out and told me he needed help because, in fact, the iconic Bernie Ecclestone would have chosen him, but Tanzi had vetoed it. What we didn't consider was that Calisto was financing *Rombo*, the competing magazine of *Autosprint*, where I worked. It was difficult to think that I could influence that negotiation with Parmalat, so nothing came of it and Ayrton went to Toleman.

Senna had not lost heart, even though Toleman was not as competitive as a Brabham might have been ...
Absolutely. Others in his place would have given up on me, but not Ayrton, who was very grateful to those who had given him credit when he was a nobody.

The subject is interesting: how open was he with those who trusted him, and how much of the freebooter (or scoundrel) was there in trying to build the career he had imagined even as a young boy? I was impressed to hear how many people received his hand-written Christmas cards at the time: the Brazilian had to spend a month preparing the cards ...

Ayrton attached great importance to the people he trusted. And his attitude was not fake, but very genuine. It was not the result of a public relations campaign, even though he had a certain innate flair for communication. One example above all? The reason why he gave up his name Ayrton Da Silva to choose his mother's surname, Senna, was due to the fact that his father's surname was as common in Brazil as Paolo Rossi was in Italy.

It was 1982, and before the F3 season started he had decided to register the trademark 'Ayrton Senna', in addition to 'Ayrton' and 'Senna' separately, for all the activities connected to him as a driver. There was a lucid and planned vision of what his career was to be ...

No doubt, but I assume he was also well looked after. Armando Teixeira, a lawyer and family friend, who later became his manager during the Lotus period, was already part of his entourage. I cannot say whether he was well advised, but one fact is certain: he started a PR campaign with Keith Sutton, a good English photographer. After each Formula Ford race, he sent a parcel to the newspapers containing photos of the race and a press release on Senna headed paper. It's a normal thing now, thanks to email and social media, but nobody did it then. Even in terms of career-building he was very strict: if he did something it was for a purpose and he didn't want any distraction from the result. I remember that, before writing a column in his name for *Autosprint*, he told me: 'If a driver wants to make bingo, he has to win everything. If you dominate a championship, but then you do so-so the next year and then come back and win the following season, you are considered ... normal. If you manage to win everything, on the other hand, you build up such an allure that you can't go unnoticed.'

Senna's rise was simply impressive ...
He took part in a Formula Ford 1600 championship in 1981 and won it. Then, in 1982 he competed in two in Formula Ford 2000 almost accidentally. In the winter he had apparently decided to stop racing but instead, when he returned to Britain he secured the Pace British and European EFDA championships, scoring 22 wins.

In Formula 3, in 1983, he won the first nine races in a row on the calendar. In F2000 he raced with Rushen Green Racing, declining Eddie Jordan's offer: the Irish talent scout offered him a long-term managerial contract, but he did not accept because he had to carry out his own business plan.

After he signed with Toleman he called me straight away, but unfortunately the deadline for that issue of *Autosprint* had already passed, so eventually the news became public with an official communiqué. On the phone he told me: 'I've signed with Toleman because it's the only team that didn't put any constraints on me.' It is incredible to think that a young driver coming to F1 from F3 was already able to negotiate his conditions. It shows how stratospheric Ayrton was. Previously I'd had a few words with Alfa Romeo and, to try to get him into the Circus, I had suggested he race in the Alfasud European Series, which ran concurrently with F1, but it didn't fit in with his plans and he dismissed the idea without even considering it: 'My objective for that year is to race in F3 and I don't want any more distractions.' The thing that always struck me most was that the world of international journalism didn't realise what was happening in front of their eyes. And even in England, where Ayrton dominated, he did not enjoy the attention that his performances would have deserved.

And what is your response to that attitude today?
He was a bit of a lone wolf who kept to himself and, therefore, did not frequent the paddock. Usually, at races, a community is created and social relationships are formed. Ayrton, on the other hand, kept to himself. He may not have been exactly obnoxious, but he certainly appeared unsympathetic. He was the one outside the group, but not out of a sense of superiority, far from it. I remember that, when he joined Toleman in 1984, someone wrote: 'Senna has a self-confidence that borders on arrogance.' In reality, he never made any statements in which he claimed to be the best, or in which he was self-congratulatory, but his superiority on the track could be seen a mile away. I remember that *Autosprint* received a piece from a collaborator who recounted Senna's first test with Toleman. The colleague reported the times with the utmost care, but without giving any emphasis to Ayrton's performance. I would have liked to rewrite the article, but I was accused of wanting to promote the Brazilian driver: instead I had simply noted that, on his debut in the TG183, Ayrton had been faster than Derek Warwick, the driver who had run the GP, on the same track. Of course one could make all sorts of considerations, stating that perhaps the car had been developed in the meantime, or the track

conditions were different, but the fact remains that someone had taken an F3 boy and put him in F1 and, at the first go, he was faster than the official drivers. This aspect was not emphasised at all.

Ayrton's ability to go fast from the outset impressed both the Brabham and the Williams staff: both were astounded by their respective tests ...
He phoned me after the test on 19 July 1983 with the Williams FW08C on the Donington track. He had made his F1 debut in the single-seater with which Keke Rosberg had won the Monaco GP, and he told me that he had felt better than in Formula 3: 'The FW08C is like a big kart: it is very positive that I felt better in a car with more horsepower. The more the power increases, the more comfortable I feel!' Of the four F1s he tested in 1983, the one he liked least was Brabham. In general, the feature that most impressed the Circus insiders was his ability to adapt to the most diverse situations. It was an aspect that characterised his entire career: already in karting, during the first lap on cold tyres, he was able to gain many positions. And everyone knew it. I remember a world championship race at Nivelles, Belgium: he had a problem in qualifying and started 16th. The announcer introduced the race by saying: in first position is this guy, in second the other guy, but watch out because in 16th position stands a certain Senna. He had seen it right, because after three laps the Brazilian was already fourth.

Senna's ability to adapt to very different cars was extraordinary, and his words bear witness to this: 'It took me a while to work out the Mercedes 190E 2.3-16, because it is a touring car with very different reactions to a single-seater, but in the last few laps I understood how it should be exploited.' Ayrton won the race that the House of the Star had organised in August 1984 with the F1 VIPs to launch the new 190E at the German GP, upon the inauguration of the renovated Nürburgring circuit. In the wet, Senna outclassed everyone, including Niki Lauda.

And how can we forget the outing with the Porsche 956 in the 1,000km of the Nürburgring in the World Championship Group C on 15 July 1984?
As cockpit mates he had Henri Pescarolo and Stefan Johansson and, although he arrived late because of his F1 tests, after a few laps he was faster than the two main drivers. In the race, after a problem with the throttle cable, he found himself last: the team asked him to drive two

consecutive shifts and he drove the Joest team Porsche to eighth place, leaving everyone speechless. And, for a change, he had mastered everyone in the wet ...

How come you didn't become Ayrton's manager, given your friendship and collaboration?
Some said I was his manager, but it was never true. And the answer is simple: I was his age and my experience in motorsport did not exceed his. I don't deny that I gave him a lot of advice in terms of communication, but at the time I didn't have the know-how to negotiate contracts and it would have been an unnecessary strain. That was the reason why we never really talked about it.

As much as he was tough, even very tough in the car, the Brazilian driver became vulnerable when he got out of the cockpit, at least at the beginning of his career: after raising the visor of his helmet, he was fully aware of certain behaviours that were not always agreeable ...
Ayrton was very sensitive to what the newspapers wrote about him. I remember that in 1985, in his early F1 days, he had already won in his second GP with Lotus, in Portugal, and then at Hockenheim, the following year, he was the protagonist of a second incident with Michele Alboreto, after the one at Monte Carlo in 1985, which caused quite a stir: at the end of qualifying, after having taken pole position, he had returned to the track with the sole intent of blocking the Ferrari driver, the only one who could have beaten him to take pole.

Senna's manoeuvre [he performed a brake test, a deliberate braking in the middle of the straight, while he was in front of the Ferrari of the Milanese driver] *had not pleased Michele at all, who went wild against the Brazilian, creating a strong media impact, so much so that ...*
In *Epoca*, a glossy weekly magazine that did not deal with F1, there was an article about the black prince [the Lotus was in John Player Special's black and gold colours] who scared the Red. In the piece it basically said that Senna was full of conceit, uncaring but also courageous: in a word, a winner. The negative connotations served to depict the uniqueness of the character, but when Ayrton saw the article he was disappointed, because he did not see himself in the role of the villain.

Could be, but when he took to the track he was anything but a malleable opponent...

He was no saint. After the Adelaide Grand Prix we watched the race together on a delayed broadcast: it was 1985 and, on that occasion, he did all sorts of things on the track, climbing the kerbs and recovering positions in a rough and spectacular way. Amongst the TV commentators was Jack Brabham, the three times world champion, a driver who used to get rough in his career, and he said: 'Senna is racing without using his brain!' Ayrton cringed at those words, he felt them inside. And I, for good measure, added to the dose by telling him that the Australian was right, because he had been up to all sorts of mischief, but he had proved a champion in difficult conditions.

Back to Alboreto, the Milanese did not forget Ayrton's bad behaviour at all, even though he later became an avid supporter of the Brazilian and was one of his greatest defenders during the Imola trial...

For a couple of Grands Prix Senna preferred not to talk about that ugly episode, because he felt it was still a hot issue. But when I asked him why he had behaved in that way with Michele, he replied: 'Peter Warr and Gérard Ducarouge, the Lotus sporting director and technical chief, ordered me to defend the pole position I had earned by creating "traffic". I didn't hesitate for a second: I entered the track and carried out the order. But then, when I returned to the pits, I rushed to tell them not to ask me to do something like that anymore, because I would never do it again in my career.' Then I asked him if he had spoken to Michele about it: 'No, now is not the right time. Alboreto is very angry with me and he's right. I have to let some time pass, then the moment will come for us to clarify.' I heard nothing more about the subject at that point, but I met the Milanese driver again when Ayrton was already dead: we were both guests at an event, sitting at the same table. Michele told me that Senna had apologised to him, even choosing the right words to do so, so much so that the two had become friends. Ayrton, therefore, had done what he told me he would. He was very careful, pragmatic: if he gave his word, then he kept it.

In 1994, did you ever talk about his move to Williams and the fact that he was not comfortable in the FW16?

No, it was a period when I didn't follow F1 and, therefore, I didn't want to bother him. I'm not the type of guy who calls just to chat, because that's against my personality. I knew I could talk to him at any time, but I certainly couldn't have imagined he would die, could I?

Nobody thought so ...
And also because ... before that, for some period I had worked for Camel, the F1 sponsor, and it wasn't such a great idea going into the McLaren pit, which was all Marlboro, so I avoided it. But that was already a very different F1.

In 1986, when he took pole at Imola in the Lotus 98T and then retired with a technical problem, he asked me to book a rental car for his parents to use after the race. So I did, but the contract was in his name, so Ayrton had to come with me to Bologna airport. The young lady at the Hertz office was explaining to us why it was so crowded that day: 'Guys, I'm sorry about the queue, but today there was F1 at Imola,' she said without recognising Senna. 'A little while ago Gerhard Berger came here and I had to keep him somehow hidden, because he had a swarm of young girls chasing him.' In the meantime, more people had gathered and someone, of course, recognised Ayrton. A young man in particular, in a very provocative way, said to him: 'Prost was strong today, wasn't he?' alluding to the fact that the Frenchman had been the winner of the GP while Senna had had to retire. His reaction was lightning fast: Ayrton gave him an unkind umbrella gesture [which means 'get lost']. The girl at the desk was speechless, both at the Brazilian's reply and at the fact that she had not recognised him: 'He is nervous', I told her, 'because he was leading the race when he had to stop.' Those were different times and there was no social media.

It can be said, therefore, that he divided the world in two, between those who had supported him before he became a champion, a personality, and those who knew him when he was already established ...
You remind me of how he behaved with Elio De Angelis after the latter's accident, during testing at Paul Ricard in 1986. The two had been teammates at Lotus the year before, then the Roman had decided to move to Brabham. Ayrton was deeply affected by Elio's accident, but was severely criticised for not rushing immediately to see him in hospital, before he died: 'You know,' he explained to me some time later, 'I never had any personal relationship, let alone friendship, with Elio and we never saw each other again after he decided to change teams. I know I would have

looked good in front of the media if I had gone to the hospital, but it would have been an act of total hypocrisy.'

He attended De Angelis's funeral, but did not visit him in hospital. I think this is proof of how he never recited a script.

When was the rivalry with Prost born? Certainly not at McLaren, where it became explosively manifest ...
I don't know, but although Ayrton considered himself the strongest, he regarded Alain as a rival to be feared.

Who were the drivers he rated most highly?
In his opinion, half the grid that was in F1 in his day didn't deserve to be there, so I assume the other half was good. In the beginning he had a very good relationship with Boutsen, but I think it was more due to the personal feeling with Thierry, who was a nice person, than his standing as a driver. He did not get on well with Johnny Cecotto, his team-mate at Toleman.

The Venezuelan, a former motorcyclist who had come to four wheels, often complained about an alleged difference in equipment, since Ayrton was always faster than him ...
Johnny simply did not realise what an opponent he had in the team. Having said that, I would add that Cecotto was perhaps the team-mate who had been the most on a par with him, excluding of course McLaren's Prost. I remember my amazement at Monaco, in a practice session, when the Venezuelan had gone faster than Ayrton. All he said was: 'Andrea, do you really believe Johnny should always drive slower? It's only fair.' It was his way, quite an indirect one, of telling me that he felt esteem for Cecotto.

At the tragic 1994 San Marino GP none of his relatives had come to support him: what was his relationship with his family?
I went to his house in Brazil with my friend Angelo Orsi: he had great respect for his mum and dad and gave the impression that his dad was the leader of the household. In the car park he had a Ford Escort which we had decided to take for a drive and he seemed very attentive to the rules of the road.

A few months earlier we had seen each other in Milan, and I was driving my car in a way that was certainly more decisive and less respectful of signs and signals: 'Have you never had an accident?' he had asked me point-blank.

'No, fortunately nothing serious, just some minor collisions, and you?'

'With racing cars I've had several accidents, but with road cars never!'

I had remembered those words and in Brazil I asked dad Milton how things really stood: 'Every week we had to take the car to the bodyshop.'

Ayrton dropped the subject with a long smile, knowing he had gone too far.

Was there ever a moment when you saw him in serious difficulty?
Yes, it happened at Monza in 1984, when Toleman decided to lay him off because he had already signed with Lotus for the following year. Ayrton was as nervous and pissed off as I had ever seen him: a person like him, who had always been in control of everything around him, didn't seem to know which way to turn. I asked my friends at the racetrack if I could use a telex to draft a communiqué [about his move], after his lawyer had sent a draft of the comment he should release. So, to cut a long story short, we proposed a series of corrections to the draft, later agreed upon with his lawyer, but at some point a journalist walked by and glimpsed the document. Ayrton got angry with me: 'This guy has just seen the document in a version that is not the final one. God only knows what he's going to spread around!' 'Calm down,' I replied, 'he barely glanced at it and may have just understood the situation, certainly he has not paid any attention to the commas you are discussing with the lawyer. Nothing has happened.'

Despite my reassuring words he was as tense as the strings of a violin.

In fact, it was the first time in his career that he had been unceremoniously dismissed...
Mentally he was not prepared for a contract termination, and at a loss to remain without a steering wheel in his hands. It took him a couple of days to seek me out, in order to apologise for being too rough on me. I actually didn't mind, considering that the moment was very delicate, so much so that we continued working and eventually sent out the communiqué. I was astonished, however, that after some time he came back to the subject, admitting his unusual behaviour: once again, he showed me his deep sensitivity.

Do you think he had an idea what he would do in life after racing?
The first time I asked him this question was after just a couple of experiences in Grands Prix: 'Something outside motorsport, something that has nothing to do with racing,' he replied. Then a few years later he changed his mind, arguing that it might be nice to stay connected to F1. In reality for him there was no afterwards, because it was a scenario he didn't even want to think about. Perhaps the beginning of his career had been very stressful for him and that is why he had pondered the idea of a break, but then he felt fully in control of the situation. It has to be said that, in the meantime, he had built up good broad shoulders and had also become politically very strong: it was just enough for me to see the ability with which he had managed to develop personal relationships with the Honda managers, who adored him, to understand what he was made of. For them, he was much more than a driver, he was a champion. An idol to whom they paid the utmost respect.

CHAPTER 3

ANGELO ORSI: AYRTON'S TRUE CONFIDANT

'IT TAKES a minute to notice special people, an hour to appreciate them, a day to love them, a lifetime to forget.'

Charlie Chaplin could not have summed up better, in one sentence, the relationship between Angelo Orsi and Ayrton Senna. But who is Angelo? Certainly he was one of the best F1 photographers from the 1980s until his retirement: he worked for the Villani Agency first and then for *Autosprint*. Many people, however, associate his name with Senna because he was Ayrton's fraternal friend. It was easy to recognise the Bolognese guy in the paddock: blue eyes, curls and a blond moustache on a powerful physique. A silent guy, who might have seemed haughty to those who did not know him, but in reality a real piece of work. A 'click' artist, accustomed to letting images speak for themselves. And photographs were his first point of contact with the Brazilian champion.

How did the friendship with Ayrton come about?
Let's start by saying that there were many people who gravitated around Ayrton, but those who had actually been *really* around him were just a few.

What was the first contact?
Paolo Bombara and Andrea Ficarelli, the two *Autosprint* contributors to the karting column, flooded us with news about this Brazilian phenomenon. Both were ready to bet that, when he arrived in Formula 1, there would be no more glory for anyone. They claimed that he would become a world champion in single-seaters.

In 1983, I was at Silverstone for the British GP; that weekend there was Formula 3 along with the F1 Grand Prix, and Senna was racing in it. Ayrton actually won and became [F3] champion. More out of curiosity than anything else, I went to the podium to take the first photographs of this phenomenon, just to have some pictures in the archive. Maybe one day they would come in handy …

Then I went back to the press room. It was a very hot afternoon: they had even run out of water supplies in England that year. While I was waiting for the newspaper reporters working with me to finish their articles and return to the hotel, I felt a tap on my shoulder. It was Andrea Ficarelli saying: 'Finally I can introduce you to the next F1 world champion.' I turned around smiling sardonically to find out who he was talking about. I thought to myself: 'Who is this blowhard going to be?' I was confronted by a beardless, thin, pale boy who wanted to introduce himself: 'How do you do, I am Ayrton Senna. I read *Autosprint*, which I consider to be the motoring bible: the magazine also follows karting with care and I like your photographs very much. I am an attentive reader, so I can say that, in my way, I know you too.'

I make no secret of the fact that I was pleased to discover that a young man was so interested in my work.

'Have a seat,' I said, signalling for him to take a seat next to me.

'Can I have five minutes of your time?' replied Ayrton, before starting a speech that left me stunned: 'I'll be in F1 next year and then I'll be world champion!'

I looked at him like an alien and replied: 'Well, your project seems to be a good one. I wish you well …'

The young man wasted no time on further pleasantries: 'Please,' he whispered, as he looked around the press room, 'can you tell me which are the best Italian correspondents who cover F1? I am Brazilian, but I consider Italy very important for motor racing, so I will have to deal with these people and I wouldn't mind at all starting to figure out who they are now.'

I was amazed, but I pointed out to him Nestore Morosini, Carlo Marincovich and Pino Allievi, who were busy writing at that moment. I noticed that he was pleased, because he would be able to remember them, when sooner or later they would have to interview him.

I thought the conversation had come to an end, but instead, Ayrton added shyly: 'I have another request to make to you and I realise it may seem embarrassing: in order to find sponsors and build up the budget I need to make my F1 debut – since my family doesn't intend to help me much – my manager Armando Teixeira and I have created a small agency in Brazil. It is in charge of sending to all the Brazilian newspapers, which are many and unfortunately don't have the chance to follow me, a short report of my race, enclosing some photographs. The objective is to build a great media visibility that will then allow Armando to ask for more money from the sponsors.'

I was amazed and almost speechless at the very clear vision that this young man had of his future: it seemed simply monstrous compared to the approach to racing that other young drivers had at the time.

So he wanted to be able to use your photos? How did you respond?
'I work for the Villani Agency,' I replied, 'which sends me to Grands Prix to supply *Autosprint* with my photos. I'll give you an answer at one of the next races, after I've spoken to those in charge in Bologna, to see if we can start a collaboration.' 'I am not too demanding,' Ayrton added, 'I understand that you can't monopolise your time for me, but of all the photographs you take, please reserve a dozen for me and duplicate them, so that I can send them to Brazil and supply the agency.'

On his return to Bologna, Angelo spoke to Franco Villani, the owner of the agency:
We agreed on a price of 400,000 lire per Grand Prix in exchange for ten photographs. It was a useful sum to lower the travel expenses for my trips. Ayrton accepted without batting an eyelid: 'Just bring me ten pictures duplicated ten times and I'll pay you back.' In short, a professional relationship was born even before he had made his F1 debut.

Two people working together are not necessarily destined to become friends ...
That's true, but with Ayrton we hit it off straight away. I'm a rather shy guy, of few words, who doesn't like F1 razzmatazz too much. And he immediately became fond of my way of doing things: essential, no frills. He liked my professional approach: on every track I got used to doing at least one lap of the track on Thursday, to find out what had changed from the year before, to look for new shots.

Nowadays all F1 drivers are used to walking a lap of the track with their engineers, but in the 1980s nobody did that at all ...
Absolutely. I was alone, very much alone. I was going in the opposite direction to the single-seaters, to find new positions from which different pictures could be taken. I had explained this to Ayrton and, very intrigued, he told me: 'That sounds like an excellent idea. In fact, would you take me with you? I don't know the F1 tracks.' In the meantime, we had begun to call each other by name, noting deeper affinities. Thursday evenings became a kind of liturgy between the two of us: when everyone else was about to leave for the hotel, Ayrton and I would set off on foot for the customary reverse lap of the track. Sometimes two laps, if not three, as in Monte Carlo.

It made sense that you ran the track against the grain, but not for Senna ...
You are wrong here: he would linger and look at the kerbs, the escape routes, the protections. He would also analyse the type of gravel, checking whether his shoes were sinking or whether it was particularly hard. I remember the first time we went to Adelaide: at the end of the lap, before the final hairpin bend, there was the pit entrance. While I was looking for a shot with good light, I noticed that he was digging the sand between the two strips of asphalt with the heel of his shoe: 'I have to remember,' he told me, 'that if someone comes into the pits and I end up long, I can get out of here easily.'

In those lonely moments, a solid friendship cemented: Ayrton would point out to me the spots that he thought could become overtaking opportunities, and even where spectacular photos could possibly be shot. A collaboration was born, which grew stronger race after race. He could rely on my experience and knowledge of the tracks, while I benefited from his eye to pick out braking points that would not have been important to others. That's how a bond was built: we became accomplices.

But who was Ayrton Senna?
A simple person who didn't like going to discos or hanging out in the evening. Someone who said to me at one point: 'Angelo, you work very hard to do your job well: you have to walk many kilometres a day and you carry the weight of cameras and lenses. How do you manage to be so fit all the time?' The answer was simple: 'I take care of my nutrition. On Saturdays I stay light, eat plain pasta and fruit, so that I don't get

weighed down and so I sleep well. This way I'm ready for a busy day on Sunday.' My way of doing things turned into his way as well. On race weekends he adopted a basic lifestyle, but if he came to visit me at my place he enjoyed tortellini Bolognese.

You saw a driver evolve into the champion he promised to be. He lived up to it, he didn't brag about anything ...
He was a simple guy who loved photography. We spent hours looking at my pictures and he acquired a certain expertise, so much so that he even started to give me advice. I remember that in 1992 (or 1993) his McLaren had a windscreen with an unusual shape, curved forward. At that time wind tunnel work was not as sophisticated as it is today. Ayrton used to complain that, when it rained, water was pouring down on his helmet and the engineers couldn't solve the problem.

What did he come up with?
'In a wet session,' he said, 'will you take a sequence of side shots? Because I want to find out where the flow of water hitting the cockpit goes.' In the pictures, in fact, you could see the spray coming off the front wheels and going onto the bodywork. Ayrton showed the photos to the engineers who figured out how to modify the cockpit to prevent the water from bouncing off the helmet. I'm recounting this episode to explain how his passion for photos drove him to solve a problem in the car.

Did he ever want to be a photographer too?
No, never. I was his eye.

The professional relationship had become a solid friendship, based on complicity ...
I never leaked anything to the others. Ayrton knew that what he told me would remain between us. I never betrayed his trust and I always saw the same person in him, even when he became the acclaimed and celebrated champion. We found each other: he was a driver, I was a photographer. We were both closed in character. Closed-minded. And maybe that's why we got along so well in the beginning. We had to learn to trust each other, but it was not difficult to find a wonderful harmony, at times made up more of silences than words.

Senna was an enterprising guy: he wanted to know every nut and bolt of the single-seater he raced in, and since he considered the magazine Autosprint *his bible, it wasn't enough for him to just have a fresh copy in his hands ...*

Just imagine: if he happened to be in the Bologna area on Monday morning, he would come to the typography department at Conti Editore to see how the magazine was being printed. Senna would come to see me, who, like the rest of the editorial staff, had stayed overnight for the closing of the issue, but also because he didn't want to miss the pleasure of witnessing the birth of a fresh magazine, perhaps even featuring him on the cover.

Between the driver who made his debut with Toleman and the three-time world champion, how much did his character change?

Well, he obviously matured over the years, but he didn't change much in attitude. He never became a star, he always continued his normal life. Sure: the number of people he had around him grew, but he always carefully selected where to go and who to talk to. He matured and never felt like a celebrity.

He remained a normal person, going out with my son Matteo and hanging out with our family when he was in Italy. In the evenings he would stay at home – which was two floors above yours, Franco – watching TV tapes with his cat, when his colleagues were perhaps going to parties. He always maintained great concentration on what was his primary goal: winning races.

I always got the idea that he was a ... nice bastard. A very tough driver on the track, with no mercy for his opponents, but outside the competition he was the same guy who did charity work for children in the favelas. *How was this metamorphosis possible?*

All drivers transform when they lower their visor and enter another dimension. And I like to tell you that, from a sporting point of view, he was polite, although he was very hard on the track, very bad. He was not like today's drivers who, whenever they make a mistake, are excused for everything and by everyone. Ayrton always had an open view of things. In the evenings, when we saw each other, I was not afraid to tell him if he had done something wrong and he accepted my opinions, knowing that they were impartial.

They hated each other in sports, but as drivers they respected each other: Ayrton Senna and Alain Prost were like cat and dog at McLaren.

Angelo Orsi, the friend of the Brazilian champion, is in the swarm of photographers who came for Ayrton's debut with Williams in 1994.

Those were also the days when drivers used to send 'messages' to each other in such a way that the FIA would never tolerate nowadays: issues were not resolved by the stewards, but directly on the track, wheel to wheel...

I remember a couple of episodes with Michele Alboreto: once Ayrton passed him and forced him on to the grass. Michele, in Austria, didn't forget that, so much so that, as he was going uphill towards the *Remus* curve, he braked in front of him, causing Senna to lose control of his car. I remember it well because I shot the whole sequence of the accident. And I'm reminded of Nigel Mansell, who arrived furiously at the Lotus box at Spa-Francorchamps, ready to beat Ayrton up after another accident on the track. But still, the two guys respected each other: when speaking of Nigel, Ayrton always told me that he was the only driver who caused him any tension: 'He doesn't frighten me,' he said of the Englishman, 'but when he's tailing you, you can see him in both rear-view mirrors! It is a feeling I never felt with anyone else.' There was a respect in it that I no longer see today. Senna was not protected, but he had to protect himself. He had people on his side who criticised him harshly: Gérard Ducarouge, the Lotus technical director, did not spare him sharp words when he did something stupid. Ayrton was vicious and aggressive, as well as extremely fast, but he had a sporting upbringing that dictated he should not go beyond certain limits.

Well that brings us quickly to the duel at McLaren with Alain Prost...
Take 1989, when the world fell in on him at Suzuka: his team-mate, Alain Prost, hit him in the last chicane and then went to file a complaint to have him excluded from the race he had won anyway, because Ayrton had restarted with a push from the track marshals. The relations between the two were already tense, and from that moment onward Ayrton no longer called him by his first name: Alain became simply 'the Frenchman' for him. He had already resented him for a while, but that gesture in Japan was the straw that broke the camel's back. The following year, again at Suzuka, Ayrton made it up to him. Like a nice bastard, as you claim.

You're talking about 1990, when Prost had switched to Ferrari and was competing for the title with Senna, who had stayed at McLaren...
Suzuka was a predictable revenge. Indeed, I would say, announced. After sealing pole position, Ayrton asked FISA if the position at the pole could be reversed, because he wanted to start on the left side of

the track, which was rubberised, and not on the inside, on the dirty side. He had been asking president Jean-Marie Balestre about this for three years, but he would not agree. Senna then declared: 'Since you say that the pole on the inside gives the right of way, I warn you that I will start straight and continue along my line, because it is the one you have chosen for me.' On the other side the reply had been clear: 'Do what you want.' Ayrton kept his word and bumped into his rival, driving him into the sand. At the first corner there was a retirement for both. The two then returned to the pits walking one in front of the other. In silence, without saying a word. Ignoring each other, as if the opponent did not exist. Unbelievable.

How did you discuss this incident, which is engraved in the history of F1, with Ayrton?
In the pit we had a raw confrontation. Senna came towards me smiling: 'I am world champion!'

My reply was harsh: 'Nice way to become world champion. I don't like that at all, it wasn't sporting!'

'You are right Angelo, but did you forget last year?'

And with that sentence he put a tombstone on the subject, before he went off to celebrate the title. And you know what? Although he had won his second World Championship by knocking out the Ferrari driver, the very same guys from the *Cavallino* [literally the 'little horse', a term for Ferrari] were there to cheer him on. Starting with Pietro Corradini, who would have liked to be his chief mechanic if he had ever gone to Maranello. The Ferrari team did not file a complaint against Senna, knowing full well that he could have easily won it. This was Ayrton, for better or for worse.

Some people harshly criticised another episode, which occurred the following year, again at Suzuka. The Brazilian champion was celebrating his third crown and, in front of the finish line, decided to slow down to let Gerhard Berger, his trusted team-mate and friend, win the Japanese GP. A gesture read by many not as generosity but as humiliation. How did Ayrton feel about it?
He was very hurt. He did not understand why people had given that interpretation. He had a great relationship with Gerhard, the two had always helped each other. Ayrton was on the verge of becoming champion for the third time and wanted to gratify the Austrian by giving him the

Suzuka success. For him, that gesture was intended as a tribute to his team-mate. He had not in the least thought that giving way in front of the chequered flag might seem like a humiliation for Gerhard.

The Austrian, in Japan, achieved his sixth Grand Prix victory, yet he always felt he was in the role of second driver with Senna ...
There was never any doubt in the team: Gerhard was slower than Ayrton. The Austrian tried to stay in front, but he couldn't and he was going crazy: 'I don't know what to do anymore,' Berger told me, 'there's no way I can put my wheels ahead of him. He's stronger and I give up.' A relationship of great complicity arose between the two off the track. They were friends and each was aware of the other's value in the car. The hierarchy was clear, very clear.

Berger got up to a lot of mischief with tSenna. There are many funny stories about them ...
Ayrton was the one who always gave way. I remember a briefcase thrown out of a helicopter while they were in the air at Monza. Inside were all Ayrton's documents. He was a bit of a sacrificial victim and didn't react much, because on the track the roles were reversed anyway. There were no arguments, because the two were genuinely friends.

True friendship is revealed in a moment of difficulty ...
I must say that Gerhard proved to be a true friend to Senna. After the tragic accident at Imola, he was the first person I met in the pits. They were transferring Ayrton by helicopter to the *Ospedale Maggiore* in Bologna: 'What do you know about Ayrton?' Berger asked me. 'Is it very serious?'

'I don't know, they took him away,' I replied.

'Then wait a minute, I'm going to make a call: should I need it, you're coming with me, we're going to the airport. Not to the hospital, but to the airport.'

He ran off in the direction of the pit and I waited for his return. A few minutes later I saw him reappear with a gloomy face: 'There is nothing more to do,' he hissed, his voice broken with tears. 'That's a pity, because I had alerted Professor Saillant [a world-leading sports surgeon]. If there had been one chance to save him, we would have gone to Paris to get the professor, who would have operated on him in Bologna. Now it's all useless. I'll see you at the *Ospedale Maggiore*.' I'm recounting this episode as a sign of Gerhard's sincere friendship.

Before moving to Williams in 1994, Senna had decided to race for one more season with McLaren, well aware that the Woking single-seater, equipped with the Ford Cosworth HB engine in the customer version [i.e. not official and, therefore, less powerful], instead of the 12-cylinder Honda they had previously used, would not be competitive. He actually preferred the Lamborghini V12 engine, which he had tested, but McLaren didn't choose it. Senna signed an agreement with Ron Dennis to race for a salary of $1 million per race, renewable after each GP ...

Senna had been shocked by the Lamborghini engine, after the first test with the Italian V12: he had asked Ron Dennis to use it on the McLaren in the last races of 1993. After the first test, Ayrton had called Mauro Forghieri and told him: 'This 12-cylinder is far too powerful. Next time give me an engine with less horsepower, but one that is smoother in its delivery: I think it is an amazing power unit.' Senna set the track record at Estoril and encouraged Ron Dennis to use that engine, because it was a winning unit. The deal would have been done if, on the Friday, McLaren had not received a phone call from Peugeot offering engines and money. Dennis called Daniele Audetto, the Lamborghini project manager, to break the deal and as a consequence Ayrton decided to sign with Williams for the 1994 season.

It was a sign of destiny: Ayrton had run his first laps in the Williams in 1983 and then died in Sir Frank's single-seater in 1994 ...

At the 1993 Portuguese GP in Estoril, Alain Prost had become world champion and announced his retirement after his fourth title. On the same Sunday Ayrton invited me not to miss the press conference in the afternoon, because there would be the announcement of his move to Williams. As we left the conference, Ayrton came up to me and said: 'Too many people around, let's not talk here, I have some things to tell you. Let's go to the car.' He took his Honda NSX and we drove two laps of the Estoril track at very low speed, just to talk freely. The best words were: 'Finally I have stolen the Williams from the Frenchman. I will be able to count on a competitive car. Then I will make you happy, because I will go to Ferrari afterwards.'

Was the ability to snatch extraordinary contracts due to the champion's determination or the desire to earn a lot of money?
Of course every driver tries to earn more, but for Ayrton having the highest salary also meant being the best. That's why he wanted to be the highest paid. When he had agreed with Cesare Fiorio, in 1990, to go to Ferrari in 1991, he had agreed on a figure of $30 million, which was accepted immediately even if nothing came of it.

In 1993 he had won five GPs and could have been fighting for the World Championship if the Ford HB engine had not broken down more often than expected: during the summer, Williams had fixed the active suspension, Prost won four races in a row and took the lead. Ayrton was happy, however, because the next year he could count on the active suspension; but the Federation instead decided to ban it, starting from 1994, with a change in the regulations. What was a perfect car was in danger of becoming an unpredictable single-seater. And not only that, being designed by Adrian Newey, it would be extreme in terms of the dimensions of the cockpit.

After Senna's debut with the Williams FW15D at Estoril, where his problem in the cockpit became evident, why didn't they make the car the way he wanted it?
The 1993 car was a hybrid version and was drivable, but Ayrton did not know what the car would be like in 1994. Waiting for it, he had disappeared to go on holiday. I received Christmas greetings. 'Look, I'll rest now, I'll be in touch when the time is right.' He was depressed, and had taken refuge in Angra dos Reis where he had a villa.

Wasn't that abnormal behaviour?
No, he liked to detach himself from the world for a month and a half, to isolate himself in his beloved Brazil. From time to time he would send postcards, as there were no social networks, unlike today. I still keep the correspondence from Christmas 1993 at home. After that, he came back only to test the FW16 at Silverstone. Anyway, I hadn't heard from him for a long time, when he surprisingly called while I was in the newsroom: 'I've just landed at Heathrow, I've come to test-drive the new car. I'll call you tomorrow night and tell you how it went. Bye.'

This was all Ayrton wanted to say: there was no way he would talk about the long period of silence. And, above all, I thought that, with all the things he had to do for the launch of the new Williams, he surely would not have had time to call me again. Instead, on the afternoon of the next day, he phoned punctually: 'Hi Angelo, I've just finished testing the car.'

'How did it go?'

'Well, just be aware that it was snowing, so I can't tell you whether the car will prove good or bad, since I drove very slowly. But one thing I can tell you for sure: they've made the single-seater to Prost's measurements and I can't fit in it. I can't even eat a sandwich because otherwise I risk not getting into the cockpit. And that's why I told them that the car has to be completely modified from the driver's seat to the steering wheel. You know I'm used to driving with a thin-grip steering wheel, but large in diameter. Well, I've got one with a big grip but small in diameter; and it stands between my legs. I am not able to drive in these conditions. Just imagine these guys: they pay the best F1 driver with the highest salary, and then give him a car in which he will perform two seconds slower. Just how do these Brits think?'

Is it true that he threatened not to drive for the team?
It wasn't a threat: it was just that he didn't fit in the single-seater! He had ruined his knuckles because they were rubbing against the carbon cover of the cockpit. Designer Newey didn't want the upper part of the body to be cut off like on the McLaren: 'This is the car,' Adrian ruled, 'the chassis can't be changed.' But then history has shown that, with the modifications made, Damon Hill went close to winning that World Championship, which Michael Schumacher 'stole' from him at Adelaide. Quite evidently, the modifications suggested by Ayrton had made the FW16 a winner. For Ayrton it would have been enough to have a comfortable driver's seat.

Actually, they then removed the carbon fibre skins from the bodywork that enclosed the cockpit in the vicinity of the hands: when do you think those modifications were made?
In preparation for Imola, not before. Ayrton also complained about the driving position at Aida. He had been knocked off the track on the first lap of the Pacific GP, but he still struggled to drive and obsessively demanded that they make the required changes. They assured him that, by the time he was racing at Imola, he would be able to use a larger steering wheel and the steering column would be moved lower. Still not

the ideal solution, but it would fit a little better. Thus, the story of the modified car started.

Let's come to Imola: Ayrton wanted the 'bumps' off the track before the winter tests ... In what psychological climate did he arrive at the Enzo and Dino Ferrari?
It was bad, but the thing that upset him most was not that he didn't have a super-competitive car, since he was sure the team would support him and they would certainly modify the car.

So why was he so agitated?
Because someone from Renault had started to make offensive inferences, such as: 'Did we get a boiled [past his best] driver?' This had reached Ayrton's ears and he was pissed off like a puma. Not only that, there was also the issue of the 'irregular' Benetton that infuriated him: according to him, Schumacher's car was completely outside the rules, because it had traction control, which was forbidden by the regulations. He had realised this at the first corner at Aida: before returning to the pits, after retirement, he stopped to watch a part of the race and noticed that, when Schumacher's Benetton came in there, the typical noise of anti-spin could be heard. This was something that irritated him, because he reported the irregularity but nothing happened. He said: 'Either they stop using it or we do the same.' Psychologically he was bothered by these two things, especially as he arrived at the San Marino GP with zero points in the standings. He wanted to win at all costs: from Imola onward he wanted to start a cycle of consecutive GP wins until the end. That was his goal.

Roland Ratzenberger died during Saturday's qualifying and Ayrton went to see for himself what had happened. The FIA admonished him and he got angry: 'When there are accidents of that kind,' he said, 'the drivers have the right to go and see what happened, to indicate whether there is anything to change.' Orsi recalls: 'On Sunday morning he was furious: I remember a very long chat with Gerhard Berger. He was returning to the pit after the warm-up. He met Gerhard and stopped in front of the Ferrari motorhome. I was there with a few others. Berger was sitting on a moped and he was standing in front, very angry at the Federation for the constraints they had put in place. With Berger, he wanted to agree on a behavioural code, since the drivers were told: "You sit in the car, we'll take care of the rest." The idea was to revive the Grand Prix Drivers' Association to have a say in track decisions. This contributed to increasing the tension.'

Some claimed that Senna was no longer serene after the death of the Austrian driver …
Much as he did not know him well and had no particular friendship with him, a colleague had died. But Barrichello's accident had already upset him, because it could have been very dangerous. And something was happening *every day* during that GP, whereas it usually happened once a year. That tragedy certainly did not help him, but it had not affected him. He was not sad – if anything, he was focused on the goal he wanted to achieve, but he was not serene for all the reasons I have listed. There was no foreboding. Nor any break-up with his girlfriend: Jo Ramirez can confirm that he had booked a helicopter to go to Faro to see Adriane Galisteu after the race.

Yet, in the pit lane, he did not take off his helmet: a strange sign ….
No, he was angry. He wanted to win at Imola, but he had Schumacher on the front row with a car he deemed should not have raced. That San Marino GP remains a big question mark for me. I have experienced 409 GPs in my career, but at Imola 1994 things happened that I cannot explain. Of all the F1 drivers I've known, I've only had four or five to call real friends: Mauricio Gugelmin, Gabriele Tarquini, Pierluigi Martini, Stefano Modena … people with whom I had an exchange that went beyond pit life. And among them the first was obviously Ayrton, with whom I also had a professional relationship.

Angelo, what memories do you have of the Imola tragedy?
My friend had an accident at a point where the drivers pushed right through, since that corner was considered a straight. But the crash would not have had serious consequences if the suspension bracket had not stuck into his helmet: almost certainly he would not have died. I considered myself the ultimate connoisseur of Imola for photographic renditions, but that day I found myself an hour before the race not knowing where to go, because during the photographers' meeting I had placed a colleague at each corner. And when I looked at the map, I saw that there was only one free position: the *Tamburello* corner. I had never shot the start

from *Tamburello*, so I thought maybe it would allow me to take a nice photo with the F1 group, with the green and the Marlboro Tower in the background. I ended up where I had never been before and my friend died right there, just a few metres away. To this day I still ask myself: why? As if someone had said to me: 'Just go there and I'll see you.' I don't know, it's strange. I've been carrying this inside of me for a long time and I've never found an answer.

Where did you position yourself?
I was on the roof of marshals' station number two: they let me go wherever I wanted, because I never put myself in dangerous spots. I had parked my moped in the little road that ran alongside the racetrack. Because from there I would then move to *Variante Bassa*.

Did you see the accident?
Ayrton had made a good start after the safety car and had given a few metres to Schumacher, because he wanted to demolish his opponent. I had seen him go straight through and, out of the corner of my eye, I caught the car sliding and then … Boom! A bang was heard and a steward shouted to me that there was a car off the track and it was probably Ayrton's … But he wasn't sure, because we couldn't see the second part of *Tamburello*. So I jumped off the roof of the stewards' station to get my moped and cover those 200m …

What were you thinking of?
Nothing. I wanted to see what had happened and I wasn't even sure it was Ayrton. As I approached, the Williams was stuck there and the doctors were already extracting Senna. Dr Salcito was taking Senna's helmet off – and doctors were not supposed to do that – because he realised it was a very serious situation. When I arrived, they were laying him on the ground. You can imagine what my state of mind was: I had the marshals updating me, but Ayrton was only a couple of metres away. I didn't see what they were doing to him. I didn't memorise the tragedy that was unfolding: believe me, I can't remember anything. I have no grim images in my memory, because there were so many people around him, doctors and marshals. I leaned my camera against the net and took sequences of shots mechanically. I had the feeling that there were very brief moments when I could see something, but I didn't realise it fully,

also because, afterwards, they shielded him from view with a white sheet and took him to the helicopter. I was petrified: the very fact that there was a helicopter on the track testified to the seriousness of the situation and from a marshal's radio I heard a message: 'Driver code three or four.' I understood that Ayrton was in a desperate condition. They took him away by helicopter. I stayed there just long enough to take a few shots of the crashed Williams and then went back to the pits, where I was mobbed by everyone who wanted to know what had happened, since I was the only one outside *Tamburello*. But I didn't know what the doctors had done and wasn't able to give precise information.

I remember a phone call you made to the editorial office and you warning me: 'You will notice a roll of photographs that I have taken in sequence. I didn't look in the frame but I don't want anyone to see them. Put them aside, we'll talk about them as soon as I get back' …
When I arrived at the pits I met Arturo Rizzoli, our journalist in charge of collecting all the rolls for development at half race. I handed him the bag with all the rolls from all the photographers, leaving out only the one that had to be delivered separately.

There was absolute silence in the newsroom. The only way not to think about the Senna tragedy was to devote ourselves to work. To prepare that issue that we would have never wanted to print. I was at the light table with Mirco Lazzari, at the time an archivist and today one of the most creative MotoGP photographers, when we were handed the big plastic bag with the pictures Angelo had hinted at: a few shots with lots of blood on a devastated face. A gag of vomit and horror: 'Those images would have added nothing to the story we had to recount that night,' continues Orsi. 'Together with the director, we decided not to show the photos, and I remain convinced that it was the right thing to do.' In Carlo Cavicchi's office we cut up those slides, shredding them after extracting them from the frames. No trace of them remained.

How much money did they offer you for those shots?
Already that evening some Brazilian agencies came to the editorial office because word had spread that I was the only one outside *Tamburello*, and everyone expected me to have scandalous photos. I must admit that, on

that occasion, I was unprofessional: I could have asked a commissioner to step aside for a moment to take the picture. I didn't. I didn't feel like it. I have always said: 'That was the only time in my long career when I failed to take pictures.'

You actually contributed to finding the truth on the Senna case, by taking the picture of the piece of column attached to the steering wheel that was lying on the asphalt next to the Williams. That shot attracted the attention of Gabriele Tarquini, who spread the suspicion that the steering wheel had broken.
Once the magazine issue was closed, with the black cover page of Autosprint, *what did you do? Did you go to the mortuary?*
Yes, at night. And it made a very bad impression on me. After I introduced myself, the doctor on duty immediately asked: 'What kind of accident did your friend suffer? All sorts of things end up here, but I have never seen a head like that.' As if a bomb had gone off. It had become huge. Ayrton was placed next to Ratzenberger.

What an absurd fate for the two drivers: the first and the last, united in a tragic fate…
They were next to each other, each one under a white sheet. I stayed there for a couple of hours, then went home to take a shower and came back early in the morning to the mortuary again, to stay until the hearse arrived: we loaded him up to take him to the airport, where an Air Force plane had arrived. The last time I saw him, they were loading him onto the plane. A caress to the coffin and my story with Ayrton ended there. I didn't go to the funeral. I went to see him at the cemetery in Morumbi the following year: I appreciated the fact that everyone who is buried there has the same gravestone, lying on the huge lawn. In the face of death they are all equal: Senna as the last *favelante*. I was very surprised that the driveway was full of shops with photographs of Ayrton, some of them were my own: they had been scanned and were being sold. I can't say whether it pleased me or not.

And how did you feel about everything that happened?
Very detached. It was a finished story. And I never heard from anyone from the Senna family, people I used to hang out with when they came to Imola. With *Tamburello* I put a stop to it.

And when they talk to you now about Ayrton, what are your thoughts?
Look, I speak very little about F1 because I follow it very little. Obviously a lot of memories come to my mind, because I had spent over ten years next to him, starting before he debuted in F1 until the end. I saw so many people who had criticised him standing beside his coffin. If you read the various accounts, on the last night Ayrton should have had dinner with at least 100 people: it makes me smile. I hear people adding some detail to the narrative each time. However, the thing that makes me happy is knowing that I had a friend, a driver in F1, who everyone still remembers. Even today, young karters say they wish they could drive like Senna. It is extraordinary, beautiful: a sign that he left something important behind, which cannot be erased.

CHAPTER 4

MANAGER RAMIREZ CAUGHT UP IN THE DISPUTES BETWEEN SENNA AND PROST

'SOME PEOPLE just want for a thing to happen, some wish it would happen, others make it happen.'

Michael Jordan, basketball ace, has always been aware that, behind the triumphs of a champion is the work of figures who are not simply 'doormats' ready to lie on the floor to satisfy any desire of a top athlete.

Jo Ramirez, the McLaren team manager, is a living example of the American basketballer's thinking. The Mexican, Ron Dennis's trusted man, experienced two unrepeatable years in 1988 and 1989, when he found himself managing not one, but two champions in the team: Alain Prost and Ayrton Senna. Two superstars on the track, with profoundly different and complex personalities, who had only one goal: to win. Jo may have looked like the crock pot between two iron pots, but only an outspoken man like him could have handled the rivalry of two titans in the same box. Ramirez learned to juggle the virtues and faults of Ayrton and Alain. After the Frenchman left Woking, a deep friendship developed with the Brazilian, which went far beyond the relationship between a driver and a sporting director.

Jo knew all of Senna's secrets: he had met him as a boy and then seen him in action at Macao in F3, gauging not only his talent but also his human depth: 'He was charismatic even when he was a nobody. He had clear ideas. I had met him in 1982 at Silverstone. I had gone to greet Emerson Fittipaldi in a motorhome. Shortly afterwards Ayrton arrived and wanted to talk to Emerson, so Fittipaldi introduced me to this young stranger. When he left, Emerson told me: "Follow this boy, because he will not only become a world champion, he will be one of the greatest in F1." It seemed an exaggerated consideration for a driver who was only racing in Formula Ford, but no one had seen as far as the Brazilian. Years later, when Ayrton was well established, I recalled this episode to "Emmo": "I have never known you to make a more accurate assessment." And he replied: "You see? I wasn't wrong at all, Senna is a pure talent."'

Ramirez was impressed by the Brazilian, who didn't put on airs, but won regularly: 'Being intrigued, I used to go and see him in action when there were F1 concurrences with F3, I would casually pass by and say hello to him. The first time we worked together was in Macao in 1983, when Ayrton came to race for Theodore Racing, where I was the team manager. Teddy Yip, the team owner, had hired the Ralt RT3-Toyota from West Surrey for the Brazilian, while in Eddie Jordan's other three cars were Martin Brundle, Roberto Guerrero and Allen Berg. The night before the race Ayrton went to dinner with his new team-mates and, in an atmosphere of camaraderie, let loose, drinking more than he should have. I don't know what they did afterwards, although I can imagine, because they returned to the hotel very late. The next morning, Senna arrived at the track at the last minute for the warm-up, but he pushed hard immediately. He seemed unaffected by the unusual evening. And yet, when the session was over, he came up to me: "Listen Jo, I feel sick and I need to go back to the hotel to get some sleep. Please come and wake me up in time for the race." And while he was explaining what I had to do, he handed me the room key: "Don't just knock on the door, because when I'm asleep not even cannonballs wake me up. Come in and stay until I'm dressed and on my feet. We'll go back to the track together." I can confirm that Senna was a real sleepyhead, I even had to shake him to wake him up: "I'm better now, let's go win the race!" Which he promptly did, as if the wild night had never happened. After that experience, we stayed in touch and spoke regularly on the phone when we weren't on the track. I was looking forward to Ayrton coming to race for McLaren. I knew it would only be a matter of time.'

What memories do you have of Ayrton 30 years later?

Well, the memories are mostly positive, although there have also been stories worth forgetting over the years. If I had to recall one in particular, I would think of the last GP he raced for McLaren. It was the 1993 Australian GP in Adelaide which, of course, he won. He was already on the grid, strapped into the cockpit of his MP4/8. I noticed that he was gesticulating and not speaking, although we were connected by radio. So I approached him. I thought he needed assistance to get his seatbelts tightened, although he usually took great care in doing this himself, pulling on them with both hands. Once I approached, he pulled me close to him with one arm: 'You know what? I am not prepared for what is happening. This is my last start with McLaren: it still doesn't seem real to me.'

'And you say that *to me?*' I answered emotionally. 'You are probably not aware that this GP has a special flavour: apart from closing the collaboration with you, there is also a statistic that will have historical value.'

He gave me a quizzical look: McLaren and Ferrari had arrived in Adelaide with 103 victories each; whoever won the Australian GP would become the leader: 'If you win this race, Ayrton, I will love you forever!'

I had barely finished my sentence when I saw his eyes become moist with tears. I thought I had messed it up, because I had upset him a few moments before the start. Ayrton was an easily emotional Latino, but he had the extraordinary ability to regain control of himself immediately. Senna, of course, did not miss the opportunity to impose himself in his own way, in a big way, by taking his 35th victory with McLaren on the very day his most bitter rival, Alain Prost, retired from F1 with his fourth world title.

That special Sunday had not ended yet, because the organisers of the Australian GP had also arranged a concert with Tina Turner. The American singer, a great Ayrton fan, had invited the Brazilian and Jo Ramirez, who recalls: 'She had reserved two seats for us in the front row. During the amazing performance, Tina came down to the stalls and brought Ayrton on stage before singing "Simply the Best". I still get chills when I think about it, because the audience went crazy and started to sing the song with an excited, a very excited Senna. That moment sublimated Ayrton's greatness, however much it marked the end of a story.'

Japanese GP 1989. Senna attacks Prost at the chicane and the Frenchman, surprised by the manoeuvre, closes: contact is inevitable.

The McLaren team pays tribute to Ayrton: the Brazilian won the 1993 Australian GP in Adelaide, his last race with the Woking team.

At this point, Jo goes quiet for a moment and, after pondering for a couple of seconds in silence, eventually adds: 'Even if he had decided to go to Williams to get into the best car, Ayrton would always remain a McLaren driver. His heart was tied to Woking. Ron Dennis and I were certain that Senna would return home sooner or later.'

Well, meanwhile, after six years your driver was leaving …
Look, you remind me of an episode: it was mid-August and we were returning from the Hungarian GP after Ayrton had retired with an engine problem. He offered me a ride to Monte Carlo on his private jet, since I was going to spend a few days with my family in Saint Tropez, before going to Spa-Francorchamps for the Belgian GP. Before I boarded the plane, Ron Dennis told me: 'Jo, you have *carte blanche* from me: convince Senna not to go to Williams. Try by any means.' I really wanted to try, but just a few words from Ayrton were enough for me to understand that I had no arguments: 'I've won with Lotus, I've won world championships with McLaren and now the time has come for me to try and win with another team.' I was taken aback: I remained mute, speechless.

Ramirez knew that Senna's idol was Juan Manuel Fangio, the Argentine who won five titles with four different teams in the 1950s. The Brazilian considered him to be the greatest driver ever, because he had been able to get into the most competitive single-seater every time, not tying his success to one team in particular: 'I believe he would have returned to McLaren after the cycle of victories in the Williams, and I would add that he would have ended his F1 career at Ferrari,' insists Ramirez. 'But there was no time to see this coming. We saw what happened …'

Was the move to Williams dictated only by the desire to get into the best single-seater or was there also a strong economic motivation?
I can say that Ayrton earned more at McLaren, it was not money that drove him to Didcot. It was even rumoured that he had offered himself to Williams for free. If I have to be honest, I have never believed those rumours, which always sounded like idle talk to me, given that, in his last year with us, he was getting paid $1 million a GP by Dennis!

In fact, Senna believed that a driver's value was determined not only by the number of world titles and victories, but also by his capability to negotiate a higher salary than anyone else. Dollars were therefore not so much a currency to spend (he did not need it), but the recognition of a status that amplified his value, not only as 'the highest paid F1 driver', but one of the best paid sportsmen in the world.

In 1993, his last year at McLaren, Ayrton agreed to race with a contract of $1 million per race. The agreement had to be renewed after every GP. Dennis did not have an official engine, since he had lost the support of Honda, but only a low-powered Ford HB customer engine, and while waiting to find another place in the Circus, Senna listened to the advice of his friend Gian Carlo Minardi to race on a 'fee' basis. 'The 1993 season was a very tough one,' recalls Ramirez, 'because Ayrton would not leave Brazil if his personal account was not credited with the agreed sum. And Ron had to make sure that the banks working with McLaren could transfer the money in time for the next race. Believe me, it was stuff for nervous breakdowns! At Imola we risked him skipping Friday practice because there was no internet, and the transfers were not as immediate as today. Ayrton made it in time to board the last flight to Rome and arrived in Fiumicino early on Friday morning, having slept little or not at all on an overnight flight.'

Dennis realised that his driver would be late for the first free practice session starting at 10am. 'Ron ordered me to pick up Ayrton with the McLaren plane,' explains Jo, 'yet they didn't let me land at Fiumicino, but at Ciampino airport, which was not far away. I had some time to spare and I took a taxi to go and welcome Senna as soon as he disembarked from the scheduled flight. The taxi driver made a good impression on me and so I asked him if he could wait for me to take Ayrton back to Ciampino, so that I wouldn't have to queue for another vehicle.

'"Fine by me," replied the driver, "but I can't stop, because I would have to respect the priority of my colleagues, so I will keep going until I see you appear from the arrivals."

'I replied, "Since you seem like a nice person, I'll leave you my briefcase with all the documents: don't vanish because otherwise we'll blow the first practice session at Imola and it will be chaos."

'I got out and ran all the way to the steps of the Varig plane, and Senna was the first to get out of the aircraft with the luggage. In a moment we were outside the airport looking for the taxi driver, but there was no sign of the car.

"'Where is the driver?" Ayrton asked. "Has he disappeared?"

"'Don't worry,' I replied, "he'll be making yet another round and he'll be here in a minute."

'And yet, after five interminable minutes, no one had showed up and Senna had become very impatient: "Let's get another taxi, otherwise you'll make me late for the track."

"'That's not possible," I replied in annoyance, "I've left my jacket and briefcase with my wallet in it and also your licence and the McLaren licence in the taxi."

"'Jo, you are crazy!" added the increasingly nervous Brazilian. "How can you trust the first Italian taxi driver you meet? We won't see him again and I won't be able to practise today!"

"'Are you kidding me? You're the one who drives us crazy at every race by leaving Brazil at the last minute! If you like to put it down hard, then let me remind you that you should have been at Imola already last night, to be fresh this morning and get in the car!"'

That was the first and only time the Mexican manager yelled at the driver he adored. Time passed inexorably and Jo realised he was in a cul-de-sac: the two of them took another taxi and were not speaking to each other again, sulking: 'I was pissed off at Ayrton,' Ramirez adds, 'but I was also very worried because I had no documents and no money. We arrived at Ciampino and the commander of our private plane had already started up the engines in an attempt not to waste time, since back then it was allowed to get as far as the plane steps with a car. Senna, despite himself, had paid for the taxi. We had just boarded the plane, when we saw in the distance a taxi rushing up, with the driver showing my jacket from the window. As I had guessed, he was an honest person, who had understood my plight and had come to Ciampino to return my wallet and documents.'

After a few minutes of mutual embarrassment, sitting opposite each other, the two, who were great friends, began to laugh loudly, almost as if to relieve the tension that had built between them: 'We had a beer in the air,' Jo recalls, 'before landing at Forlì, where a helicopter would take us immediately to Imola. We arrived at the racetrack just in time for the start of practice.'

Ayrton ran to change at the McLaren motorhome, while the team manager went to the stewards to complete the checks. 'The session was short-lived,' Jo continues, 'because Ayrton spun after a few laps. He had slept little and was suffering from jet lag. He was also still very nervous about the adventure we had experienced in the morning. But the important thing was that we had arrived on time.'

In 1993 Senna was astonishing, because with the McLaren MP4/8, equipped with the Ford HB engine capable of just 720 horsepower, 50 less than the V10 Renault mounted on Alain Prost's Williams FW15C, he won five GPs, finishing second in the World Championship: 'It was all down to him,' Ramirez recounts, 'and he had reached the top in the European GP at Donington. In the dry the Williams were uncatchable, but at the start it was raining and Ayrton was only fifth immediately after the start. In the wet Senna had no opponents, he was overwhelmingly superior. He overtook all the others like they weren't there and, after giving us the best first two laps in the history of F1, he took the lead with an embarrassing advantage over the Williams. That was his masterpiece race: he left us speechless, in awe of his astonishing talent.'

The Mexican manager was a great supporter of Senna. He knew his immense talent, but also his flaws. Ayrton knew how to take to the limit virtues that, in certain cases, could turn into problems. Ayrton's driving philosophy can be summed up in a famous phrase: 'There is no corner where you cannot overtake.' For the Brazilian, this was a mantra that characterised his career from his karting days. It was an attitude that made him relentless with his opponents: 'He won many races with this determined approach,' continues Jo, 'but he also lost some, because every now and then he brought out one of his flaws: he was terribly impatient. In 1988 we would have won all the GPs of the season with the MP4/4 if, during the Italian GP at Monza, he had not wanted to force an overtaking move on Jean-Louis Schlesser, who was lapped, at the *Prima Variante*. He had such an advantage that he could have waited to get out of the corner, but instead, Ayrton came in hot and clumsily clipped the back of Schlesser's Williams, forcing his own retirement. He got caught up in the rush! Something similar had happened before in the 1990 Brazilian GP with Satoru Nakajima. The Japanese driver in the Tyrrell ruined the nose of Senna's car, forcing him to make a pit stop while he was in the lead, so Ayrton had to be content with third place, leaving his rival Prost with the win.

Tina Turner during the concert after the Australian GP called Senna on stage, dedicating the song 'Simply the Best' to him.

Jo Ramirez was the team manager to whom Senna was closest: the Mexican remained a great friend even when the Brazilian had left McLaren.

In 161 GPs, the Brazilian won 41. But some mistakes have become famous, as well as some of his legendary wins. The most clamorous case remains his retirement at the 1988 Monaco GP: the Brazilian had humiliated Alain Prost on the streets of the Principality, giving him an impressive 1.427 seconds lead in qualifying with the same car. His pole position lap of 1:23.998 remained an example of his driving perfection, so much so that Prost, although second, had not even seen him through binoculars.

'In the race,' the manager recounts, 'Ayrton took the lead and, with a furious pace, built up a margin of almost a minute over Alain, who was slowed down for a long time by Gerhard Berger's Ferrari, which had preceded him at the start. Ron Dennis shouted at him repeatedly over the radio: "Slow down, slow down!" but Senna did not heed the order until, on lap 67, he slammed his McLaren into the Portier corner.' A wheel bent against the barriers and he was furious at having thrown away a certain victory. Instead of taking the pit road to explain the mistake to Dennis, he took the opposite direction, going straight home, since it was not far away: 'He did not want to admit he had made a mistake. Ayrton was living the Prost obsession: when he had arrived at McLaren, the Frenchman was the acclaimed number one, so Senna wanted to destroy his team-mate. When Alain had got past Berger he had raised his pace and Ayrton immediately retaliated by setting the fastest lap. But then he went too far: he knew he had messed up and hid. I only managed to talk to him late in the evening. I found him in tears and repeatedly calling himself stupid. He was merciless when someone in the team made a mistake, so you can imagine what he was like when he had to judge his own mistake.'

Senna and Prost? Like cat and dog ...
They did all sorts of things to each other, but I assure you that deep down they respected each other, and they did because they knew they were the best.

At least at the beginning of the story, at McLaren it seemed that the relationship between the two was collaborative. Then there was the rift in the 1989 San Marino GP.
At Imola there was an agreement not to battle in the first lap until the *Tosa* corner, then it would be open race. At the first start, Alain was in

front with Ayrton behind, but there was an interruption of the race due to Gerhard Berger's bang at *Tamburello*, which set his Ferrari on fire. At the second start Alain did not do well and Ayrton passed him before the *Tosa* braking, thus infringing the agreement. Alain was very disappointed and took it as a discourtesy. Prost got so nervous that he spun, but our McLaren was so superior that the Frenchman still managed to climb to second place. I remember that he refused to go to the press conference: 'I don't want to see anyone, because what I would say to journalists could be something wrong. I'd rather pay a fine, but I don't want to talk, I'll leave and run away from here. And I don't want anything to do with *that one* anymore.'

Ayrton had won his first GP of the season with McLaren: an important success to gain influence within the team, but one that risked having many drawbacks. How did the Brazilian justify himself?
He claimed he had understood that the pact allowed them to fight all the way to the *Tosa* corner, whereas the agreement was *after Tosa*. He had broken it, but Ayrton was a terrible liar. When he did tell one, it was in his eyes.

It had been up to Dennis to try to reconcile the rift between Prost and Senna, but that row at Imola created an incompatibility that later degenerated into a deep rivalry ...
Ron asked both of them to go to a test in Wales, because he wanted to talk to Senna and make it clear what the team's priorities were. The situation seemed to have formally improved, but from that race on, it was as if we had two separate teams within the same team. In the briefings, Alain's engineers spoke in whispers, so that Ayrton's engineers would not hear them and vice versa. In short, there was a practical risk of exchanging no data for the development of the car. In reality, the war was only being waged by the drivers: since the engineers worked for McLaren, as soon as the two left the circuit the engineers would then talk to each other. Believe me, it was not easy to manage that situation.

In 1989, the season did not start in the best way, because of an engine problem that was later brilliantly resolved ...
At the Brazilian GP, which opened the championship, we had brought as many as five single-seaters, two old MP4/4s in addition to the new

MP4/5s, because we wanted to offer the maximum to these two drivers fighting against each other: it was an enormous effort for the team, which was not understood. Ayrton, despite his difficulties, had taken pole, but after a collision with Berger he began to lose performance and positions, also due to an alleged engine problem. He got out of the car and left, furious, at the end of the race, without speaking to anyone. A journalist who saw the scene put a microphone in front of my mouth and asked me what had happened: 'There is nothing wrong with the car,' I replied in annoyance. Later, after Ayrton had heard my statement on the radio, he immediately called me on the phone shouting at the top of his voice: 'Jo, what do you know about the problems on the car? Was it you in the cockpit? You can't say such things!'

My reply was as calm as possible, because he was furious: 'Dear Ayrton, I stated what you heard because you did not want to tell us anything. You slipped out of the cockpit and left without wanting to talk to anyone. What was I supposed to do?'

The next day he showed up at the track as we were packing everything up: 'Ayrton, if you think I made a mistake, give me a punch …'

For a moment I thought he was going to punch me, but instead, he hugged me tightly and then we burst out laughing like a couple of kids. The bond that had been created was too strong: it could not be broken by one accident, but believe me, he was not an easy person to please.

How did such an easily susceptible guy react to Nelson Piquet's repeated accusations in the paddock that he was gay?
I never discussed it with him, because it was a subject that bothered him. It was a personal matter, very sensitive. I can assure you that Ayrton was not gay, because he had relationships with many women. If I had to give you my opinion, I would say that Nelson provoked him because he knew he was not as strong a driver as him, and Ayrton had a presence and a charm that Piquet did not have. Nelson had women because he was an F1 driver, Ayrton would have had them regardless. He was simply jealous. Full stop.

Jo Ramirez is one of the few people who got to know all the facets of Senna's complex personality. The now 83-year-old Mexican was not just the team principal of McLaren for Ayrton, but a sincere and trusted friend. The bond remained intact even when the Brazilian switched to

Williams. 'We had maintained an excellent relationship and spoke to each other at every race. On the Saturday before that terrible day he had sought me out: "Can I ask you a favour, Jo? We work in different teams, but we are friends. At Williams I'm probably the highest earner, but in the team there's no one to help me solve even the smallest personal problems. I would ask you if you could book me a helicopter to go to Forlì after the race, where my plane is. You know everyone here and speak the language well, do me this favour."

'"Of course, Ayrton. We are friends regardless of the flag we work for."

'And the next day I had seen him again at the drivers' briefing after the warm-up: he seemed charged up from having taken pole on Friday. The atmosphere was heavy because of Roland's death, but when I saw him hint at a smile, I approached him to dictate the helicopter's initials and the name of the pilot I still remember: Fumagalli. That was the last time I saw him. He was convinced he could take his first win for Williams. And Michael Schumacher, not far from us, commented that Ayrton was driving the car beyond its limits. And, unfortunately, in the afternoon we saw what happened.'

The Circus on Saturday at Imola was very shaken by the terrible qualifying accident in which Roland Ratzenberger, the Austrian driver in his very first Formula 1 season, had died ...
The front wing broke off and ended up under the front wheels of the Simtek: Roland crashed because the single-seater could no longer be steered. The driver had not wanted to return to the pits to do a check after a spin, we all thought that it was a shame to die for such a trivial reason. Having dinner with the McLaren engineers, we discussed the episode among ourselves and concluded that such a thing could never have happened to Ayrton, a driver with ten years' experience in GPs.

Why did you mention Ayrton?
Roland had passed away while he was in one of his first F1 races. And I don't know why the talk went to Ayrton: at the table we wondered what would happen if something similar had happened to Ayrton. It had been 12 years since Riccardo Paletti's death in a GP and eight since Elio De Angelis's death: nobody thought that people could still die in F1. Unfortunately, the Roman driver had had his accident during a test at Paul Ricard, without the rescue services normally in place at Grand

Prix races. If there had been a rapid fire service available on the spot, Elio would have escaped that accident and lived. I wonder why we came to talk about Senna?

In your opinion, did the steering column modification on the Williams take place at the factory or on the track at Imola?
I don't know, but for sure Alain also didn't like the closed cockpit that covered the steering wheel. Patrick Head [the Williams technical director] has a strong character and had told Prost that he had to drive the car as it was. To Ayrton, he had repeated the same thing: 'The steering wheel you like is too big, you have to adapt.'

Senna had reacted: 'I'm not driving this *fucking car!*'

So they had to modify it for him. He had told me about it, at a test I think, but I didn't give it any weight until the accident happened. They had worked on the column to avoid having to change the chassis but, unfortunately, the modification didn't work.

If the Brazilian champion had not been stabbed by the blade-shaped suspension arm, how would he have reacted?
Today I believe that Ayrton's fate was to be fulfilled on 1 May. Immediately after the crash I noticed a movement in his helmet and I was convinced he had got away with it. Then I went back to work, because I believed that the race would start again. I thought Ayrton might have a big headache, but I was sure he was OK. I turned a deaf ear to what they were saying around. It was Keke Rosberg who gave me the news: 'Have you heard? Ayrton is dead.'

I didn't want to believe him. I didn't want to see him, I preferred to remember him smiling. My imperative became to get away from Imola as soon as possible. There was an F1 charter leaving to Heathrow, and that journey was difficult. Later I decided to talk to Ayrton's father and mother, but it was a painful call. Milton was devastated.

Now that the pain has subsided, what remains of Ayrton?
Thirty years have passed, but his memory has not faded. On the contrary, even young people know Senna, a sign that the Brazilian champion is a myth that is passed on from generation to generation. He is still, as Tina Turner sang, 'Simply the Best'.

Is it true that Senna's relatives poked their noses into his romantic relationships with Adriane Galisteu and Xuxa Meneghel?
Ayrton's family had a bit of a problem, because they had not accepted Adriane, who was a model and had no blue blood, while Xuxa was a marketing operation. She was helped by Pelé: when you watched the programmes she did for the children she was a charmer. And I thought: '*Mamma mia*, this woman will be great for Ayrton.' But then, when I met her in person, I discovered that she was completely different. It was a relationship that served as publicity for both of them, but it was not destined to last. The relationship with Adriane, on the other hand, was very strong. I helped the director who made the film about Senna, and when I asked him why Adriane wasn't mentioned, he told me that Ayrton's family didn't even want to hear about it. But when you make a documentary about the life of a legend you cannot hide the truth: I was sure that Ayrton would have married Adriane. That's why I wanted nothing more to do with this film. And I heard that Alain also felt bad about how he appeared in that documentary, as he had also collaborated on the script. The villain of the story should have been Balestre [FISA president], not Alain.

And what about the affair with Carol Alt?
It lasted a while. She never came to any competitions so we never talked about it. We knew she was there. Adriane was also very reserved, she spoke Portuguese, a little bit of Spanish and Italian, but not English. So when she came to a GP, she felt out of place at McLaren. Ayrton's dad wasn't comfortable there either, he always preferred to go to Minardi.

Jo Ramirez is like Ayrton, he has eyes that speak. He is always cheerful and smiling, grateful for what life has given him, but when certain topics are touched upon he becomes serious, his words become more sparse and his gaze moistens. And it is best to leave him to his deepest memories, which he will never want to recount ...

CHAPTER 5

ASCANELLI AND THAT SILENT LAP IN THE HONDA NSX AT SUZUKA

'THE BEST way to find out if you can trust someone is to trust them.'

Ernest Hemingway never experienced the world of racing, but he was able to sum up in a few words such a complex relationship as that between driver and track engineer. It is a bond, indeed a mutual complicity, which is not easy to introduce into a simple working relationship. The driver usually does not choose the engineer: he finds him in the team where he decides to race. Only the best – and Ayrton Senna belongs among them – have the charisma to bring along their own trusted engineer, to create a climate of familiarity in the new team, with operating methods known and developed over time.

Once the engine has been switched off, the driver is called upon to explain his feelings about the car to the track engineer: in the briefing he has to describe, in as much detail as possible, the strengths and the flaws of the car, analysing its behaviour curve by curve, in order to suggest the changes the engineer should make to it, with a view to improving its performance or drivability. Some drivers just stick to transferring precise and analytical information, while others, based on the experience they have gained, even dare to suggest solutions. Some other drivers are particularly sensitive in their analysis of the vehicle, and are capable of being so precise in their information, that their meticulousness could 'split a hair in two'. And finally, there is no lack of natural talents, drivers of few words, who know how to cover up the shortcomings of the car with their acrobatic driving skills.

The relationship between driver and engineer has changed over time, with the introduction of ever more technology capable of reading and diagnosing data from hundreds of functions controlled on the car with sensors. Today, during a GP, there is not just a track engineer at work, but a whole group of about 50 engineers not operating physically in the paddock, but located in the team headquarters – the so-called 'factory' – in an environment called the 'remote garage', where they are following the car on monitors. A sort of *sancta sanctorum* where the individual vital functions of the single-seater are monitored in real time, thanks to high-powered computers connected in a network that also includes the car itself.

Ayrton Senna lived through the transition between old-fashioned motor racing, in which the driver's word was law, and an F1 with the most extreme telemetry. In the era of active suspension, bi-directional adjustments had been introduced, whereby engineers were not limited to reading information, but could freely intervene to modify set-up or engine parameters. In short, from the pits it was possible to change the behaviour of the car, thus altering the confidence of the driver, who would find himself racing a single-seater with different reactions to those he knew. This could become very dangerous: one wrong command was enough to cause an accident. Fortunately, the FIA has long since banned bi-directional telemetry, so that, today, drivers make the changes using the steering wheel computers at the radio suggestion of the engineers.

Senna was the prototype of the driver who contributed to the development of technologies: being a champion he was very fast, but he had acquired an extraordinary sensitivity that did not only show on the track, but also in the briefings, which could last hours with him. Fussy, perfectionist, by then devoted to that motto which, as already said, he had made his own: 'Driven to perfection'. A reminder that details could make all the difference.

At McLaren, the Brazilian had met engineer Giorgio Ascanelli. A native of Ferrara with a background in Ferrari, Benetton, McLaren, and then Ferrari again, before Prost GP and Toro Rosso, he has been nicknamed the 'engineer of champions' because, in addition to Ayrton, he has worked with other top drivers, including Nelson Piquet and Sebastian Vettel.

I didn't decide to involve Giorgio in this book because of this definition, from which he shies away, but because Ascanelli was among the first engineers to connect a computer to a single-seater, thus interpreting the role of track engineer in an innovative, modern way. Just the way the Brazilian liked it. Giorgio is a man of few words – resistant to gossip – who, at the age of 64, decided to retire: in the last chapter of his professional life he was the technical director of Brembo, the Bergamo-based multinational leader in braking systems, but he spent most of his working life out on the racetracks of the world.

Should the driver trust the track engineer?
I don't believe in a relationship established according to the roles. It is always a matter of people. There are people you get on with and others you don't. The driver has to decide whether he trusts the track engineer or not. We have to be aware of the fact some drivers always keep an ace up their sleeves. The same applies to the track engineer, for sure. Let's say that, even in modern and very recent times, this 'non-definition' of responsibility, this inability to define objective roles is a major limitation in operations. I am reminded of some lines from the film *A Few Good Men*, with the great Jack Nicholson and Tom Cruise, when they say: 'Have you ever served on the forward lines?'; 'No sir'; 'Have you ever put your life in someone else's hands?'; 'No sir'; 'In that case I don't give a shit what you do.'

There is a relationship of mutual trust to build. Sometimes it substantiates, sometimes not.

I called Ayrton a 'nice bastard': very tough with his visor down, an amiable and extraordinary man outside the cockpit. What was he like during the briefings? That's a part of his character we couldn't find out about ...
I disagree with the assessment that he was a big bastard when he lowered his visor. I think the best thing about Ayrton's life is summed up in a sentence in Bruce McLaren's book, when he talks about Timmy Mayer: 'In any kind of sport there are people who want to excel!' Does excelling mean being a bastard? Let's say we are part of a different world. And as Paolo Conte says, '... it was a grown-ups' world and you made mistakes in a professional way'. There was no room for ambiguity. If you could do something, you tried to do it to the best of your ability. Full stop. I remember a lovely person like Lee Gaug, head of Goodyear Sporting Activities, who grabbed Nigel Mansell by the neck when he spoke badly

about his tyres at Spa. It was another world. And similarly, it was Nigel who also grabbed Senna by the collar for a borderline manoeuvre. We are talking about another era. So much for the ethical world. It was a different one. I don't think they were bastards. Some were trying to do things the best they could, because it was terribly difficult to even try. You became manic, because it was like being at war. And then, at the end, you looked each other in the face: you said *bravo* to the winner, while the loser would try to do better the next time. Those were the rules that attracted me and that brought Ayrton into the sport. And 'Beco' [another nickname used among those who were close to the Brazilian] was able to do things better than the others.

How was your relationship in 1993?
The [mutual] appreciation came after we worked together for a while. It was obvious that he was not happy with the person who was there [at McLaren] before me. Ron Dennis sought me out twice to go and work for him: in the first case, when I left Ferrari in 1989, he didn't have a vacancy for me, so I chose to go to Benetton, while later I joined, because I was going back to work with Berger, who had left the *Cavallino* to go to Woking. Gerhard had the idea that McLaren's track engineers had something to learn from me and so I went there. And when Ayrton requested a change of engineer, Berger mentioned my name and he came looking for me.

When did you meet Senna for the first time?
It all started by chance and on a beautiful occasion. I think it was at the launch of the Honda NSX in 1989: the car was on display in the pit lane at Suzuka, and I liked it a lot. I remember I had scrutinised it carefully: I had been lying on the ground, I had looked at it from the front, underneath, to the side and behind, and after a while, when I had already resumed work, I saw this car arrive in front of the garage. The door opened and a finger beckoned to me as if to say: 'Get in with me?' It was Ayrton inviting me to take a lap of Suzuka in the NSX. That's how we met. It's something I've never told …

What made him do that?
It was obvious that I liked the car. The link was the new Honda. We didn't say anything in particular to each other, except comments about

the Japanese car, which was extraordinary. I was not even in my thirties and I was travelling the world to see how it span around. I can say that Ayrton drove the whole lap in a very responsible manner, devoting all his attention to the car.

When did you start working together?
The debut with Ayrton was in a test at Silverstone, before we left for South Africa. We started to talk to each other and get to know one another better. The relationship started off well: 'More wing, less wing. Lower, higher. Softer, harder.'

Was it the driver who dictated the solution to the problem, or did he point out the behaviour of the car and then wait for the track engineer to find an answer?
Ayrton would tell you what he had on the car and what he wanted on the car, except when he wasn't sure. Everything developed quite quickly, because the MP4/7 was late and the MP4/6 was not good enough to challenge Williams, although it had won the World Championship the year before. I remember one Saturday afternoon after qualifying – at that time you could still change the set-up before the race – he said to me: 'I want to have this, that and the other thing done.' I took note in silence. Only after a long pause did he ask me: 'But what's your take?'

I replied: 'Half of the things you proposed make sense, the other half I would throw away and do differently.'

'When were you planning to say it to me?' he replied, and then I said: 'When you felt like listening to me!'

'Why don't we start right now?' Ayrton queried.

That's how our beautiful collaboration started. You need to build up a relationship. You may disagree with a driver about his choices, but you've got to say it in the right way: if you disagree with them, you have at least to make sure you are right, or at least not wrong too often. You can't do any harm that way. It's statistics.

Is there always a fine line to maintain?
Um, 'always' and 'never' are words I hardly ever use. It depends on the driver standing in front of you: some just didn't want to poke their noses in my things. 'You're the engineer, I am the driver: you do it.' Some other drivers didn't accept the roles and got hurt. As for me, at the end of qualifying that day Ayrton had started with his barrage of requests,

and at that moment I hadn't understood yet if I was allowed to have an opinion or not.

Ayrton, therefore, was a driver used to dictating his list of changes. End of story?
A driver dictates the list when he doesn't trust who is around him. Fair enough. But I don't think that Ayrton was the only one to have this characteristic. It is a starting point for all drivers.

Until a relationship of trust is established with the track engineer...
This is bullshit. Because the question I have been asked more often is: 'Who decides when it's time to change the tyres and do a pit stop?' My answer has always been simple: 'The one who knows best.' There are things you know that the driver doesn't, and there are other things the driver knows and you don't.

And how do you resolve that?
Making decisions with sound judgement. There is no time for press conferences, you have to have trust. Can you imagine what would happen otherwise? What happened with Senna in the 1992 Belgian GP, which was also Michael Schumacher's first victory with Benetton on the wet track: Ayrton did a stint with slicks on the water, in which he was extraordinary. While the other drivers had pitted, he had decided to stay on the track because, according to him, the sun was about to come out again, so why would he go back into the pit lane to change tyres? He made a choice and he made a mistake. But it fitted. What didn't fit was that immediately afterwards the grumbling began.

Even the great can make mistakes...
At Donington 1993, in that fantastic lap that has gone down in F1 history, Ayrton had set the fastest lap going through the pit lane, but I have never said he was screaming on the radio because he wanted new tyres. We had already replaced them three times and we told him no, even though Prost in the Williams had stopped seven times. It's clear that if you say no to Ayrton Senna who is fighting to win an epic Grand Prix, then you'd better win it, because if you're wrong, then you've burnt your credibility. I remember when Ron saw Prost come back he signalled something to me but I shouted, 'No!'

1993 European GP at Donington: Senna's masterpiece race, in the wet, leaving every other driver trailing in his wake. Here he is overtaking Prost driving the Williams and beginning his solo ride.

THE BEST WAY TO FIND OUT IF YOU CAN TRUST SOMEONE IS TO TRUST THEM.

You overrode the team principal's opinion?
No, Ron was evaluating his feelings, while I took responsibility for the decision. And in that moment either you are right or you're wrong. There is no alternative. It's like when you play cards: if you can remember all the hands and how your opponent behaves, knowing which cards have already been played, you can find ways to win. And if you can't find them, you'd better get up from the table and go do another job.

We can say that Ayrton changed the way he worked with the engineers: while other drivers finished their briefing with them and went on to something else, can it be said that Senna was willing to stay at the racetrack until the evening?
This is a very important aspect: he gave total availability. Perhaps Beco's most distinctive point was that he could maintain a high level of concentration for a very long time. For him, any detail could be important to do better. At the end of one of his quarter-hour speeches in which I hadn't understood anything, I might even say to him: 'Please start again.' And Ayrton would start from scratch. He always took his time, because he was aware that he would need it. He understood that communication alone was not enough. If you want someone to do something for you, you have to take the time to make them understand what you want.

When complicity was established between you, did the method of communication change?
No, because Ayrton was a person used to working in a structured way. It's customary for a driver to jump out of the car and tell you immediately the thing that bothers him most at that moment, which isn't necessarily the most important or the right one. Let's not forget those were the early years when we had started to have telemetry data. Before that there wasn't much in the way of data. That was my strength, if you like. In 1982 I had graduated in mechanical structure assisted performance, so I was involved in mathematical models, physical models, calculation, computers and data. Engineering is nothing more than measuring variables to find performance as a function of how things move. So I was playing on home turf from that point of view. Certainly, I was the first one in F1 to bring my computer on the track to connect to the car [in the pits]. The others didn't have it.

When did it start?
In 1987, before the McLaren experience. I was known as 'the man with the computer'. But the relationship of trust is a human aspect that is won with time, day by day. I was very close with Gerhard and still am today. We are friends. During the Covid-19 period he used to call me and start the conversation like this: 'Are you still alive or dead already?'

A good start to touch base again …
Well, you know, I was the one who sent him against the *Tamburello* wall in 1989 …

It seems to me a somewhat extreme description: the front wing had broken on the Ferrari 640, causing Berger to go off the track. That accident, perhaps, finds some analogy with that of Roland Ratzenberger …
But that was my car; that was his car …

Giorgio, you give me the shivers listening to you …
What shivering are you talking about? We must tell the truth and the facts speak for themselves.

Sure, but hearing Patrick Head, or reading Adrian Newey's autobiography and his take about the Senna tragedy, I didn't get the feeling that either of them thought of the FW16 as 'my car'.
My father was born in 1922 and on 7 September 1944 he delivered the *Fortezza dal Basso* into the hands of General Alexander [Italian anti-regime militias had liberated Florence, and symbolically delivered the city's iconic *Fortezza* to the Allies, led by Alexander]. He was 22 years old. Full stop. I jealously guard a photograph at home. The buck-passing ends here. There are always things that can be done better and more accurately. I still have in my eyes the moment when Gerhard returned to the track at Fiorano, 30 days after the accident, on 23 April 1989. He put on the suit, which incidentally was the same one from the crash. I turned white and got goose bumps. I'm not a genius, I'm a clown who collects memories.

The last time Ayrton was tempted to go to Ferrari, it seems he wanted Giorgio Ascanelli on the team …
I don't know. I have no idea if this was really the case.

Yet Senna would have wanted to count on people he could trust in Maranello...
I can believe this. He trusted me, as I trusted him. Full stop. It happened with Piquet, with Berger. With Beco to a greater extent, with others to a lesser extent. It depends on your interpretative ability, but it's better not to build a case on this rumour, because I really don't know a thing about it.

But, who was the Ayrton you met?
A very intelligent man. Not one who changed whether he wore a helmet or took it off. He was one inspired by his motto: 'Driven to perfection'. He tried to do everything well. Humanly speaking, he was very enjoyable to know, when he got to the point of trust. Someone as famous as him knew very well that he could not give too much away. He did not reveal himself too often, because he knew that he could be attacked. It fits for a character who has always lived in the public eye.

He would open up only with people he trusted...
This is the behaviour of great people, who have a very high public image and who are not fools. Why would he expose himself to petty controversy over confidences to the wrong people? I agree with his attitude. Besides, the man was very reserved. Precisely because he was very exposed, he liked to be cautious.

You mentioned Nelson Piquet earlier, and to me he doesn't seem to fall into this category...
Nelson is a jolly fellow, in the end he was not so different from Ayrton, although he was a talkative guy...

The two could not stand each other, in fact, perhaps they hated each other...
They did not. Of course they were taking the piss. Which of them was the fastest gun in the West? Nelson was great, but with the arrival of Ayrton he had begun to suffer. A younger Brazilian driver had arrived in F1 with a higher appetite for risk than he had. It is clear that they played psychological games with each other in the press.

Well, Piquet's play when he had called Ayrton 'bicha', homosexual, was very heavy...
I don't know the full story. Nelson wanted to hit and Senna cashed in, but I don't think they hated each other. Piquet is irreverent and you have

to take him as he is, otherwise you have to ignore him. But I remember that, in 1990, at the Japanese GP, during the drivers' briefing in the presence of Jean-Marie Balestre, FISA president, while commenting on the events of the year before, Nelson said that the world title had been stolen from Ayrton. And this was not a joke, but an important stance. And it was certainly not an action against Senna. Great personalities must be allowed to play. Great rivalries are built when you build a good story. But how real such rivalries are is not easy to fathom.

Did you also get to see Alain Prost up close?
Alain knew how to play with words. If I remember correctly, the discord between the two had begun at Imola: after a restart, Senna passed Prost before the *Tosa* corner, while there was an agreement that they would not battle until after that corner. Ayrton didn't have this kind of ... finesse, but then he learned it.

After Suzuka 1 [in 1989], *Alain had made the episode weigh heavily on Senna* [by getting him disqualified] *but he received a reaction the following year at Suzuka 2 ...*
Well, sure, we discovered another Ayrton in the Suzuka episodes which decided the two world championships, but with another style, in his own way. The difference was great. A guy who doesn't take his foot off the accelerator and then gets out of the cockpit and says: 'Some win a World Championship in the Japanese GP at the last corner of the penultimate lap, some others win it at the first corner of the first lap.' There was a totally different approach. One whines, cries, calls his mum, the other is silent. To my friends, to my colleagues, to my fellow travellers I have always repeated it like a mantra: 'Think about the facts, never think about emotions.' Facts are already difficult, don't waste unnecessary energy chasing emotions as well.

Races are characterised by facts, but they are driven by emotions ...
Everyone does what is in their own capabilities. I think a lot of energy is wasted chasing emotions that could better be used by just dwelling on the facts. I believe that things need to be resolved regardless of who is at fault. Someone said: 'To forgive is for kings, to forget is for fools.' It is so ...

When you saw Ayrton's accident what did you think?
We knew something serious had happened, because he didn't restart. I had a race to run. I asked what was going on and the thing that comes to my mind, thinking back to that moment, is no different from what I remember about 1989 [Berger's crash at *Tamburello*]: total silence on the circuit. Everyone was silent. But then we had a job to do, and we did it. I realised that Ayrton had died only when I was on the plane: Ron told me. That is also part of the job. It is not cynicism. Far from it. The person who was closest to me in those moments was Tyler Alexander: on Monday I processed the tragic news very badly. The next day was very difficult for me. We, at McLaren, were testing a power steering system that we hadn't used yet: we found ourselves race-testing after such an accident. We did it, but it was hard, very hard …

CHAPTER 6

FIORIO: HERE'S HOW I CONVINCED SENNA TO COME TO FERRARI

'NOTHING IS easier than disappointing oneself. For man believes true what he desires.'

Ayrton Senna did not pay heed to Demosthenes, the greatest Greek orator. The Brazilian's story with Ferrari never blossomed, although, as we shall see later, several attempts had been made over time to bring Magic to Maranello. If Enzo Ferrari's first call in 1986 had seemed premature, Cesare Fiorio's in 1990 had given hope. The first one had come unexpectedly, which is why Ayrton had preferred to stay for a third year at Lotus. However, the 99T equipped with the V6 Honda Turbo seemed less brilliant than the single-seater of the previous year: in qualifying he had achieved only one pole position compared to eight in 1986 and seven in 1985, but Senna nevertheless managed to finish the 1987 season in third position, behind Nelson Piquet (Williams) and Nigel Mansell (Williams), thanks to two wins and eight podiums.

It was Ron Dennis who benefited from Senna's decision: he persuaded Ayrton to join McLaren instead and the Brazilian would become world champion for the first time with them in 1988. The extraordinary MP4/4 dominated the World Championship, winning 15 out of the 16 GPs on the calendar: eight wins for Senna against the seven of his team-mate Alain Prost, a tough adversary who felt himself ousted in the hierarchies of the Woking team by the newcomer, starting a deep no-holds-barred rivalry that would animate F1 for years.

In 1988, at the venerable age of 90, Enzo Ferrari died: he went quietly, while the whole of Italy was on holiday. He died on 14 August and in his last will and testament, penned in purple ink, he had ordered the funeral to be held at 6am. It was mid-August, and only relatives and a very small group of friends and collaborators attended.

Ferrari, therefore, had to change its skin: it was no longer the founder's baby. It had to find a new dimension without betraying its history, which had made King Enzo a myth even in his lifetime. Less than a month after the engineer's death, an unexpected victory arrived with a one-two finish by Gerhard Berger and Michele Alboreto at the Italian GP.

The surprise victory aboard the F1/87-88C was dedicated to the *Commendatore Enzo Ferrari*, while the undisputed leader of the race, Senna, had been forced to retire due to an accident that had occurred two laps before the chequered flag. The Brazilian, in fact, at *Prima Variante* had suddenly found the Williams of the lapped Jean-Louis Schlesser in front of him – an admired French driver in Endurance races, who was making his debut in F1 – and had not managed to avoid the collision. Schlesser, considering the type of car he was used to and his driving style, was a fish out of water, while Ayrton, on that left-right bend of the circuit, did not want to lose any time, even though he had a big advantage over his pursuers. Waiting was not his style and aggressiveness was his strength. If he spotted the slightest space he had to jump into it. Most of the time it suited him well, but not in this case, at Monza. Schlesser had arrived long on the braking with smoking tyres and, instead of going straight into the escape route, had tried to turn into the chicane, hitting the right side of Senna's car. The Brazilian, following the contact, had gone into a tailspin and his McLaren had gone off the track, perching on the kerb with its wheels off the ground. Ayrton had not taken his opponent's possible mistake into account and paid heavily for his exuberance.

In March 1989, Ferrari appointed Cesare Fiorio as head of the team, to give the sports team management a new look. Before his death, Enzo had appointed McLaren's John Barnard as technical director, while the drivers were Gerhard Berger and Nigel Mansell. The Englishman had won the Brazilian GP on debut with the famous 'duck', the single-seater equipped with a semi-automatic gearbox with two paddles behind the steering wheel, without the traditional lever

NOTHING IS EASIER THAN TO DECEIVE ONESELF. BECAUSE MAN BELIEVES WHAT HE DESIRES TO BE TRUE.

on the right side of the cockpit. A revolution that would set a standard, not only in racing cars.

At this point Angelo Orsi, photographer for *Autosprint* and a trusted friend of the champion, was called into action. Cesare Fiorio was trying to establish contact with Ayrton, without creating too much fuss: 'The idea had originated as soon as I arrived at Ferrari in 1989,' explains Fiorio, 'because Ayrton was the best driver around for me: not only did I want him as a driver for the *Cavallino*, but I also wanted to take him away from the competition.

'I received a call from Franco Liistro, head of communication for the Fiat Group Sporting Activities,' recounts Orsi. 'I was informed that Fiorio wanted to meet Ayrton with the intention of bringing him to Ferrari, but the contact had to remain secret, otherwise a big mess would have arisen. I took a few days and talked it over with Ayrton, who made himself available for a meeting on the Friday of the Monaco GP. That

GESTIONS SPORTIVES S.A.
############
############
SWITZERLAND

9th July 1990

Ayrton Senna da Silva
Apartment No 3
Block B
9th Floor
Houston Palace
2 Avenue Psse Grace
Monte Carlo
Monaco

Dear Sir

Following our various meetings we hereby summarise the current position of our negotiations for you to drive exclusively for the Ferrari Team in the FIA Formula One World Championships in 1991 and 1992.

We have reached agreement in principle on the following points:-

1. You will be paid consideration of US$ ######## in respect of the calendar year 1991 and US$ ######## in respect of calendar year 1992.

2. You will be paid a bonus of US$ ######## each time you win the FIA Formula One World Championship in 1991 or 1992.

3. You will be provided free of charge at the Ferrari Factory with the following new road cars:

   1991: An F40 and your choice of a Testarossa, a Mondial, and a 348;
   1992: An F4? (or equivalent car of your choice) and your choice of a Testarossa, a Mondial and a 348.

4. You will be provided free of charge with a Ferrari Formula One car utilised by you during the 1991 season. This car to be provided in full working order and bearing race identification at such time as it becomes no longer directly technically relevant to the future development of the Ferrari Formula One car.

Cont...

Ayrton Senna/Page 2 /9.7.90

The following issues remain open and subject to resolution to our mutual satisfaction:-

a) Nacional:

b) Steve Nichols:

c) Insurance:

d) Nigel Mansell/the length of your commitment:

e) Formula One car 1992:

We confirm that this document sets forth the current position in our negotiations and does not create any binding legal commitment. However we would be grateful if you would sign the enclosed copy of this letter and return it to us to confirm your interest in proceeding with negotiations on the terms set forth above.

Yours faithfully

FOR AND ON BEHALF OF
GESTIONS SPORTIVES S.A.

AYRTON SENNA DA SILVA

The draft contract that Fiorio proposed to Senna to become a Ferrari driver in 1991. The Brazilian had set five conditions, but nothing came of them.

was the day off, when F1 wasn't practising, so in the afternoon I had nothing to do.'

It was not going to be easy to organise a meeting that had to remain top secret in the middle of the Grand Prix weekend ...
It was actually less complicated than it seems. I knew Fiorio, who was a great friend of Carlo Cavicchi, editor of *Autosprint*. At 4pm sharp I went to *Rascasse* in my car, since the track was not closed and the circulation was free. I waited for Cesare to come out of the paddock and we went to Senna's home together. I parked in front of the Houston Palace on Avenue Princess Grace, where Ayrton had a flat on the ninth floor. We walked along until we were sure no one was around, and then we got into the lift to Ayrton's place, and he was waiting for us at the door. After a brief formal introduction, I left the two of them in the study, while I went to the terrace so that they could talk freely. The conversation was very brief, just a few seconds. When Cesare came out of the room, he told me he did not need to be driven back, because the Ferrari hotel was close by and he would walk.

It had been a lightning-fast meeting. After the hesitations with Enzo Ferrari, the second approach from Maranello had been more than rapid ...
'I offered him a contract,' Fiorio says, 'but he replied that he already had an agreement with McLaren for 1990 so he couldn't back out, but he was very interested in coming to Ferrari and we would talk about it again.'

Senna was very impressed by Fiorio: 'Gee! He's a determined guy, your friend from Ferrari!' he said to Orsi. 'It's not a finished conversation, because we will talk again.'

The photographer then left the scene. He had done his part, so that the two could catch up with each other without the need for intermediaries. The year 1989 passed in anticipation of more propitious moments. Cesare Fiorio, meanwhile, took on Alain Prost, who had left McLaren, slamming the door and taking the number 1 with him to Maranello, to be affixed to the bodywork of his single-seater as reigning world champion.

The 1990 season was only just beginning, but Fiorio did not want to waste any time in securing the services of the best. The Brazil GP was the second on the schedule after the opener in the United States at Phoenix: at Interlagos Alain gained his first success with Ferrari, aboard the 641.

'While the team was returning to Maranello,' Fiorio reveals, 'I remained in São Paulo and on Monday I went to Senna's house for an exchange of ideas: I wanted to have him in the team in 1991. The most incredible thing about that meeting was that he didn't turn up with a manager, a lawyer or a consultant. He was alone, as I was alone. There was no one else in the house, so we talked freely. It was a very deep negotiation, in which we identified the points of contact that we could develop. We agreed on almost everything, except for a couple of aspects that could not be discussed. The first concerned a sponsor that Ayrton had on the chin guard of his helmet, Nacional: I had to check if it could be accepted by Marlboro, therefore that aspect would have to be discussed with Philip Morris [International, which owns Marlboro]. The other issue we couldn't define concerned the car designer: Senna wanted to bring Steve Nichols to Ferrari at all costs. In the meantime, however, I had already made a super-secret contract with Steve, which obviously could not be disclosed immediately, otherwise the switch from one team to another could be blown. Only Steve and I knew the detail of the agreement: Nichols came to Maranello afterwards and duly fulfilled the contract.'

And what happened with Ayrton?
Senna sent me a draft contract with all the points we had discussed. Back then there were no emails, documents were sent by fax. He sent it to me from Monte Carlo, a clear sign that he had accepted my proposals.

But was there a date for this agreement?
Sure enough, 17 July, after the French Grand Prix, another race Ferrari won. It was held at Le Castellet and, instead of going directly to Paul Ricard, I went down to Nice in a rented car to meet Senna again at his home in the Principality, where we also defined the contractual aspects that had remained pending in Brazil.

It all sounds simple: the negotiation was very straightforward, but there was a problem…
Before activating this operation, at a meeting of Ferrari's board of directors, I had presented this idea of mine, which was accepted, but with a budget limit set at a certain figure.

And what was the size of the budget?
I don't want to divulge the figure, but I can say that I only offered Senna 30 per cent of what was authorised to me by the Ferrari board.

Although 30 years have passed, Cesare Fiorio did not want to talk about money, but at the time there were rumours in the newspapers of around $15 million per season. A record amount, but the Piedmontese manager had an enormous margin for negotiation.

'Yes, it is true,' he confirmed, 'because I had gambled on a couple of benefits that interested Ayrton: he wanted an F40, a car that he liked very much, and a specimen of the F1 single-seater in which he would have raced, coming to Maranello. We defined in the agreement that he would only get it a few years later, when it would no longer be replicated as a concept. Those were the aspects we had focused on.'

Was Ferrari's chairman at the time, Piero Fusaro, fully aware, being part of the board of directors, that this negotiation with the Brazilian champion existed?
Of course he knew, but in his heart he didn't believe I would complete it. And here's the sequel to the problem: Fusaro was going through a moment in which he was particularly 'suffering', let's say, because he was at the top of the *Cavallino* but no one was considering him.

Did everyone want to talk only to Cesare Fiorio?
When it comes to Formula 1, certainly yes.

So what did he do?
Since I had completed this super-secret negotiation, Fusaro thought it best to call Alain Prost to tell him that his team principal, as we say today, was plotting behind his back. Obviously the Frenchman didn't like it, and then Fusaro also thought it best to warn Philip Morris, who were sponsors of both Ferrari and McLaren. Fusaro set off a bomb, promising Alain that as long as he was president of Ferrari, Senna would not set foot in Maranello. I suddenly found myself in great difficulty, because the man who was my chosen driver at the time could no longer have any trust in me, and there was turbulence within the team as well.

But was the initial idea to form the Senna-Prost pair that had already exploded at McLaren, or to bet on Riccardo Patrese to be put alongside the Brazilian?

Prost would never have agreed to race with Senna again so I had put all my eggs in Riccardo's basket, who had won two world titles with my cars in the Prototypes, and with whom I had established an excellent relationship. Ayrton would also have appreciated having him as team-mate. I remember that more than once Senna said: 'In spite of the past, I want a very fast team-mate, because if I were to finish behind him in qualifying, that would mean that I haven't done my job properly.' I had proposed Riccardo to him and he had supported this candidature, also because he held the Paduan in high esteem.

Once again, the dream of bringing Senna to Ferrari was shattered at the moment when it looked likely to be achieved.
The situation at Maranello had deteriorated and I realised it was better to leave the Prancing Horse.

Ayrton wasted no time, because on 17 August 1990 he extended his agreement with McLaren.

In the August 2020 issue of *Quattroruote*, Carlo Cavicchi revealed a tasty behind-the-scenes story in which Piero Fusaro himself explained that '... Prost had asked Gianni Agnelli, the *Avvocato* [literally 'lawyer', the head of Fiat and Ferrari], for a private interview and obtained reappointment for 1991. It was the *Avvocato*'s decision. It was not possible to bring Senna with Prost's confirmation, given the bad relations between the two after their years at McLaren, so everything was off.'

Cesare Fiorio, even today, disagrees with this interpretation of the facts: 'No, it can't be. Maybe people don't know it, but I was on very good terms with Gianni Agnelli and he would certainly have told me about such a thing. I absolutely exclude that there may have been such a contact. It's more likely that Fusaro organised a meeting between Prost and Cesare Romiti, but certainly not with the *Avvocato*, with whom I used to speak at least once a week.'

The Piedmontese adds: 'Fusaro can tell people around whatever he wants, but I can say that his position in this affair was as negative as possible, and when I realised that I could no longer act as I had always done in 40 years in this capacity, I decided to leave Ferrari. The result was that Ayrton did not come to Maranello.'

So your exit from Ferrari, after just four GPs in the 1991 season, was caused by what happened with the Senna deal?
Of course. I realised that Fusaro had set me against Romiti, Marlboro and the driver, as well as part of the team. I had been totally delegitimised in my role, so I had no choice but to leave Ferrari.

Has Alain Prost never held this episode against you?
After I left Ferrari, the team had a three-year blackout of victories. Later that year also Fusaro and Alain were dismissed. However, I didn't leave F1 for good, so much so that in 1994 I was called to manage Ligier. Flavio Briatore, who had taken over the team, alongside Bernie Ecclestone probably, needed a manager to run it, so he sought me out. I accepted the proposal, but at some point the team was taken over by Prost. And everyone started telling me: 'Now you'll see that Alain will kick you out right away!' On the contrary, the French champion came to the Ligier factory and we sat around a table: he wanted to tell me his version of the facts about what had happened at Ferrari.

What was Prost's account?
Simply, Alain had been warned by Fusaro that I was taking on Senna. And I must say that he never made any hostile manoeuvres, although it was clear to me that he had suddenly become less cooperative with me than he had been up to that point. At the end of that very frank talk, Prost asked me to stay and work with him. In fact, we worked together for another year and a half.

Paradoxically, therefore, a relationship of trust was established in spite of what had happened at Ferrari: it was certainly an unusual ending …
Alain understood everything. And we moved on without having to talk about the past.

Back to Ayrton: how attracted was he by a Ferrari that had a semi-automatic gearbox, with paddles behind the steering wheel, instead of the traditional lever?
That was not the decisive element. For Ayrton what mattered, after the first months of inevitable poor reliability of the car, was to have a competitive single-seater, and above all one capable of winning races. Out of 36 GPs that I experienced at the head of Ferrari (mind that at the time there were not 23 or 24 races a season as there are now, but at most 16),

I had won nine, and 25 times we had got on the podium. It was a sign that we were always competitive.

Senna considered Ferrari ripe to aim for the title: the driver was a great supporter of Juan Manuel Fangio for his extraordinary ability to win five world championships with four different single-seaters. Ayrton would have liked to equal and beat the Argentinean's record...
That's right, and he had identified Ferrari as a team that would lead him to victory.

Too bad that even the second attempt to make the 'red dream' come true ended up in a cul-de-sac for Senna. For him, the possibility of joining Ferrari thawed like snow in the sun; while, at the end of 1991, Piero Fusaro and Alain Prost were also kicked out of the *Cavallino*, in addition to Cesare Fiorio.

Luca di Montezemolo was then called back to Maranello, but that's another story.

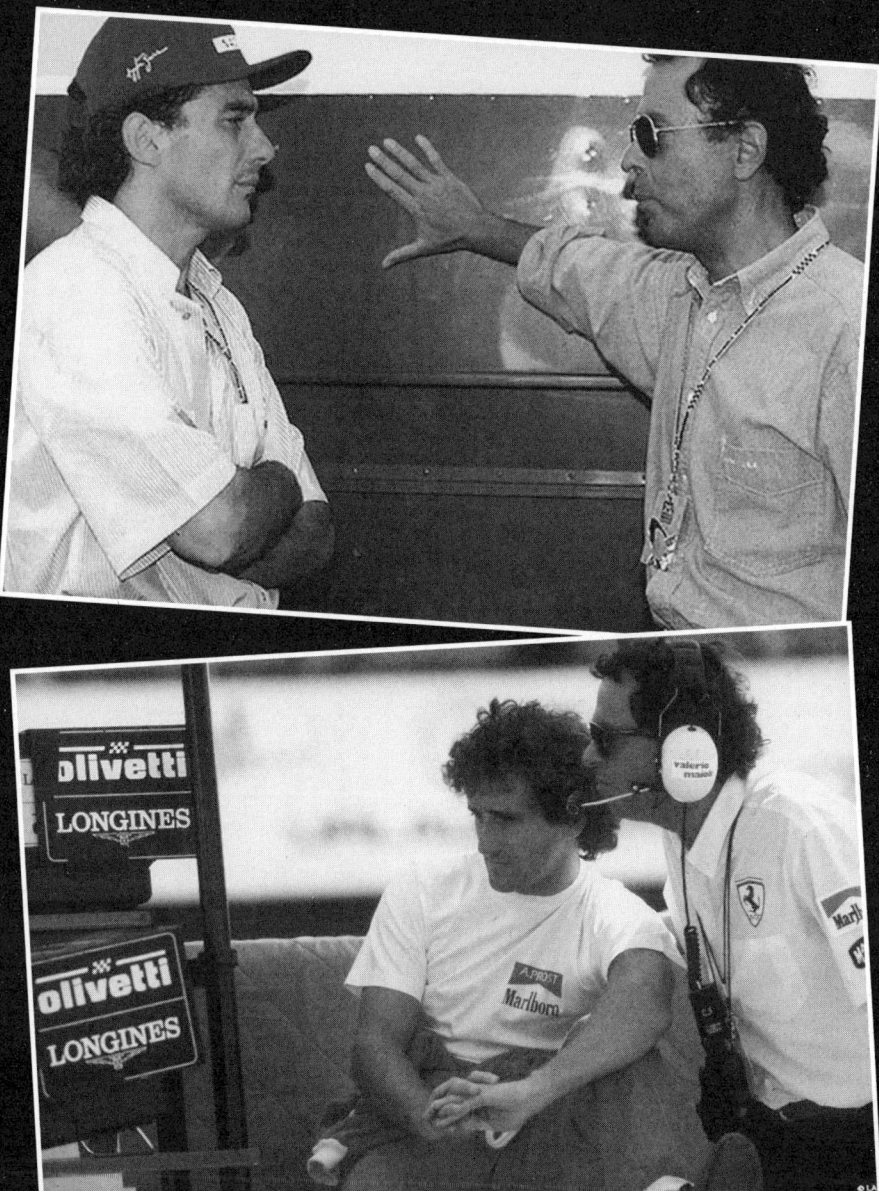

Senna talks to Fiorio: the Cavallino manager wanted to bring Magic to Maranello in 1991. Everything fell through when the deal seemed to be done...

Fiorio and Prost at the Ferrari pit wall: the two did not have a good relationship in Maranello, but Alain later called Cesare to manage his team.

CHAPTER 7

COMAS: SAVED BY SENNA, BUT HELPLESS IN THE FACE OF AYRTON'S TRAGEDY

'FATE SHUFFLES our cards and we play them.'

Arthur Schopenhauer, the 19th century German philosopher, had his own view on fate. Man does not govern fate, at most he suffers it. Ask Érik Comas to believe that.

Now 61 years old, the French driver from Romans-sur-Isère had a less than radiant career in F1. The F3000 champion in 1990, he spent four seasons in GPs with transalpine teams: two seasons with Ligier, in 1991 and 1992, and as many with Larrousse in 1993 and 1994. His *palmarès* lists 59 appearances in F1 with a best finish, a fifth place, in the 1992 French GP with the Ligier JS37-Renault.

Érik's story is strange, because it is intertwined with that of Ayrton Senna, in a cruel game of life and death. At the beginning of 1992, Comas seemed destined to be left stranded, because Guy Ligier had offered his cockpit to Alain Prost, a driver with more emblazoned honours than him, despite the fact that Érik had a two-year contract just like his team-mate, Thierry Boutsen. Comas was mothballed because he cost less than the Belgian. Alain had kept the team on tenterhooks throughout the winter, taking part in pre-season tests, only to decide, shortly before the start of the championship, to give up the position.

'A week before the start of the World Championship at Kyalami,' Érik recalls, 'they called me from Ligier because they had not reached an agreement with Prost. They put a private plane at my disposal to fly to South Africa and prepare my seat. I had kept myself in shape, even though I had not put my butt in a racing car that year yet. On debut I finished seventh, doing better than Thierry.'

That was as far as Ligier were likely to go, although the team had strong support from state sponsors, such as the tobacco brands Gitanes, Seita, and the Elf oil company. Ligier was supposed to be the expression of French *grandeur*, but the results were not coming. 'F1 was in a phase of technological transition: the top teams already had semi-automatic gearboxes. Williams had active suspension, ABS and traction control, while we still had a manual H gearbox. Although the budget was adequate, the team had not grown in the right way, because there was too much anxiety to become a top team: we suddenly grew from 70 to 200 people, but it didn't affect the issue of not being a British team, which at the time was considered to be more effective. Frank Dernie was hired as technical director, but there was too much confusion in the team: you wouldn't just talk to your track engineer for every decision, you also had to talk to the aerodynamics and car development people. In short, there was too much bureaucracy, not to say politics.'

In Canada, Comas won his first point for Ligier in a year and a half and, in France, he finished fifth, after having been fourth for a long time, until a problem with the drive-by-wire [the potentiometer that controls the opening of the accelerator without a cable control] had forced him to slow down. It seemed, however, to be the beginning of a more favourable period.

'The next race was at Spa-Francorchamps,' the driver continues, 'where I had always run good races: for example, in 1989 I had fought with Jean Alesi for victory in the F3000 race. Unfortunately, during the third lap of Friday's free practice at the Belgian GP, I had a very bad accident. I was lapping with an almost full tank (about 180 litres of fuel) and, therefore, my single-seater was a bit heavy. At *Blanchimont*, the car in front of me closed its trajectory too much on the inside of the bend and brought dirt onto the track. On the sides, in fact, the kerbs used for touring cars during the 24 Hours had not been repositioned, so much so that the F1 cars tended to climb on them with their inner wheels and take off dangerously.'

The most famous parts of the Spa-Francorchamps track are *Eau Rouge* and *Raidillon*, the two uphill left-right corners, but for connoisseurs

Blanchimont is the most challenging bend. 'It's a blind turn,' confirms Érik. 'Once you set a line, you can't change it. It's a corner you go through in sixth gear at high speed in an F1 car and, after two laps of tyre warm-up, you're already in full throttle. I was on the third lap and had no problems with tyre pressure, but I suddenly found myself on the dirt, losing control of the Ligier JS37 and crashing into the guardrail on the outside. I must admit, I can't remember anything about that very violent bang, because I lost consciousness immediately. The single-seater bounced back on the track and was left with the throttle stuck, perhaps because a foot was caught between the pedals. The 3.5-litre Renault V10 engine howled at full power, right up to the rev limiter. The situation was very dangerous because the car was battered and leaking water and oil: the risk was that the engine could explode at any moment, catching fire.'

At that moment Ayrton Senna arrived on the scene with his McLaren: the Brazilian saw the wreckage of the Ligier and looked for an opening on the right to pass, but immediately pulled the MP4/7A over and stopped. He unbuckled his seatbelt and ran back towards Érik, even before the marshals intervened. 'In those dangerous situations every second could be important,' Comas explains. 'Ayrton had heard the engine screaming at full throttle and had noticed that I had my head tilted to the side, so he instinctively decided to intervene. He rushed towards my Ligier, while the race directors were showing the red flag to interrupt the session. In the meantime other single-seaters were arriving at that blind spot, so the situation was terribly dangerous not only for me, but also for Senna. Ayrton did not evaluate the risks he was exposing himself to, he acted instinctively, without thinking in the slightest that, not being visible at that point of the track, he could have been mown down by another F1 car coming in. He first turned off the engine, then held my helmet up to the side to reduce the strain on my neck, while he waited for the rescuers to arrive. I can say that he probably saved my life!'

After being rescued, Eric was transferred to hospital where, fortunately, he regained consciousness quickly. The Frenchman escaped with few physical consequences, but appreciated his great fortune in escaping the accident: 'I was discharged from hospital the day after the crash and immediately returned to the paddock to thank Ayrton. I was amazed by his reaction, because for him the rescue operation he had performed was simply normal, there was nothing heroic about it. For me, however, it had been extraordinary: a champion who had cared about a colleague.'

Larini with the Ferrari cannot avoid Senna's Williams at the first corner of the 1994 Aida GP – Érik Comas passes shortly behind with the Larrousse LH94.

Senna is the first to help Comas, who is unconscious during free practice for the 1992 Belgian GP after a serious accident with the Ligier JS37 at *Blanchimont*.

'In this regard, I must recount an episode: when I won the F3000 championship and the doors of F1 were opened to me, no one had words of congratulation for me in the Circus except Senna, who came up to congratulate me on the title I had won. He was not just the first colleague to congratulate me, he was *the only one*. This gesture struck me emotionally: after all, Ayrton was not only the champion who won F1 world championships, but also a fan who followed the young talents as early as F3.'

Érik, what did that accident mean to you psychologically?
I have no memory of that day on the track: I lost my memory of the period from the moment I left the hotel in the morning until I woke up in hospital. I reconstructed the crash from stories and videos. But I can say that it was not without psychological consequences: it took me three months to fully recover. I can't say I was scared really, but it wasn't easy to regain my usual feeling in the car and my self-confidence until Suzuka.

Comas concluded his adventure with Ligier at the end of 1992 and joined Larrousse, a team with smaller financial means, so much so that in his second year he was not paid even a franc of the promised salary. With the LH94-Ford he only picked up two points, at Aida and Hockenheim. But the watershed of the season and of his F1 career was that damned 1 May 1994, the day of the San Marino GP.

'At the start there had been the accident between Pedro Lamy and JJ Lehto. During the safety car laps I felt a bump from behind and after the restart I noticed a strong vibration in the rear [of the car]. After what had happened in the previous days, with Rubens Barrichello's accident on Friday and Roland Ratzenberger's death on Saturday, I didn't hesitate for a moment to go back into the pits for a check-up. And, in fact, the team replaced my rear wing. While I was in the pits, Ayrton's accident happened. We did not understand what had actually taken place, because the team was working on my car. At the time there wasn't all the data on the team monitors – the kind the TV now broadcasts live: we only understood that there had been another accident, after the one at the start, but nothing else. We imagined that the race would start again. "Amen," I thought. The GP had been interrupted by the red flag, but as the pit lane had remained open with the yellow light flashing, I decided to return to the track to line up on the grid.'

At the end of the pit lane the light was yellow and there was no one to stop the drivers who wanted to return to the track ...

I had no idea what could have happened. But after a few hundred metres, when I arrived at *Tamburello*, I saw the rescue vehicles and even the helicopter on the track. There was great confusion and I approached to find out what had happened. I stopped the Larrousse and got out of the cockpit: I immediately caught sight of Ayrton. He was lying on the grass next to the Williams that had been destroyed at the front right. Once out of my car I wanted to get closer, but a doctor stopped me and invited me to sit in an ambulance. I immediately understood there was not much I could do for the Brazilian champion.

I would have liked to give him a hand, as he had given it to me, but the doctors and helpers who had intervened were already active in a way that was certainly more competent than what I could have done, but that vision was heartbreaking for me. I was looking inertly at the person who had saved my life two years earlier and I, at that moment, could do nothing for him. It was very hard, psychologically it was much more devastating than my own accident could have been. When you see a colleague die on Saturday and then, on Sunday you see someone go who was ... a god to us drivers at the time, you are left scarred.

That 1 May 1994 changed my life: there was a before and an after Senna's accident. When I returned to the pits, I said goodbye to Larrousse and the team and literally ran towards the airport. I couldn't stay one minute longer at Imola. At the time I had decided to stop, not to race the next GP. Then many people called me: Patrick Tambay, René Arnoux and Jean-Paul Driot, persuading me that it was not right to retire after an accident. So I finished the 1994 season, but in my head I was no longer an F1 driver.

It was a nightmarish weekend. F1 had not suffered a fatal accident since the death of Elio De Angelis in the 1986 tests, and to remember the last one in a race, you had to go back to 1982, when Riccardo Paletti was killed at the start in Canada. Since I had begun racing single-seaters in 1985, I had never crossed paths with death. Rubens Barrichello on Friday had been a miracle, considering his terrible accident. On Saturday Roland died: I had strange feelings in my soul. On Sunday morning I was sitting next to Ayrton at the drivers' briefing in the Marlboro Tower and I remember him saying to me: 'Érik, we have to intervene to change something in this F1: we haven't realised it, but it has become dangerous.

We must meet in London before going to Monte Carlo.' Holy words, which remained an unheeded alarm. There was no time to intervene. The increasingly strong carbon fibre cockpits had deluded us that we had become immortal. And instead, if you look at the footage from 1994, you discover that we had our shoulders out of the chassis and we had no side protectors, no Hans collar. We were driving in a dangerous situation, but we were not aware of it. At the weekend of the San Marino GP we came up against that harsh reality and had to deal with destiny. Imola changed my approach to life in a profound way.

A real sliding door ...

CHAPTER 8

THE COVETED LAMBORGHINI V12 AND THE SECRET TEST IN INDYCAR

1993 WAS a year full of travails for Senna: he no longer felt like McLaren was his home, even though 'the Frenchman', as Ayrton used to call Alain Prost in a derogatory tone, wasn't in the team anymore. His rival had snatched the Williams, the most competitive F1 car of the moment, equipped with active suspension.

The FW15C was a perfect car that led the French driver to his fourth title, even though Ayrton won five GPs with the MP4/8 equipped with the Ford Cosworth HB, a customer engine not even comparable to Prost's Renault.

1994 was the year when McLaren had to find a new engine supplier, and Chrysler, owner of Lamborghini, contacted Ron Dennis's team to explore the possibility of collaboration. A chassis of the MP4/8 was adapted to house the V12 from Sant'Agata Bolognese, and the day after the Portuguese GP in September, Ayrton Senna took to the track in a car with a white livery, devoid of any sponsors.

Ayrton was shocked by the Lamborghini engine. He called it the most powerful engine he had ever driven in F1. He immediately called the designer Mauro Forghieri to compliment him, even claiming that the V12 had far too much horsepower: 'In the next test,' Senna explained to the ex-Ferrari engineer, 'I would prefer an engine with less power and smoother behaviour: this unit is simply amazing, but brutal in its delivery.' The Brazilian considered Lamborghini's V12 to be a winner and would have done anything to have it immediately.

Senna set a new track record at Estoril. He was so enthusiastic about the Lamborghini engine that he began to press McLaren team principal Ron Dennis to use the 12-cylinder in the last GP of the season. The English manager said a flat 'no' to this request, because in the meantime Peugeot had stepped forward, and, in addition to supplying a V10, was willing to put up money that, at the end of the day, made a big difference.

Disappointed, Ayrton decided to leave McLaren and agreed to drive for Williams in 1994, after negotiations with Ferrari had broken down. But how might F1 history have changed if the Brazilian had been able to race with McLaren-Lamborghini, in an all-Emilian derby with Ferrari? Ron Dennis had chosen Peugeot and its money, but had found himself with a 'deflated' and unreliable engine.

Senna had hoped to go to Williams in 1993, but the door had been closed to him by Alain Prost, who had signed a contract for that season well in advance. At the end of 1992, Senna agreed to try out a Formula Cart in America. The team was Roger Penske's which, like McLaren, wore the red and white colours of Marlboro. The tobacco sponsor did not want to lose the three-time world champion, who was being offered a deal with Rothmans, a competitor on the market. Penske's official driver was Emerson Fittipaldi. Ayrton liked the idea of driving a single-seater without the electronic devices such as F1's active suspension, and made himself available for a secret test, enticed by the idea of making a jump to the American series, just as Nigel Mansell would do, later winning the title on his debut with the Lola T93/00 of the Newman-Haas team.

The track chosen for Senna's try-out was Firebird Raceway West, located in the desert near Phoenix, where Penske was to carry out a three-day comparative test between the new PC22 and the single-seater that had raced in 1992. On that Sunday Ayrton, accompanied by Philip Morris boss John Hogan, arrived at the circuit while Fittipaldi was sorting out a basic setup (with the team): it was 20 December and it was freezing cold.

From Arizona, Senna leaked to his friend Angelo Orsi that he would be driving a Formula Cart: in the editorial office of *Autosprint* it was already the afternoon of the closing day of the next edition. The editor Carlo Cavicchi was forcibly absent because of a leg injury and, therefore, the responsibility of closing the issue was mine, as his deputy. The news of Ayrton in the Penske PC21 was an exclusive that might have deserved the cover, although we also had the first images of the new Ferrari F1 car, the F93A. It is fair to say that, at the time, image transmission technology was not what it is today: there were no smartphones, so if we wanted to come out with the story of Senna in the Formula Cart we would have had to get photos taken on the other side of the ocean, before the cover of *Autosprint* went to the printer.

At my side was Roberto Boccafogli, today head of strategic communications at Ferrari and at the time head of service, a real hound in the hunt for news. We both wanted to make a good impression with director Cavicchi and not squander the news of the day.

Although we were aware of the technical difficulties, we did not give in. We researched whether there was an agency in Phoenix equipped with a tele-photo transmission system, since at Conti Editore, always at the cutting edge, we had the special equipment to receive that type of material. Nothing was digital, but the original image was broken down into its basic colours (magenta, cyan and yellow) by means of three photographic reproductions, which made it possible to obtain negatives for the recomposition of the shot in three printing phases.

In the Arizona capital, Boccafogli had scouted out the Associated Press (AP) office. After several attempts, the still half-asleep editor on duty answered the phone. He was a journalist, but we needed to find a photographer who could transmit the images via tele-photo. The colleague on the phone, consulting the AP's directory, had found the phone number of a photojournalist. His name was Trojanos, a Puerto Rican who normally covered news events and who had never even seen a racing car through binoculars.

'Hello? Is that Trojanos the AP photographer?' said Boccafogli. 'I'm calling from Italy, from the weekly *Autosprint* and I need an exclusive shoot.'

'Who the hell is speaking?' replied a hoarse voice on the other end. 'It's Sunday morning and I'm not on duty today. You have to ask at the agency. I don't even know why I answered the call, I want to rest. In fact I'm going back to sleep.'

'Please don't hang up,' replied Roberto firmly, 'it's true that it's a holiday, but we could repay you with a big fee. You won't regret it.'

Trojanos's tone of voice suddenly changed and he seemed to be more present: 'But what do I need to do?'

'You have to go to Firebird Raceway West, you'll find F1 driver Ayrton Senna performing a test in a red-and-white single-seater,

Senna driving the Penske PC21 Formula Cart during a test at Firebird Raceway West in December 1992.

with Marlboro lettering: take a few photos without being noticed and then rush to AP and send us a couple of colour pictures via telephoto. Our hours are numbered, since we are keeping the cover of the weekly open.'

'I have no idea who this Ayrton Senna is,' added the Puerto Rican, 'but how much are you willing to pay me for the service?'

'$500 for two pictures,' Roberto replied dryly and, switching to a more colloquial tone, he added, 'And if you want to claim the money you'd better get a move on, because if the pictures arrive with the cover closed, we won't be able to do anything with them.'

'OK, guys. I'll get moving right away, but I hope there's not the usual Sunday traffic coming out of Phoenix.'

In the meantime, alongside the graphic designers of *Autosprint*, I prepared two covers: one with just the Ferrari, which was ready to be sent to the press, and the second with the red single-seater at the bottom, while in the middle we had left a large empty box, but with a giant headline next to it: 'Scoop! The photos of Ayrton Senna's test in F. Indy'. Everything was ready: the only thing missing was the photo.

'You guys are crazy!' commented Giordano Capelli, head of graphics. 'Are you really waiting for a Puerto Rican across the ocean to send you

pictures of Senna in a Formula Cart? You believe in fairy tales: those pictures will never arrive. It's better we release the cover with Ferrari now, without going late, because then you'll hear from Cavicchi.'

But for us it had become a challenge. A 'mission impossible' that went against all logic, but why not try?

From the switchboard came a call: 'There is a certain Trojanos on the line, do you know him? Shall I put through the call or tell him to call back?' the receptionist asked.

'Nooo, pass him on to me now!' replied a galvanised Boccafogli, and then to the photographer: 'Where are you?'

'I am at the only pay phone in the deserted paddock,' replied Trojanos. 'I can see a driver with a yellow and green helmet about to get into a red and white car. Shall I go and take a shot? Is he the one you are so interested in?'

'Yes!!! Run, that's Ayrton Senna!'

Click, that's all he wanted to hear.

Then, a long wait began. We were hanging by a thread without a net – until the cyan image of a racing car began to appear on the tele-photo drum. It was like a sudden apparition of the Virgin Mary. It took a few minutes of transmission for each of the three images to come through and it would only have taken the slightest jump in the line to have to start all over again, making it all too late.

'Hi, Bob!' It was the legendary Trojanos on the phone. 'I understand that the transmission is completed: have you seen the photos?'

'Good job, you just earned your $500.'

Ayrton had started to drive with a certain circumspection after Fittipaldi had checked that everything on the car was in order: the Penske was heavier than an F1, while the responsiveness of the turbocharged Chevrolet engine was appreciable. The Brazilian champion made no mistakes, although he had to get to grips with the sequential gearbox he was not used to. Initially he drove a series of 14 laps, with a best lap time of 49'51. Then, after a stop for a few adjustments, he managed 49'09, showing a very convincing pace with the old Penske, taking into account that Emerson had ended the day with a 49'7 on new tyres and on the more promising PC22.

'Thank you,' Ayrton said, handing his helmet to Penske's track engineer Nigel Beresford, 'it was an important session, because I understand everything I wanted to know.'

It was not the time to bet on America.

Senna explains to Fittipaldi, Penske driver, his thoughts on the PC21 after the test at Firebird Raceway West.

The 12-cylinder Lamborghini engine that Ayrton had tested experimentally on the McLaren: he considered it the most powerful in F1.

CHAPTER 9

MINARDI AND THE MILLION DOLLAR PIECE OF ADVICE

'EVERYTHING IS made up of three points of view: mine, yours and the truth.'

Oriana Fallaci could have ideally summed up with this phrase the disinterested and sincere bond that united Ayrton Senna and Gian Carlo Minardi. Two very distant figures, yet capable of attracting each other. Gian Carlo Minardi was the talent scout of young motor racing hopefuls, or the team manager who for 21 years led an F1 team with means immensely inferior to those of the top teams, putting Pierluigi Martini with the M189 on the front row at Phoenix 1990. He is among the men who brought the Imola GP back to the F1 Circus in 2020, after a 14-year absence. President of Formula Imola, the company that manages the Santerno racetrack, and a charismatic figure in both the ACI [Automobile Club of Italy] and the FIA, the man from Faenza became the narrator of a slice of Ayrton Senna's story. He was friend, advisor, confidant and trusted inspirer of the Brazilian champion: he had won his trust without seeking the slightest benefit from such a prestigious acquaintance, establishing a truly special relationship.

'I had met Ayrton in the spring of 1982: I was at Thruxton at Easter, a day when there was no racing in Britain: qualifying took place on Saturday and the races on Easter Monday. Paolo Barilla, the driver who was paired with Alessandro Nannini in my F2 team, told me: "Go and watch the Formula Ford race, there is a driver who will become world champion in my opinion. It's a Brazilian who is often in Parma." I went to see this young guy, he was already in his twenties, because racing drivers didn't start as early as they do now. He had impressed me straight away: he

Senna with Minardi and Martini: the Brazilian had promised his friend from Faenza that he would end his career in F1 by racing a season with the Romagna team.

Ayrton in the Minardi motorhome with his friend Orsi and Gian Carlo: Senna was often a guest for lunch at the Faenza team, where he felt at home.

took pole position and then dominated the race in the rain, almost giving everyone a lap. I was blown away, but since one swallow doesn't make a summer, two weeks later I went back to watch him at the Nürburgring, where Formula Ford was still concurrent with F1. In Germany he took pole and then won the two races. At that point I invited him to dinner at our hotel, close to the circuit. Senna accepted the invitation and was very nice, so we started talking.'

Gian Carlo, in addition to being the owner of his team, was always appreciated for his ability to 'sniff out' up-and-coming young drivers, earning himself the role of acute talent scout. 'At the end of the evening I had offered him a contract to race with me in 1983 in Formula 2 and Ayrton shocked me with his reply: "I thank you, but I already have my own programme: in 1988 I have to be F1 world champion." I was speechless because that guy already knew where he wanted to go. In that meeting an atmosphere was established which immediately went beyond the relationship between driver and team manager. He came to see me every time we went racing in Britain, even if he wasn't busy there. He really liked pasta, a food that was a must in our hospitality, so the relationship was consolidated over time even outside of racing.'

In short, a friendly atmosphere had been established with this Brazilian, but nothing had worked out professionally ...
I was impressed by this young man who was carrying out the programme he had launched for his approach to F1. Ayrton was one of the few who could read the future both in racing and in the management of his life. He was incredible, it was something I had seen in very few drivers because, even during the race he was running, he was able to explain to you over the radio what was happening in front or behind. I don't know if he was watching the big screens or if it was his own feeling.

Over time, Minardi became a focal point for the Senna family at Grand Prix ...
After I landed in F1, dad Milton often came to my motorhome: he was happier staying with me than at McLaren, where his son raced, so a relationship of mutual respect was established with Ayrton, so much so that more than once he asked my opinion on what I thought about various issues, before making his own choices independently.

He considered you a reliable and credible figure...
He told me repeatedly: 'You were the only one who immediately offered me a professional racing driver's contract, while the other team managers always asked me for money to race, at least until I became "Senna". And this gesture of yours I will remember for the rest of my life.' A relationship born from a job offer that turned into a friendship, so much so that in 1993, when he didn't know which way to turn with McLaren, he called me quite often to hear my opinion.

Ayrton, at the end of 1992, had been caught off guard: Alain Prost had blown him away with the Williams, which was the single-seater of the moment, equipped with sophisticated driving aid systems such as traction control, ABS and, above all, active suspension. Senna's McLaren MP4/7A had been the last using the Honda engine and, despite having the electronic throttle and chassis-integrated bodywork, it had failed to match the pace of rainbow winner Nigel Mansell. Without the Japanese 12-cylinder, it would have been impossible to counter the French rival in the Adrian Newey-designed car, especially as Ron Dennis, his boss, had tried to reduce his salary when he realised that for Ayrton the Williams door had closed and he would have no viable market alternatives. Not only that: he would have to counter 'enemy' Alain with a McLaren deprived of an official engine, using an eight-cylinder Ford HB customer.

Senna was on his toes because, for the first time in his career, he was not in control of the situation and found himself as if at the mercy of the waves, tossed between them. He considered giving himself a sabbatical year and had not even discarded the idea of racing a season with Gian Carlo: 'In order not to lose form.' Ayrton proposed, 'I could come and race a year with you.'

Minardi would have had the chance of a lifetime: his team, last only for lack of adequate resources, would have been able to race a three-time world champion driver and, perhaps, thanks to Ayrton, the team would have found the support it had always lacked to attempt the great leap forward. But the time available was very limited and the risks of the operation very high.

The Faenza man's reply was more as a friend than as a team manager: 'I thank you for the thought, but you can't lose a year of your career, you have to find the best solution for you.'

And it was Gian Carlo himself who launched the idea of running with McLaren with a token contract, perhaps overpaid. If he had Ayrton in his team, Minardi could have proved a point to Ron Dennis, who had never been enamoured of the Romagnolo team manager. 'We never got along: Ron didn't like the fact that I didn't speak English. And we hadn't taken to each other since the Formula 2 days.'

Dennis was repeating to the press that he did not like Minardi as a neighbouring pit team, McLaren being a top team and the team from Faenza the poorest in the Circus: 'It's an attitude I never liked either. But, in fact, the rift had started in F2, when in one race Miguel Angel Guerra didn't see the chequered flag and ran an extra lap. Dennis personally had come to protest, complaining about the "usual Italians, spaghetti-eaters". They had to stop me, otherwise I would have thrown a hammer at his head!'

Senna's tug-of-war had gone on throughout the winter and the phone calls with Minardi were increasingly frequent. The climax was reached, however, on the last day of Carnival in 1993 ...
It was evening already and I was attending the Mardi Gras party at the city club I belonged to, I was not wearing a mask but a dinner jacket. The party was being held in a historic building in Faenza, where there was no mobile phone reception.

Were mobile phones already available?
Well, perhaps it is more accurate to say one of the first 'giant mobiles'. Ayrton called me at nine o'clock at night and I remember that it was freezing cold. To answer him, I had come out of the building and leaned against a pillar to listen to his words. And for the umpteenth time he raised the idea of coming to race for Minardi ...

But wasn't it his intention to come and race for you in the last year of his F1 career?
That was his intention, manifested in a previous episode: we were having lunch in our hospitality area with Angelo Orsi, dad Milton and a friend of Ayrton's, alongside the Brazilian champion, of course. On that occasion he said for the first time: 'I'm going to win five world titles and then make Minardi great: before I close with F1 I'll come and race for you.' It may have sounded like a 'casual' remark, but it was uttered by a person who

normally didn't bullshit. It filled me with joy because of the way he had said it, adding that he was indebted to me because I had offered him a contract as a professional driver. I never told that story until daddy Milton brought it up in an interview with the *Gazzetta dello Sport*, more than a decade ago. I had been dumb as a post, just as I will never recount what we said to each other on the Saturday before the tragedy. All I can say is that he was not serene: he was not happy with the car, because his knuckles were touching the bodywork, while McLaren was open. I didn't know what change he had asked the Williams engineers to make, otherwise I would have told him he was crazy if he wanted to move the steering wheel, which actually his team had just about finished to integrate in the new car bodywork he was about to get into shortly afterwards.

In fact, Williams was ready to call up Riccardo Patrese, who was fresh out of F1, to ask him if he wanted to help develop the FW16 for Senna ...
Well, I might add that Riccardo, after the tragedy, was also approached to replace Senna, but he did not feel like taking Ayrton's wheel.

At this point in the story Minardi falters. He seems ready to reveal what they had told each other on that Saturday, but then Gian Carlo, after a fleeting mention of the affair in which Senna allegedly was having disagreements with his family, clams up to keep his pledge not to reveal that secret. 'That evening Ayrton was not serene, not only because of Roland Ratzenberger's death, but also because it was the very first time there was no one from his family to follow him. And at this point I don't want to add anything else, because I think it's a private affair: in short, the family disagreed with him on a certain matter ...'

Apparently, father Milton did not like his son's relationship with the model Adriane Galisteu, who had taken the place in Ayrton's heart of Xuxa Meneghel, a Brazilian TV presenter, actress and singer, whom he had met during a Christmas programme for children. The Senna family was crazy about Xuxa: they already imagined the Brazilian champion as her husband, while Adriane in their eyes was nothing more than an opportunist, although Senna had chosen her as a possible life partner.

It should come as no surprise, then, that the anachronistic dualism culminated on the most painful day: at Ayrton's funeral, the Senna family wanted Meneghel to accompany the relatives, while

Adriane was prevented from taking a place at the head of the cortège, forcing her to follow the coffin at a safe distance, amidst the beloved champion's fans.

But let's go back to the Saturday of the San Marino GP, because the subject of safety was back on the F1 table: at the start of the 1994 season, the drivers had realised that they were once again crossing that invisible line which allows each driver to seek the limits of the single-seater without fearing for their own safety. 'During pre-season testing at Imola,' says Minardi, 'there was a meeting between Ayrton, Michele Alboreto and Pierluigi Martini. Under discussion were the bumps in the track. One bump was due to the road subway, so there was little we could do to eliminate it, but there was a way to intervene on the others. I am aware that the drivers wanted to make demands on safety in general. When Michele lost his wheel in the pit lane on the restart from the pit stop, a massacre was avoided only because he was not driving down the pit lane at high speed – as he would have been allowed to do at the time – but restraining himself, with my consent.

'The safety alarm also went off after Barrichello's accident and Ratzenberger's passing. There were several meetings to discuss the problems on the table.'

Ayrton was greatly affected by the death of the Austrian ...
Sure, but I think in the end it had a bit to do with everything, even personal emotions. Daddy Milton didn't come to Imola ...

Gian Carlo, tell me about the phone call you had with Ayrton before the start of the season in the cold of Faenza's ancient city centre ...
Ayrton finally gave up the idea of coming to Minardi. I advised him to try and get Dennis to sign race by race: 'In my opinion you will do very well with McLaren,' I explained to Ayrton. 'Maybe you won't win the World Championship, but you will win GPs. You could ask for $1 million per win. In fact, you could ask for $1 million per GP!'

Was that a shot, a random guess?
No, in my opinion Ron did not want to give Ayrton the salary he was asking for, but he would have been willing to discuss a points-based contract. And, even with an unofficial engine, Senna would have been

able to earn a good amount of money … The Brazilian, at the end of a tough negotiation, had won over Dennis: he would have earned $1 million per race. And he was grateful to me for that result. Want to know something? He showed me his thankfulness in a blatant way: at every Grand Prix, the first time he drove past my pit box in the McLaren, he would give me an OK sign. And that made me very happy. With two prima donnas like Senna and Dennis, it was not taken for granted that the agreement would hold for the whole season: there was no contract valid for the entire championship, but it was renewed race after race. And Ayrton would not move from his home unless he had received a $1 million bank transfer from McLaren into his account. In short, the two were no joke at all, but both benefited from the tug-of-war: Senna had won five GPs and McLaren had finished second in the Constructors' Championship. The Brazilian only won one pole position, but with a Ford HB customer engine it would have been too much to expect to challenge Alain Prost's Williams FW15.

Ayrton always told you his confidences, but did you ever talk about the Williams FW16 that was unsuited to him?
He complained about his knuckles rubbing on the bodywork, but we never went into detail about his technical problem. We used to joke about his affair with Carol Alt, but the main issue was that he had to win at Imola after two retirements at the beginning of 1994: 'If I want to fight for the World Championship,' Senna said, 'I have to impose myself in the San Marino GP, because afterwards they will give me a new bodywork and there will be no more hope for anyone.'

The FW16 had suffered from the abolition of active suspensions decided by the FIA, but Senna suffered from that closed and cramped cockpit. Could the last modification to the steering column have been made at Imola?
Yes, at least as far as I know. It is possible that they lowered the steering wheel at Imola and those are jobs you don't usually do at a track if it can be avoided. They may have made one last attempt to put Ayrton in a position to drive at the limit. After the accident I followed the case very little, because I wanted to detach myself emotionally from it. That disgrace made me feel very bad.

What do you miss most about Senna?
More than the driver, the friend, because of the sincere and deep relationship that had been established. And I must confess that I had experienced such intense moments with him that it would have been difficult to establish even with my drivers. There are emotions that I savour more now at the Historic Minardi Days, than in the 21 F1 seasons: that was a time when there was little room for talks. That's why I consider the one with Ayrton a different relationship. After the accident it was hard for me, because I had to tell Michele and Piero over the radio that Senna's condition was less serious than it unfortunately was – I played the part at least until they retired [from the race] and finally touched on the tragic situation. It was stressful to stay in the paddock and talk to the media as well. One of the rescuers was a resuscitator from Faenza, who had informed me of what, unfortunately, was the reality. And I immediately felt a strong sense of loss.

How did you experience the return of death to the paddock?
We realised we had gone too far. The cars weighed less than 500kg. We had started crash tests for the deformable nose structure, but it was laughable stuff. We were still going off the rails, with elementary choices. Senna's death forced the FIA and the constructors to revise the rules. A team as small as Minardi underwent three changes in safety regulations in one season: in a budget as tight as mine, I was short by almost two billion lire. We went beyond all forecasts, but nobody complained, because the safety regulations that led to modern F1 were born at that time. That's why I often repeat that Ayrton is always with us: apart from the Jules Bianchi tragedy, fortunately we have not paid any other tolls. With Ratzenberger's death alone, the rules of F1 would not have changed so profoundly. Ayrton's death forced a change. Adrian Newey built the cars around the driver, but even in our team Christian Fittipaldi struggled to get into the cockpit, while Martini and others more than fit. A virtuous mechanism was triggered for which Senna must always be thanked.

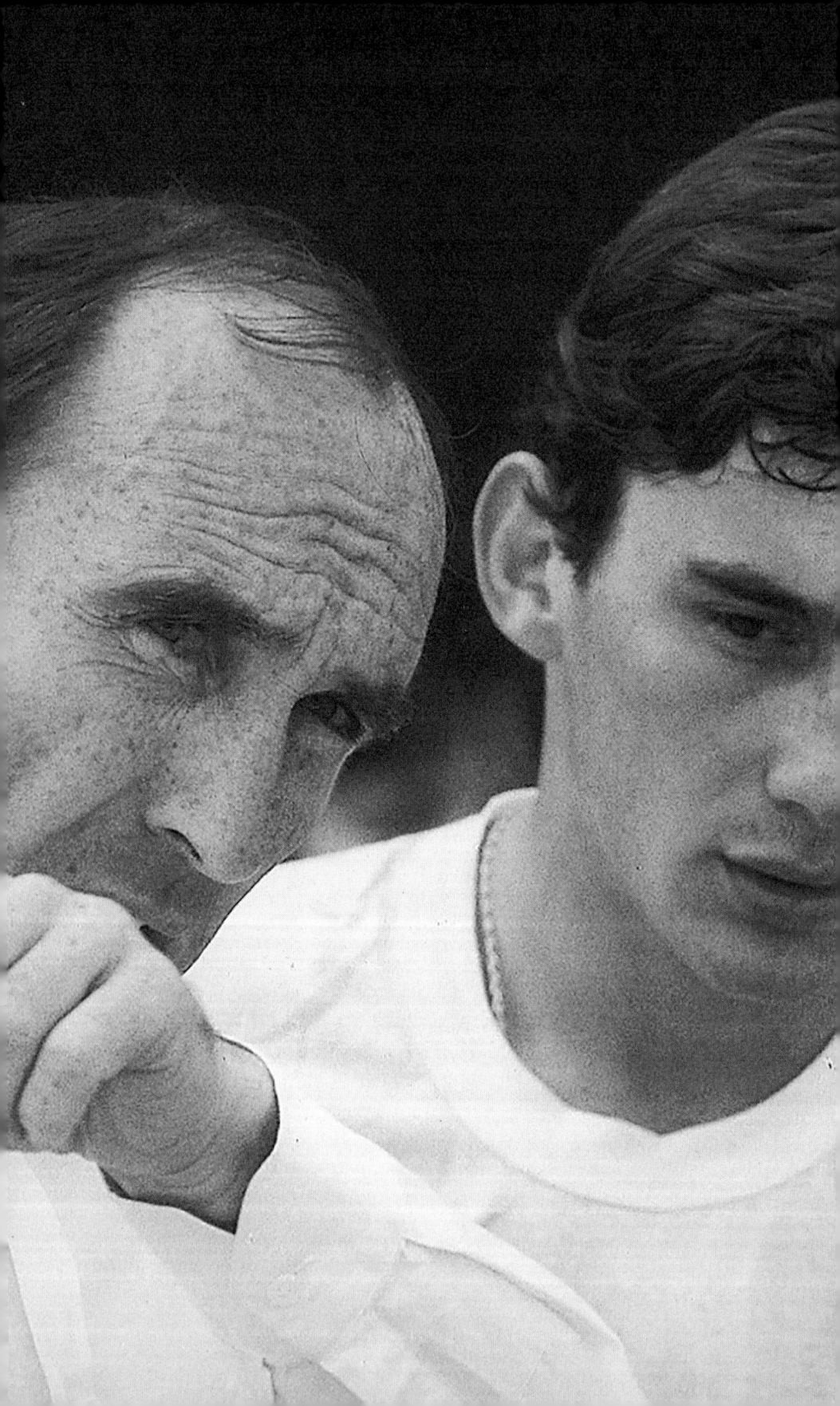

CHAPTER 10

WILLIAMS: FROM BEGINNING TO END, THE DRAMA OF A CIRCULAR STORY

'ON A circle, every starting point can also be an end point.'

Heraclitus, a pre-Socratic Greek philosopher, is considered an obscure thinker. Among his sometimes cryptic oracular aphorisms, this one stands out with crystal clarity and identifies Ayrton Senna's circular story with Williams.

His debut in a Formula 1 car happened on 19 July 1983 when he took part in a test session with Williams, then it took 11 years to see him back in Sir Frank's court. In short, the beginning and the end: 1983–1994. In between came three world drivers' titles and 41 successes. None with Didcot's team. A nasty twist of fate. The void, indeed the abyss, after the fullness. Yet, the first outing with Williams had been full of hope, just like the arrival, ten years later, at the team that was dominating the World Championship.

At Donington, on that summer's day in 1983, Ayrton knew that his immediate future would not be with Williams, as the starting drivers for the 1984 season would be Keke Rosberg and Jacques Laffite. On the English track, which ten years later would propel him into legend in an epic wet race, he wanted to make a good impression in the FW08C, the car derived from the world champion single-seater with Keke Rosberg aboard.

The Brazilian was 23 years old and still biting at the English Formula 3 title with a Ralt Rt3-Toyota. Initially, he seemed intimidated by the jump in power of an F1 car, but it only took him a few laps to realise that with the Ford Cosworth DFV he was even more at ease, managing the 500 or so horsepower at his disposal with great talent. Frank Williams arrived slightly late for the Donington appointment and Senna, in the meantime, had already won over the mechanics of the rainbow team. At each pit stop he knew how to describe the behaviour of the single-seater, giving them information with a meticulousness that not even certain seasoned drivers were capable of transferring to the technicians. He knew how to separate the aerodynamic analysis from the mechanical one, just as he was able to interpret tyre wear, recommending appropriate set-up changes as the degradation of the Goodyears increased.

By the end of the day Ayrton had covered 83 laps, a distance that had put his lean, not to say puny, physique to the test. It was a problem that also affected other young drivers, who were unaware of how fatigued their muscles would be, particularly in the neck, if not adequately trained to the loads exerted by F1s when cornering and braking. Ayrton had shown an unquestionable natural speed, combined with a refined knowledge of technique, the result of a superfine sensitivity that had left the incredulous Williams open-mouthed.

The team principal was aware that he had a blossoming star on his hands. For Senna, Williams would be his first F1 drive but not the only one, because the Brazilian had decided that his growth programme in motor racing, meticulously planned years before, would take him into the world of GPs from the 1984 season. Later he would also test a McLaren, Brabham and Toleman, eliciting identical judgements from those who had been able to appreciate his skills behind the wheel. Usually a young driver finds it difficult to convince a team to allow him a test, especially if not aimed at driving for the season, but Ayrton had the opportunity to try no fewer than four different single-seaters before making a decision. He did not want long contracts: he did not want to put his career in the hands of those who could then decide his future.

So, in the end, the only door that opened on his terms was that of Toleman. He had presented himself in his own way: he had immediately outclassed the titular driver, Derek Warwick, and had won over Rory Byrne, Toleman's car designer. At Brabham, Nelson Piquet had already created an obstruction as he was very much against a compatriot as a team-mate, not to mention the veto of the sponsors, in particular Parmalat, who wanted an Italian driver.

The path back to Williams became long and convoluted. Senna found his 'kennel' at McLaren, after a rapid rise in the F1 firmament that, from Toleman, had taken him to Lotus. With Ron Dennis he began to cash in with victories and titles, while fighting an old-fashioned duel with Alain Prost. With Honda's withdrawal from F1 the tables turned and Williams was experiencing what seemed to be a winning cycle, so the two great rivals had both set their sights on the Didcot team to build their future.

With a shrewd move, played in advance, the French champion managed to win the 1993 Williams cockpit, forcing Senna to stay at McLaren on a 'token' basis, with a salary of $1 million per GP. Yet, it was clear to everyone that Williams's technical pairing of Patrick Head and Adrian Newey was simply extraordinary. The logical rationality of the former, combined with the technical imagination of the latter, had made the Didcot team the benchmark of F1.

If he wanted to be in the hunt for a fourth world title, Ayrton would have to settle down with Sir Frank, who was thrilled to finally be able to meet again the skinny guy who had become Magic, the undisputed number one in GPs for everyone.

This time Senna had to act cunningly, taking the seat away from Prost. The transalpine, on the day he won his fourth world laurel at Estoril, announced his retirement, because the Brazilian had 'snatched' the Williams from him, repaying the Frenchman with the same coin that had been reserved for Nigel Mansell, world champion in 1992. The Briton, in fact, had been forced to move overseas, to the world of Indycar, with the Lola of the Newman-Haas team, because his steering wheel had been promised to the Frenchman. Williams has never cared for human relations with its drivers, often putting them in a tussle with each other, in the conviction that 'divide and rule' was the best way to manage top drivers.

The first outing with Williams was set for Tuesday, 18 January 1994 at the Estoril track. Two days of work behind closed doors to take photos and television footage with Ayrton Senna and Damon Hill for the presentation of the team. Rothmans, the sponsor who had wrested the Brazilian champion from the 'red and white tobacconist' with a munificent two-year contract, appeared on the bodywork with its logo, so the event was to have worldwide resonance.

The single-seater used for the occasion was not the one to be used in the championship, which was still under construction at Didcot, but the FW15D, i.e. the car with the active suspension switched to passive for the occasion, so as to comply with the FIA regulations, that had banned electronic control of the kinematics and the use of traction control, the infamous anti-skid system.

Senna's debut was entrusted to the head of the test team, Brian Lambert. The others would show up when it got serious, i.e. from Thursday, when the 'cinema' would give way to a four-day test session, with five teams and a total of eight drivers.

Williams, after the presentation, left Damon Hill free, putting test driver David Coulthard alongside Senna instead. The Brazilian's approach was gradual: every track entry was prepared with almost maniacal meticulousness, looking for the smallest details to be addressed, so as to transfer all the useful information to those who, at the Didcot headquarters, were completing the assembly of the FW16.

Ayrton made no secret of the fact that he was uncomfortable in the cockpit. After the seat tests, which had already taken place in the factory, the engineers had decided to remove a portion of carbon from the upper part of the cockpit, where the fairing was closed in, unlike the open cockpit he was used to in McLaren. Senna was initially forced to use a small steering wheel, which suited Prost, but was not to his liking; the Brazilian in fact preferred a large wheel, which he felt was more precise in its graduated use.

To some it might have seemed just whimsical, but as was later discovered in the events at Imola, that basic requirement immediately expressed by Ayrton was not understood at that juncture. In reality, the technicians' attention was focused on the passive suspension and the new Renault RS6 engine that the French manufacturer had prepared for the 1994 World Championship.

Ayrton returned to driving with a V10 engine. Over the course of four days, he had the opportunity to test both the old (RS5) and the new (RS6) versions, expressing favourable opinions, but immediately giving Bernard Dudot's staff useful pointers on the power delivery, so that the torque curve could become more linear.

Senna made his F1 debut with Keke Rosberg's Williams FW08C at Donington: he immediately went very fast.

CHOOSING WILLIAMS, HE DIDN'T KNOW HE WAS ABOUT TO ENTER A BLACK HOLE.

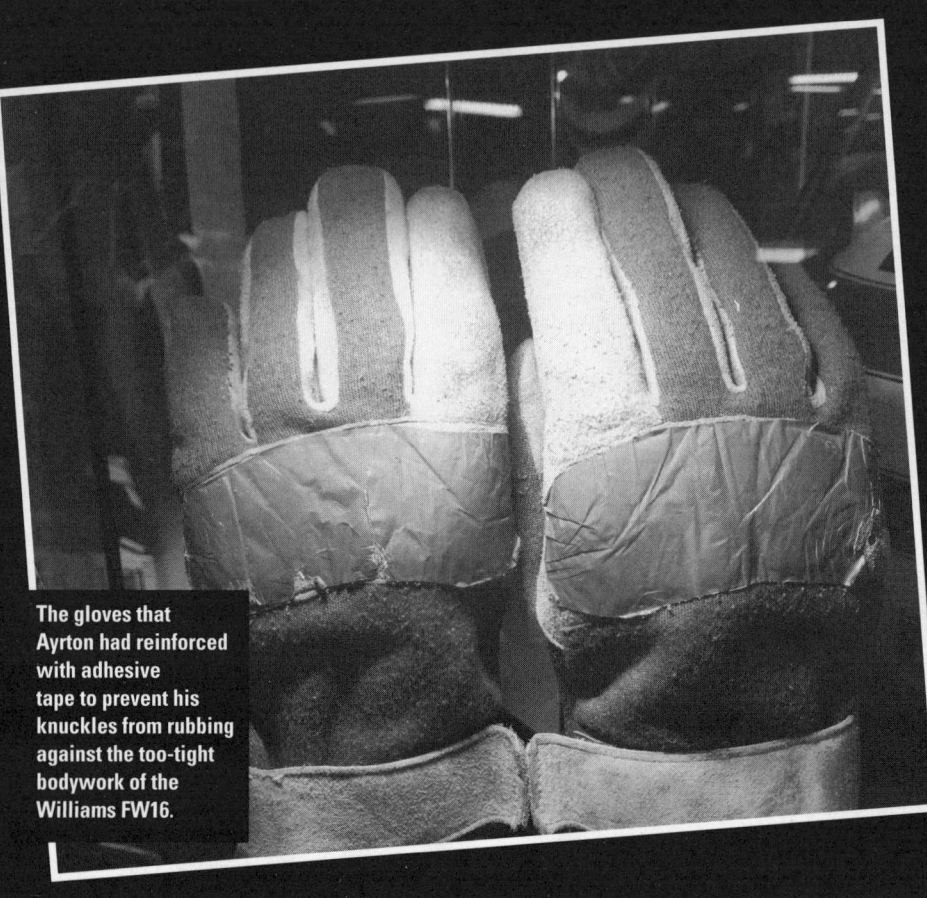

The gloves that Ayrton had reinforced with adhesive tape to prevent his knuckles from rubbing against the too-tight bodywork of the Williams FW16.

Not only that, the fussy three-time world champion also recommended modifying the management software of the semi-automatic gearbox to make the shifting of gears smoother. In short, Senna presented himself with his very resolute 'temperament' and a manic approach that kept Alain Prost's old habits very much alive. Technical director Patrick Head took note of all the requests; it was clear that he was particularly keen on the reactions of the FW15D on the track – a 'hybrid' car on which many solutions had been simulated which would only be seen on the new car.

Senna closed the four-day Portuguese test with the best time, repeating on Sunday the same performance as on Friday, with a peremptory 1'12"49. The Williams seemed high performance, but rather difficult to tune and control in the changes of direction. On the second day, Ayrton had had his first mishap with the FW15D: he went off the track at turn three, a corner that was tackled in second gear after a stretch from fifth gear at over 240 km/h: 'The car spun and I ended up crashing into the barriers with the right side.' He had escaped without any physical issues, but had damaged one side and the flat bottom. The spin, unusual for a meticulous and precise driver, testified that the package he had at his disposal was not yet up to what he could have expected when he joined F1's flagship team.

There was a lot of work to be done before the start of the 1994 season, but going round the track had never frightened him, at all. What worried him was a second spin on Sunday, in the same spot as Friday's crash: this time he managed to avoid impact in the barriers and damage, but it made it clear that the car's behaviour had not improved over the two days of testing.

Ayrton had joined the rainbow team, but he still felt like an outsider in a system that had given itself different priorities from those that the Brazilian was accustomed to. It would take some time to find the right harmony: in the meantime, surnames were abolished in communications between the team's top management. Everyone called each other by first name only, as if that was enough to make it easier to get acquainted with the other team members. Formally it was right to break down all divisions, but the climate between people remained quite frosty, even in the presence of a pale, typically wintry sun.

His debut at Estoril was intended to be the beginning of a new cycle in Senna's career, that of the definitive consecration among the greats of F1. Three world championships were not enough for him. He wanted to reach at least Juan Manuel Fangio's five. The Argentinean had been an ace on the track, but also in knowing how to sniff out the best car around. Ayrton was convinced he had made the right bet by choosing Williams. Little did he know that he was about to enter a black hole.

CHAPTER 11

WILLIAMS FW16: THERE WAS SNOW ON THE SILVERSTONE DEBUT

THERE WAS fog and also snow on the sides of the Silverstone track. It was very cold. After all, what could one expect in Britain in the middle of winter? It was 24 February 1994 – the day had finally come to put the Williams FW16-Renault, which had just been completed at the factory in Didcot, on the track. It was the only F1 car from the top teams that had yet to be seen and it was the most eagerly awaited. Ayrton Senna's dream was materialising in a strictly closed-door test: the Brazilian had left McLaren after six years and three world titles, in the certainty of having landed at the best team. He was very excited and curious about starting a new chapter in his career.

The International Federation had made important regulatory changes: namely the abolition of active suspension and the introduction of refuelling which required the design of different single-seaters to those of 1993, as the tanks, with a capacity of 220 litres by regulation, were never filled with more than 140 litres.

In his autobiography, *How to Build a Car*, the Williams chief designer Adrian Newey explained that the FW16 was an evolution of the FW15, because he didn't think it was a good idea to come up with a completely new concept unless one was needed. However, the English 'genius' had to do without the intelligent suspension, which, thanks to a sophisticated electronic control system developed by Williams, had allowed the car to maintain a constant ground clearance, ensuring maximum aerodynamic load and the performance that had enabled Alain Prost to win his fourth Drivers' World Championship and the team's sixth Constructors'. The roughness of the track had been effectively nullified by the system, because the shock absorber excursions were managed in real time by a computer, and the driver could count on a car capable of maintaining a constant set-up, as low as possible, thanks to which more downforce could be generated, preserving tyre wear.

Didcot's team had reached a level of active suspension development that gave it an indisputable technical superiority over the competition. The president of the FIA, Max Mosley, had launched a campaign to get control of the single-seaters back into the hands of the drivers, renouncing electronic aids (traction control had also been abolished, i.e. the engine system that cut power to prevent the drive wheels from skidding under acceleration), but underneath this he had the aim of breaking what was to become a Williams hegemony.

Newey admitted (in his book) that he had spent more time looking for the best aerodynamic configuration than adapting to the outlawing of active suspension systems and said it could be argued he didn't put enough work into that area. With a much smaller fuel tank due to the compulsory race refuelling, it became very important to design a very small car with reduced drag that would facilitate the pursuit of high top speeds. Hence the need for a chassis with the minimum dimensions imposed by the International Federation. Adrian had retained the enclosed fairing cockpit on the FW16, so the driver's hands were inside the cockpit, and used just two carbon skins instead of the usual three on the upper part of the body – a bold choice that allowed for a lighter and more profiled chassis. Adrian could not have imagined that this option would be the main cause of Ayrton's complaints. The Paulista (a person from São Paulo) immediately understood that the space available to him was too tight, but Newey did not worry about that at the time, because in the past he had always forced his drivers to adapt, ensuring the car's superior performance in return.

At the front, the FW16 looked very much like the world champion Williams, with its high Benetton-style nose, while at the rear, it included a completely innovative concept, the result of the inventiveness of Adrian, who is very good at reading the regulations in their most hidden folds, drawing often imaginative interpretations that are very much on the

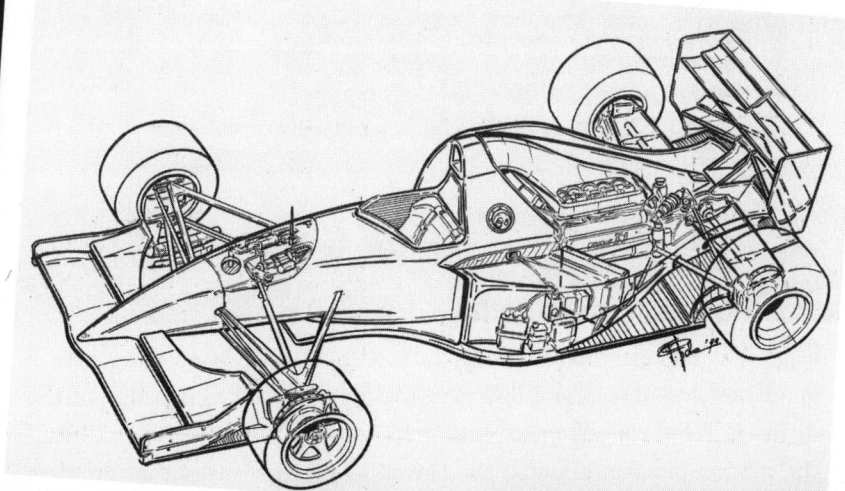

Patrick Head, Williams's technical director, analyses the times with Senna: the Brazilian had complained from the beginning that the FW16 had been built on Prost's jockey measurements.

The Williams FW16 in the design of Giorgio Piola: the single-seater had been adapted to the return of passive suspensions, although it had been designed for active ones.

First race of the 1994 season at Interlagos. Senna, after taking pole, was forced to retire on lap 55 after spinning while chasing Schumacher in the lead.

limit. His main aim was to tidy the air flow to the beam wing, which generates downforce and low pressure above the trailing edge of the diffuser. Wind tunnel tests found the 'dirty' air from the upper arms of the rear suspension affected the flows, so Newey solved that problem by lowering the wishbone by about 12cm, so it enclosed the driveshaft.

It was a very brave choice that would have put a lot of strain on the suspension, but freed up flows for a great aerodynamic advantage. The suspension would have taken the shape of an airfoil: something never seen before.

However, Adrian had to convince the technical director, Patrick Head, who was overseeing the design of the mechanical parts. The two, after a long discussion, did not waste much time in finding the most effective solution: not metal arms, but a composite structure in a trapezoidal shape, capable of encompassing the axle shaft.

The idea was futuristic, so much so that after the release of the first images, a great deal of controversy was stirred up, with some claiming that it was illegal. Some felt the futuristic suspension arm was nothing more than a mobile wing system, which was forbidden by regulations.

The solution, in reality, did not generate any aerodynamic load, the profile being neutral, and therefore, after thorough checks, it was accepted by the FIA.

There was, however, another detail of the car that could have sullied that clean line sought in the wind tunnel. The regulations stated the car had to have a square 'rain light' of 100x100mm, to be used in the wet when spray was being generated. However, if it was placed in its usual spot beneath the beam wing, it interrupted the air flow. Newey found that getting the wishbone out of the way gave the space to put the light above the gearbox, where it was part of the engine cover. In his book he recounted how the FIA argued it meant the light was obscured by the pylons that held the wing in place, unless you were directly behind the car, but they could not stop Williams from placing it there because it was acceptable within the letter of the regulations.

With the rear end finally free of blockages, an anhedral lower wing was adopted, i.e. an inverted V shape, higher in the middle and lower at the ends.

Williams used to introduce only ultra-tested solutions into the car, but every time Newey managed to get his creative flair over Patrick Head's rationality, dictating very innovative concepts from the aerodynamic point of view, they then found themselves having to reckon with cars that were extremely fast, but very difficult to fine-tune on the track. In short, it was up to Patrick to dampen Adrian's excessive leaps forward – a role that the grumpy technical director succeeded in by nature, being a very decisive and resolute character.

At Silverstone, in those dramatic weather conditions, Senna just got to grips with the FW16: he only completed about 20 laps on grooved Goodyear tyres: 'I only did six consecutive laps,' Ayrton commented to the media, 'but they were useful to understand that everything was in order in view of the next tests at Paul Ricard. I've considered it more important to work with the engineers in the pits, with repeated stops. The car is very original at the rear, with extreme aerodynamic solutions. I would say that it is a car made to measure. I can't gain a single kilo of weight, otherwise I won't fit in it.'

These conciliatory, not too polemic words were utterly different from the more peppery ones reported to the team and to his friend Angelo Orsi: 'I want to use the steering wheel I have always used. We will have to work a bit to get the right position in the cockpit, but we will find a solution.'

Ayrton was unhappy with the small steering wheel, which was mounted lower down than he was used to, but Newey felt it was too late to do anything about it. Both Senna and Damon Hill found the car unpredictable in testing. The Brazilian did not want to begin the new chapter of his career on the wrong foot, but the start of the 1994 season was likely to be complicated, much more difficult than expected.

He had waited for that debut like a child waiting for Christmas: but after just a few laps he had already realised that he had an extreme car on his hands, complicated to handle, and also very uncomfortable for him. Moreover, the coldness of the men in the pits was equal to the winter weather. It was not the best debut for someone who wanted to build a lasting relationship of trust.

Ayrton could not have imagined that 24 February would represent the beginning of the end ...

CHAPTER 12

TWO POLE POSITIONS AND TWO RETIREMENTS: A DISASTROUS START

AFTER THE shakedown held at Silverstone with snow on the sides of the track, Williams was in a hurry to assess the true potential of the FW16, the weapon with which Ayrton Senna was to attack the world title. Didcot's team chose to go to Paul Ricard, the French track completely devoid of grandstands, since it had been transformed exclusively into a test-track. Four days of testing starting on 2 March. Even in winter, the weather there is mild, given the proximity to the sea in Marseille, and the long straight of the *Mistral*, before the insidious *Signes* curve, is ideal for evaluating a new single-seater.

Renault, who supplied engines to Williams and Ligier, had a hangar at the end of the straight, so the FW16 could be developed away from prying eyes. The start of work was positive, even if the car proved to be difficult to drive: Ayrton complained about the turbulence that affected his helmet and asked Bell (the helmet supplier) if he could try an Indycar type, used by American drivers on ovals, with a flap in the chin area: 'This test did not work,' Senna later explained, 'because the flap generates too much load and crushes the head at high speeds.' Then, several windshields made of dummy materials and scotch tape were tried, before deciding on the least-worst version: 'I'm struggling to read the instruments on the dashboard,' continued the Brazilian, 'and my belt buckles hurt.' In short, Ayrton could not get into symbiosis with a car that, on the track, seemed to have good potential. In the evening the quiet atmosphere changed and faces became tense: in the Renault hangar the Williams technicians discovered a small crack in the rear left suspension arm, the famous wing profile containing the axle shaft made of carbon.

Patrick Head and Adrian Newey stayed for more than half an hour analysing the part that had broken, chatting amongst themselves. Then they decided that the car would not run the next day, because metal reinforcements would arrive from Great Britain to remedy the problem. The technical director wore a grim expression and Newey was worried: the fear was that the structural calculations had been wrong, and there was a risk that the old FW15D would have to be used for the World Championship opener in Brazil. Who would have told Ayrton? From Didcot came two triangles reinforced with an unattractive metal plate below and the carbon profile above.

On the third day, Ayrton was ready to return to the track, but in the hangar the tension could be cut with a knife. David Brown, the track engineer, warned Senna over the radio: 'Take a slow lap, then increase the pace slightly and come back to the pits for a check-up. We don't want to take any risks. We'll go step by step at first.' The driver nodded his head in affirmative response.

The FW16 took to the track under the attentive gaze of Head and Newey in religious silence. The Brazilian made his way back to the hangar: after a brief check he set off again. Everything seemed fine. One lap to warm up the tyres and then he began to push. On the first pass he had slightly lifted his foot off the gas at the fearsome *Signes* corner, but by the next lap he was already in full throttle, at 318 km/h to close the run with a time of 1'03'40. The blond engineer put his hands in his hair, while Head and Newey regained their smiles.

The danger was averted, the modification was holding, and a strengthened composite triangle would arrive for the next test at Imola. At the end of the day the Brazilian came in at 1'03'16, doing immediately better than Alain Prost the year before, with a completely different car. It should be remembered that Senna had not lapped with an empty tank and a qualifying set-up, but constantly had 50kg of petrol on board: 'I could have gone a second faster,' he admitted to *Autosprint*, 'but I preferred to concentrate on the race pace, because there is still a lot of work to do.'

Two pole positions and two retirements: a disastrous start

In particular, the car was still not balanced and had sudden offsets at the front.

The next day, while the team followed Damon Hill's work, Ayrton took off in his plane from the adjacent airport and passed over the Renault hangar.

'Celso Itiberê, the Brazilian correspondent who was following F1 for *O Globo*,' recounts Paolo Bombara, journalist for *Autosprint*, 'had looked up at the sky following the aircraft and came out with: "Boom! Can you imagine if the plane exploded now?" I was chilled by that joke, but if I think about what happened less than two months later at Imola, I still get the shivers.'

The start of the World Championship was approaching – there was only the Imola session left to deliberate on the FW16 before the inaugural trip to Brazil, and above all, to find out what its potential was in direct confrontation with the rivals. The response from the track after four days of testing had been clear, very clear: Michael Schumacher in the Benetton B194-Ford was fastest in 1'21'078, while Ayrton Senna in the Williams was second at 166 thousandths, with team-mate Damon Hill over half a second behind the Brazilian. Flavio Briatore's team had a very competitive driver-car combination and the B194 immediately seemed more on point. However, the FW16 scared everyone because, while still a very nervy single-seater to drive, it was able to keep a very interesting pace, with unloaded front wings, a sign that it was the car bodywork that generated the load. To improve the behaviour on uneven asphalt, new Ohlins shock absorbers were introduced during the Emilian tests, made exclusively for Williams: they were miniaturised, with the gas tanks mounted at the sides, to favour the design of a very profiled chassis at the front.

The wing rear suspension had brilliantly passed the stresses of the Enzo and Dino Ferrari, so concerns about the reliability of the solution designed by Adrian Newey ceased, erasing fears that had emerged at Paul Ricard.

The opening of the World Championship was at Interlagos, Ayrton's home track: the people of São Paulo descended on the venue to see Senna's debut with Williams and the general expectation was that he would seal pole position and win the race. In his autobiography, Newey reported that

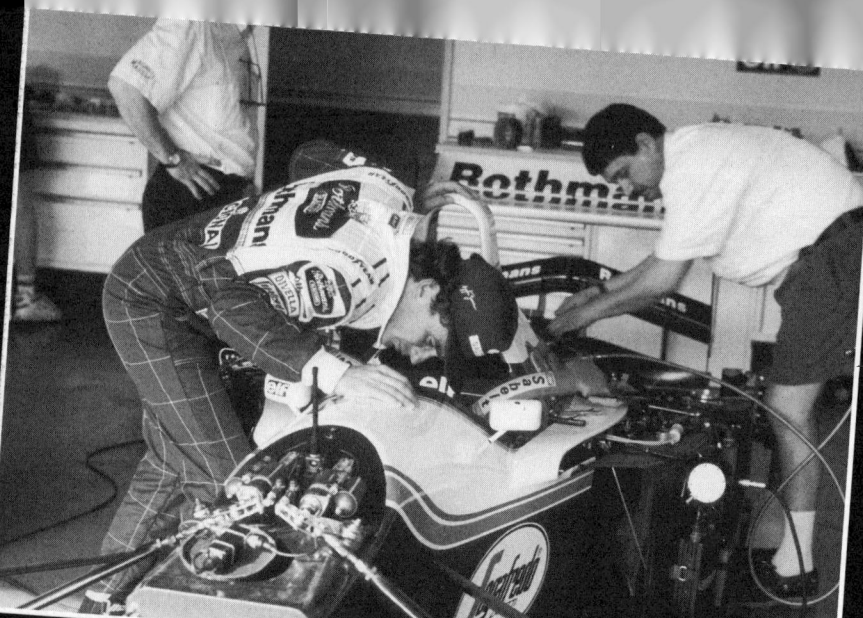

Ayrton checks out the cramped cockpit of his Williams FW16 that prevented him from using the larger diameter steering wheel he preferred.

Detail of the revolutionary rear suspension of the FW16: after a failure during the Paul Ricard tests, a metal reinforcement was introduced.

Two pole positions and two retirements: a disastrous start

AYRTON HAD HELD FIRM AND, THANKS TO HIS PHENOMENAL CONTROL AND SKILL, HAD MANAGED TO PUT THE CAR IN POLE POSITION.

Senna had achieved the first part of that double aim, saying: 'His starting position was very much a measure of his ability rather than of our car's superiority.' A change had been made to the set-up, with the return to Penske dampers, but Senna still drove brilliantly.

His 63rd pole start, 159 thousandths off the track record set by Mansell in 1992, speaks volumes about the Brazilian's commitment not to disappoint his public, despite a car without active suspension and jumping like a cricket.

In the race, Senna was authoritatively in the lead for 21 laps ahead of Schumacher, until the pit stop for the tyre change and refuelling, when the German took the lead. The team believed Ayrton could reel him in but on lap 56, on the exit from the last corner, the Williams spun. Was it a mistake by the driver, too hasty in going on the accelerator, or yet another demonstration of an unpredictable FW16?

The fact is that, coming out of the *S-Senna* corner, named after him, the Brazilian was left with the engine running and with the gearbox stuck in third gear. He tried to restart but the Renault engine stalled, causing him to retire. The immediate effect was that the packed grandstands began to empty: the home idol was out of the race, the show was over for them.

Schumacher won, with Hill second, but like all pursuers he was a lap behind. It was clear from the outset that the 1994 World Championship would be a two-way game between the up-and-coming German and Senna. The Brazilian's start could not have been worse, with a retirement and zero points in the bag. Adrian revealed in his book that Senna had admitted the spin was his mistake and nobody in the team crucified him; the engineers were aware that there was work to be done on the behaviour of the FW16 and the team scheduled three days of testing at the Jerez track from the following Monday, 4 April. The Andalusian track was ideal, because the asphalt had many bumps.

A spare bodyshell was brought to Spain, as the others were already on their way to Aida, Japan, and an old FW15D was also dusted off for comparative tests. Test-driver David Coulthard lapped on the first day, on Tuesday Senna and Hill alternated, and on Wednesday only Senna tested, comparing the two single-seaters. Coulthard spoke of a step forward in development, while Ayrton complained of understeer, despite using the mechanical power steering he had already used in Brazil.

The FW16 continued to be tough, all the more so as the Brazilian was forced into a cockpit which he continued to find tight, and the feeling was that the FW15D, the car made 'passive' in suspension from the year before, was doing better.

At the Williams headquarters it was clear that the reigning world champion team was experiencing a difficult moment: the FW16 was only a fast car in very limited conditions, and then it became grumpy, even for a champion like Senna. So it was decided that Adrian Newey would not go to Japan for the second GP: the engineer from Stratford-upon-Avon would remain at Didcot to study in the wind tunnel what was wrong.

F1, meanwhile, had gone to the Tanaka International Circuit in Aida for the first Pacific GP. The TI Circuit was new to everyone. Senna achieved his second pole position of the season, ahead of an increasingly consistent Michael Schumacher, while Damon Hill was on the second row, still struggling with the same transmission problems he had experienced in Brazil. Williams was innovative, but continued to experience tuning problems. The two drivers were in serious trouble in the slower parts of the circuit, and both were unable to avoid a spin during free practice, despite the fact flaps had been fitted to the sides of the nose that were supposed to improve corner entry.

Ayrton again complained about the car to Pierluigi Martini, as he walked down to the circuit from the small houses which hosted the entire Circus. With the two drivers was team principal Gian Carlo Minardi and Gabriele Tredozi, a technician of the Faenza team.

'Ayrton was disappointed, very disappointed,' Martini recalls. 'His Williams was unstable and it jumped a lot. He confided to me that he was still not comfortable in the cockpit with the position of his arms, but the team had repeated to him that, if that cockpit had previously suited Prost, it had to suit him too. And for this imposition, talking to me, he threatened never to race with his team again.'

Was this harsh response the result of a moment of discouragement? 'I replied, however, by telling him that if he was complaining about a car that was in pole position, could he imagine how much mine was jumping?'

The Japanese interlude ended with a quip from the Brazilian: 'Piero, if you are used to ugly women, it's not my fault, I only date beautiful ones.'

Senna left with a sardonic smile: 'It stayed in my mind,' concludes Martini, 'because we know what happened at Imola.'

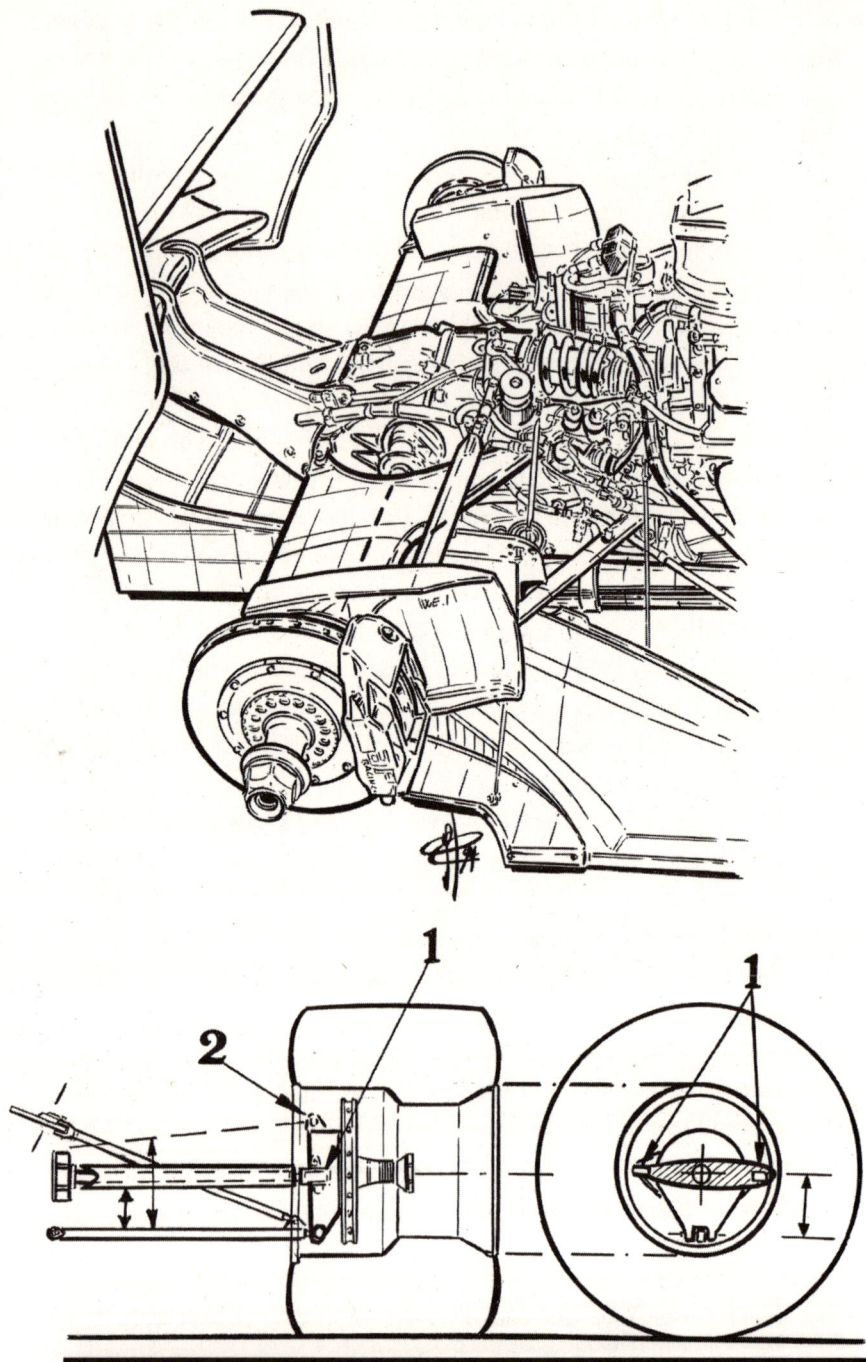

The rear suspension of the FW16 was highly innovative: Adrian Newey had devised a neutral wing profile that contained the two wishbones and the half-shaft.

Two pole positions and two retirements: a disastrous start

The race had an antecedent: the grid drove the reconnaissance lap preceded by the safety car, to prevent gaps from opening up too much as had happened in Brazil. In short, it was not poleman Senna who dictated the pace, so the Brazilian was unable to warm up his tyres as he would have liked. And, in fact, he got off to a bad start, causing the rear tyres to skid. So, into the lead went Schumacher, tailed by the McLaren of Mika Häkkinen who, at the first corner, crashed into the Williams, sending it into a spin.

There was chaos in the pack and Nicola Larini, making his debut in Jean Alesi's Ferrari 412 T1, completed the disaster by hitting the Williams at the edge of the track. It was retirement for both. Schumacher thus easily won the second race and already had a 20-point lead over the Brazilian. The season could not have started worse.

To heat up the atmosphere, there were also the rumours that filtered through Bernard Dudot, Renault's technical manager and a friend of Prost, who expressed the doubt that Williams had taken a 'boiled' driver (one who is past their best). The rumours reached Senna's ears, and took it very badly. The wind of controversy made it even more difficult for the Brazilian to live with a team in which he was not as comfortable as he had been at McLaren.

Williams's main focus was on assessing the FW16's instability problems and not on putting Ayrton in a position to drive better. Newey said in his book that he knew there was an instability in the aerodynamics. He feared the car could suddenly have a loss of downforce and become unpredictable, and this phenomenon usually happened at high speeds.

Williams tested again at the bumpy Circuit de Nogaro in south-western France, with Hill driving. The Englishman reported the car was jumping around violently, and Adrian saw it with his own eyes by following on a scooter. He returned to the wind tunnel to try to uncover the issue, but found nothing to indicate any problem with the front wing.

He realised the blockage had emerged under the leading edge of the sidepods. The separation was such that the diffuser almost completely stalled. 'It was a proper Eureka moment! The issue was a simple geometrical problem requiring a simple geometrical solution,' Newey said in his book. The long sidepod needed to be swapped for a shorter one which would mean a lower peak downforce, but which would prevent the front of the floor getting close to the ground and causing the stall.

THERE ARE THOSE WHO WANT SOMETHING TO HAPPEN, THOSE WHO WISH IT WOULD HAPPEN, AND THOSE WHO WORK HARD TO MAKE SOMETHING HAPPEN.

Two pole positions and two retirements: a disastrous start

Between the Pacific and San Marino GPs, Newey designed a shorter side that was sent into production. The mechanical part of the FW16 did not have to be changed, but new underbody and bodywork were needed.

Ayrton and Damon, therefore, would still have to face Imola with a single-seater that could stall on bumps. It was a macabre omen ...

CHAPTER 13

RATZENBERGER THE DAY BEFORE, AN ALARM UNHEARD

'THE DAY we fear as our last is only our birthday for eternity.'

Seneca, the stoic Roman philosopher, understood how death is a thin line that divides the passing of time from the perpetual. Some are doomed to oblivion, and some find a kind of immortality: 30 years has now passed since the tragedy of Ayrton Senna. Many F1 fans were not even born on that cursed 1 May, yet they have come to know and love the Brazilian champion. It is a media phenomenon that sooner or later will have to be studied, because the myth is handed down from one generation to the next and remains intact in its essence. Certainly, Magic has struck the collective imagination: there are films, books, DVDs and editorials with reconstructions and behind-the-scenes stories of an extraordinary career.

It is normal, it will be said, that Ayrton has reached an eternal dimension, while it is much less obvious that Roland Ratzenberger has somehow achieved it too. A minor character, another 'knight of risk' – as the master of journalism Marcello Sabbatini admirably defined drivers – who only became famous with his death.

The Austrian's 'birthday for eternity', if I may be allowed this reference to Seneca, was the day before Senna, on 30 April 1994. And it is perhaps for this reason that Roland will never be forgotten, because his dramatic end in the qualifying of the San Marino GP should have been a warning, but the Circus did not heed it: F1, in 1994, had crossed the safety threshold and, unknowingly, was playing with the imponderable. And the first one to suffer its consequences was the Austrian.

Roland was a good professional driver, not a champion. He deserves great respect, because he was the last underdog who stubbornly earned a place on the GP grid. It is sad to admit it, but it is fair to think that the course of Formula 1 history would perhaps not have changed if, on that accursed weekend, only Roland had tragically perished. Probably his bloody end on live TV would only have lengthened the list of drivers who have died in F1, men who, to follow their passion, play with their destiny by paying the highest price. But on that fateful San Marino GP weekend, a series of facts concatenated to make one think that God had decided that F1 should no longer be talked about.

On Friday, there was Rubens Barrichello's 'flight' over the protections of *Variante Bassa*, with his Jordan 194. I was at the Renault hospitality, on the second floor in the pit lane: it was in a very coveted spot, because it overlooked the pit lane entrance, so with one eye you had a perfect view of the last chicane and with the other you could watch the time monitor. The ideal position before going down into the pits to talk to drivers, managers and engineers.

The entrance to *Variante Bassa* was characterised by a very high kerb, designed to prevent the drivers from getting too confident at a point where, in fact, there was no escape route. For Barrichello that kerb became a sort of launching pad: the right rear wheel touched the kerb and the Jordan took off. There were moments of terror, because the single-seater went over the rows of protective tyres. Rubens looked like Spider-Man, clambering over the track fences with a car that had turned into a ground-to-air rocket: but it wasn't the special effects of a Hollywood film. It was all terribly real. The fences, fortunately, withstood the impact. The scream of the Hart V10 engine died in the air, leaving only the sound of the crash. The dull thud of the bodyshell crushing its nose on the asphalt, before turning over several times, brought us back to reality. The Enzo and Dino Ferrari plunged into a gloomy silence. Not a fly could be heard. Rubens was underneath his car with the wheels in the air, but he was a walking miracle. He spent a night in the Bellaria Hospital in Bologna for observation. He got away with a few bruises, a small fracture of the nasal septum, a few cuts on his mouth and a conspicuous bandage on his right arm, but clearly that was not 'his time'. Sid Watkins, the FIA's medical neurosurgeon, rightly did not allow him to race that GP. Better to take a break as the shock had been severe anyway.

A generation of F1 drivers had grown up without knowing what death on the track was. The last racing tragedy had been that of Riccardo Paletti, at the start of the 1982 Canadian GP. It cannot go unnoticed that, among the 28 drivers entered in the 1994 San Marino GP, only Michele Alboreto had experienced the drama of the death of that young man who had come to the Circus more to indulge his father's passion than his own. Four years later there had been the crash of Elio de Angelis during testing at Paul Ricard with the Brabham BT55. The rear wing had come off Gordon Murray's 'sole-fish', and the Roman driver rolled over before the single-seater caught fire. The rescue was very slow, because Grand Prix-standard safety measures were not required at private sessions. Elio could have been saved, but instead he passed away the next day, from the hot fumes he had breathed in for seven minutes. The stark lesson taught the Circus that the same safety standards had to be guaranteed in testing as in races. And, despite the frightening accidents that had followed over the years, the common feeling was that F1 had reached a standard that transformed drivers into immortal 'Highlanders'. This was not true.

Just like De Angelis, Ratzenberger's fate was determined by a wing. Roland was born in Austria on 4 July 1960. Already as a child he had used his imagination to build his own carts. He had breathed the air of the Salzburgring, one of the fastest and most dangerous circuits, where courage counted as much as clean driving.

He was not a champion, but he was talented and deeply motivated: he had managed to turn his visceral passion for racing into a profession. He had started out penniless, a heavy handicap for a driver with high hopes. Yet, with Van Diemen, he won the Formula Ford Festival at Brands Hatch in 1986, which at the time was considered a kind of world championship with small training single-seaters. Ratzenberger had beaten 126 opponents, just like some 15 other winners who had later gone on to F1: the last ones had been Mark Webber, Jenson Button and Anthony Davidson. These drivers had found a quick route to the Circus, while Roland's path was longer and more tortuous.

He worked his way up through the ranks in English Formula 3, then sought a place in the DTM, the German touring car championship: compatriot Helmut Marko entrusted him with a Mercedes 190E 2.3-

16 to race at the Nürburgring. But Roland could not break through: he decided to go to Japan, to compete in the F.3000 Japan, first with the Noji International team, then with Stellar International.

Away from home he started to win and, in the East, he became famous, finally earning his first money. In the land of the Rising Sun, Ratzenberger's esteem was growing, so much so that he was called into Toyota Team TOM'S, the official team of the Japanese giant, to compete in endurance races. In 1990 he won the 1,000km of Fuji and the following year the Suzuka race, and placed in the 24 Hours of Daytona with a Porsche 962. In 1993, he won the C2 class at the 24 Hours of Le Mans in a Toyota Sard, shared with Mauro Martini and Naoki Nagasaka.

He divided his existence between Japan and Monte Carlo. In the Principality he met Barbara Behlau, a beautiful lady who managed sponsorships and who found him the budget to make the leap into F1. The resources were sufficient to start the 1994 season, covering five Grands Prix, to begin with.

His single-seater was the Simtek S941 with Ford HB 3.5 V8 engine, designed by Nick Wirth. It was an immature car, modified in a hurry because it had been designed with active suspension, which was then banned. It was destined for the last rows of the grid. The technician was the godson of the FIA president Max Mosley. They had worked together at March, before setting up Simulation Technology Research Ltd, a consultancy firm that later built the Ligier wind tunnel, with subsidies from the French government, and conceived two F1 projects: for BMW, in 1990, and for the Bravo GP, two cars that never saw the light of day.

However, Nick Wirth did not want to waste the experience he had gained: with Jack Brabham, the three-time world champion, he therefore founded Simtek Grand Prix to take part in the 1994 World Championship with the support of MTV. One driver in the team was David Brabham, son of the Australian partner; the other was Roland, who brought in money from sponsor Russell Athletic.

Ratzenberger, a perceptive and intelligent boy, immediately understood where he had ended up: all resources were reserved for his team-mate and he would have to make do with the material they made available to him. In Brazil he did not qualify, but he then fulfilled his dream by making his debut at Aida, a track he knew well from his long experience in Japan: he was 26th on the grid in the Pacific GP, but passed the chequered flag in 11th position, finishing last of the classified drivers,

The impact of Ratzenberger's Simtek S941 against the barriers of the *Villeneuve* curve during the qualifying of the 1994 San Marino GP.

Roland's car stopped at the *Tosa* curve and the driver was helped by the marshals and the CEA Lions: it was immediately clear that the situation was serious.

Ratzenberger touches a kerb and cracks the front wing of his Simtek S941: he did not stop in the pits to check if there was any damage and went for another lap, the fatal one …

five laps behind the winner Michael Schumacher. It was a kind of miracle with a patched-up car, especially when you consider that David Brabham, in a full season, would not finish higher than tenth place (in Spain) and Jean-Marc Gounon, who took over from Andrea Montermini, the driver who replaced Roland, would peak with a ninth place in France.

In short, the boy who had studied mechanics at the Salzburg Vocational Institute, and who had also been a mechanic at Walter Lechner's school in order to race, had achieved his goal: to become an F1 driver. To his father Rudolf, half seriously, he repeated that sooner or later his name would finally appear in the legendary Marlboro Guide, the 'bible' of F1 statistics before the advent of the internet, edited by Jacques Dechenaux, which only took into account drivers who had competed in at least one GP.

'The mountain rat' – the literal translation of the Austrian's surname – did not know that Aida would mark his first and only appearance and his destiny would be fulfilled in the cursed San Marino GP.

A background incident unknown to most people was revealed in Adrian Newey's book *How to Build a Car*. The designer of Ayrton Senna's Williams FW16, recalling the nefarious Imola weekend, told of a puzzling episode that speaks volumes about how the minor F1 teams fared in those days. He said he remembered the front wing coming off one of the Simtek cars (he couldn't recall which) and he was then approached in the paddock that evening by the Simtek team manager, Charlie Moody, who he knew quite well. Moody said Nick Wirth had asked him to fix the front wing and he wanted some advice from Newey. The Williams man was bemused, as he knew Moody was not an engineer, and he asked him where Wirth was, only to be told he was at a sponsors' dinner. Newey said he couldn't help as he didn't know anything about the design of the Simtek and he told Moody he needed to get Wirth back from the dinner to do the work. In his book, Newey said the conversation worried him.

The broken piece, as it later became clear from the investigators' research, was Roland's.

How and when that wing was repaired is not known, but even during Saturday morning's free practice session, there was a misunderstanding between the two Simtek drivers at the *Tosa* corner, so much so that David Brabham ended up long in the escape route after avoiding his Austrian team-mate. They just grazed each other and it seemed that the episode ended there. In the pits, once the S941 had been recovered, the mechanics cleaned David's car of sand, checking that there was no damage before qualifying. Everything seemed fine, while on Ratzenberger's car there was a small crack in a flap support. Nick Wirth decided to replace the whole nose with the last available new part.

Roland wanted to prove that he was capable of getting on the grid even on a fast track like Imola, even though he knew his V8 Ford HB D6 engine was decidedly less powerful than the more recent versions. After a first run of three laps, the Austrian asked for more aerodynamic load at the front, so the incidence of the flaps had been increased.

Returning to the track after a launch lap, Ratzenberger ended up spinning at *Tosa*, the corner that was evidently hostile to him. It would have been just a small mistake without consequences, if on restarting he had not 'pinched' the front wing against the very high kerb. Roland was convinced he had not suffered any damage and, instead of returning to the pit lane to check that everything was OK, he chose to set another timed lap with that set of Goodyear tyres which was still fresh, even if no longer at peak performance.

As the team's telemetry later showed, the Austrian did not realise that the front wing had already shown a small failure when exiting the *Acque Minerali* bend. The driver did not notice any strange behaviour on his Simtek, until, in the higher speed section, on the straight that leads from *Tamburello* to *Villeneuve*, a piece of the front wing came away and flew off like a seagull. The increase in downforce at 308km/h had produced a sudden tear. Part of the profile stuck under the car, so that the front wheels lifted off the ground and lost contact with the asphalt.

That is the worst thing that can happen to a driver, along with a broken steering column, of course.

Roland did not panic: he instinctively applied the brakes violently (the telemetry speaks of a deceleration of between 2.0 and 2.2 G). The braking, however, was not as effective as usual because only the rear tyres slowed the single-seater down, as the front ones were raised. Ratzenberger managed to reduce his speed to 228km/h, but he had now become a helpless passenger in his uncontrolled single-seater. He could no longer steer, he could no longer do anything. A situation similar, very similar, to the one that the next day would make Ayrton Senna's blood run cold, with a broken steering column.

Roland crashed into the *Villeneuve* wall aware of his tragic fate: he stared death in the face. The violent impact was fatal. Tremendous. While his Simtek pirouetted, disintegrating all the way to *Tosa*, Roland's helmet, in the red and white colours of Austria, flopped back and forth as if there was a puppet and not a man in the cockpit.

The carbon bodywork had a huge hole on the left side. The effects of the crash had been destructive: chest compression, fracture of the skull base and exsanguination by laceration of the aorta. The doctors who rescued him were faced with a frightening sight, as blood pulsed profusely from the visor of his helmet. He would have died on the spot. A heart massage, however, revived him for long enough to be flown by helicopter to the *Ospedale Maggiore* in Bologna, where he later died. If he had died on the racetrack, it would have been temporarily closed by the legal authorities. And the show, probably, would have stopped.

ANOTHER KNIGHT OF RISK WHO BECAME FAMOUS WITH HIS DEATH.

Another alarm bell had rung, after Barrichello's bang, but F1, again, did not listen. Only Senna was concerned; he wanted to understand what had happened to Ratzenberger. He went to talk to Sid Watkins, the FIA doctor, and argued with the stewards who wanted to prevent him from going to *Tosa*. He 'stole' an official car to make an inspection of the track. Ayrton understood.

On that Saturday, the 'unknown soldier' of F1 died. He would probably have been forgotten. However, Magic's sacrifice the next day brought Ratzenberger into the pantheon of the gods of risk.

CHAPTER 14

TWO FLAGS IN THE COCKPIT FOR A TRIBUTE THAT NEVER HAPPENED

AYRTON SENNA had no ominous forebodings before the start of the San Marino GP. The Brazilian champion, after two pole positions and as many retirements at Interlagos and Aida, was still on zero points in the Drivers' World Championship standings. Imola, therefore, was to be the revival appointment in the championship, to stem the rise of Michael Schumacher with Benetton, who had won the first two rounds.

The Brazilian, of course, had been shaken by the dramatic Imola weekend, but he never, ever, thought of not racing there, or retiring. Clearing up any doubts is the account of Senna's friend Angelo Orsi, who reveals some details of an episode that has somewhat entered the legend of the Brazilian champion.

Senna, who had achieved his third pole position with the Williams FW16-Renault on the banks of the Santerno, had decided that, after winning the San Marino GP, he would do the lap of honour while waving both the Brazilian and Austrian flags in front of the Italian public, in honour of Ratzenberger. It was not just an idle thought, but a very serious intention of the Paulista. Ayrton did not question the victory in the slightest, so much so that he had carefully planned the project in detail. Angelo Orsi was to be his 'accomplice' and he had been properly instructed.

Angelo explains, 'Senna told me, "I'll be waiting for you at *Tosa*. I want a photo taken by you from the car with the Imola crowd in the background as I wave the two flags: the Brazilian and the Austrian in memory of Roland."

"'Ayrton I can't,'" I replied firmly, "the FIA will take away my pass if I dare to get on the bonnet of your Williams. And do you know what that means? That I won't work in Formula 1 anymore, not to mention what they might do to you. You've seen what's happened to you before! No one forbids you to wave the two flags on the return lap, but I won't be allowed to get onto your car to photograph the lap from *Tosa* to the *parc fermé*.'"

The South American champion did not listen to reason, telling Angelo he would refuse to race if they took his pass away. 'I am Ayrton Senna … don't worry, they won't take your pass away. We will do something extraordinary!'

They discussed and drew up a precise plan. 'He insisted so much,' Angelo continues, 'that he convinced me: I gave in because I saw how much he liked the idea, and the more he talked about it, the more I began to like it too. Undoubtedly, it would have been a unique thing that would have caused a sensation. So, from words to deeds, I made an agreement with the marshals at *Tosa* to allow me to go to the edge of the track with them when they waved the flags at the winner of the GP. Ayrton would stop and I would sit on the bonnet of his Williams, with one leg tucked into the cockpit.'

Not an easy task to accomplish …
I was very apprehensive about this photo, because I had taken laps in an F1 car before and I knew it was no picnic. Doing a lap in a car driven by a friend who had just won the San Marino GP was a bit scary for me. Ayrton had also thought about the framing: him waving the flags against the backdrop of the passionate Imola crowd. We had also looked at the point where we could have the light in our favour.

Where did the two flags end up?
I never had them. They were in the car, Ayrton would take them out at the moment of victory, which he took for certain. He wanted to celebrate his success at Imola, he was sure he would win the first world championship points that would [help to] take him to his fourth title, and he wanted to remember Roland. This was supposed to be my GP at Imola. Instead, we know how it turned out.

Two flags in the cockpit for a tribute that never happened

The Brazilian and Austrian flags disappeared before the FW16 was seized by the judicial authorities. They disappeared just like the driver's left glove, which was stolen and has never reappeared, even among collectors ...

The memory of Ratzenberger has never faded: at the *Villeneuve* chicane his fans left testimonies of affection for the Austrian driver who died in qualifying for the 1994 San Marino GP.

CHAPTER 15

THE SAFETY CAR DRIVER: THE LAST PERSON TO SEE SENNA ALIVE

'HE JUST looked at me. That look told me everything there was to say.'

Charles Bukowski, the cursed American writer, captured the essence of the drama suffered for years by Massimiliano Angelelli, the driver of the safety car in the San Marino GP, the last one to meet Ayrton Senna's eyes alive.

Massimiliano 'Max' Angelelli is more famous in the United States, where he trained as a professional driver, than he is in Europe. Born in Bologna in 1966, he has won the 24 Hours of Daytona twice, coming second on seven other occasions. A specialist in endurance racing, he has become a reference figure for Dallara in the world of sports cars, as well as a valued manager. In 1994, he was an official VW driver in German Formula 3, having won the Italian title two years earlier; in short, he was the Bernd Mayländer of the time, anything but unprofessional.

I know Max well, because I followed his rise from Formula Alfa Boxer, where he began his career in 1987 like many other talented young Italian drivers. His father, as well as being in charge of track operations at Enzo and Dino Ferrari, was at the time one of the owners of AB Motorsport, a team for which I also raced in the Civt with a Peugeot 205 1.9. If there was a car available, during the breaks in the German F3, Angelelli would join the group of drivers competing in the Turismo championship for pure fun, and he never missed an opportunity to race at Imola, on his home track, which he knew like the back of his hand. It should come as no surprise, therefore, that the young Bolognese driver was chosen to drive the safety car in the 1994 San Marino GP. The car intended for the purpose was an Opel Vectra turbo with permanent four-wheel drive and self-locking differential. It had a 2-litre front transverse four-cylinder engine, capable of 204 horsepower at 5,600rpm, with torque of 280Nm at 2,600rpm. The manual transmission was six-speed, while the weight was 1,350kg. In short, it was a sedan that was anything but sporty.

'When they showed me the car, my blood froze,' Angelelli says. 'It wasn't suitable for running in front of F1 cars. So I went to Charlie Whiting, the FIA's technical delegate, and explained my doubts to him: that car wasn't powerful enough and, above all, it didn't have an adequate braking system for track use.'

Angelelli then decided to do a short test: a couple of laps of the Enzo and Dino Ferrari, just to understand how the Vectra behaved in practice. 'I wasn't wrong: it was a real disaster. On the two downhills you had to throw an anchor to stop it. Already at the end of the second lap, the brakes overheated and the pedal became spongy, lengthening the braking distances. I was worried and saw that my fear did not elicit any reaction.

'I then decided to go to the Porsche Super Cup paddock and ask if they had a 911 with roll cage and trim, and with road tyres. It didn't seem real to them to eventually have one of their cars appear on live TV in front of the F1 grid. I was proud of my choice and set about transferring the safety car signs and the in-car camera into the cockpit of the Porsche. When everything was ready, they explained to me on Saturday morning that I would not be able to use the 911. I was still young and didn't understand certain dynamics and certain balances: evidently there were some commercial agreements I didn't know about. For me, simply, the Opel Vectra was not suitable as a safety car, so I had looked for a more suitable car, which was the Porsche. Without giving me any further explanation, they told me to take everything out of the 911 and reinstall it into a three-box Vectra. I realised that what should have been fun, could turn into a nightmare.'

And so it was: at 2pm on Sunday, 1 May, the San Marino GP got underway: shortly after the start, there was an accident between the Benetton of JJ Lehto, who was stationary on the grid, and the Lotus of Pedro Lamy...

Everything happened suddenly and I was not ready, in the sense that I had not put on the upper part of the fireproof suit and I had not yet put on the helmet, which was placed on the back seat. The accident took me by surprise, but it was my own fault. Charlie Whiting received the order over the radio and told me to start: to enter the track we had to go through the pit lane.

Charlie kept control and dictated the orders in a calm voice: I knew him quite well, because he was the race director in Macao, where I had raced several years in F3. He was sitting in the right-hand seat and was not wearing a helmet, because he had a headset in radio connection with the race director to carry out the instructions. We entered the track and slowed down, waiting for the single-seaters behind to arrive, which in the meantime had reduced their speed after the safety car signs had been displayed from the marshals' stations.

With a glance in the rear-view mirror, I saw Senna's Williams arriving, which was in the lead, so I picked up speed, and, well aware of the car's limits, I did not go looking for 100 per cent performance, especially as I had no idea how long I would have to stay on the track before the race could restart. I knew that the brakes would not hold up for more than a couple of laps, so I tried to be conservative on the braking, while under acceleration I pressed the accelerator pedal so hard that I could have made a hole in the floor.

Angelelli was as focused as if he were involved in an F3 race: 'Imola did not put stress on the Vectra in acceleration, at least not until you got to the two climbs. The most critical point was coming out of *Acque Minerali*: on the ramp towards the *Variante Alta* the Opel was almost stuck, I couldn't go over 130km/h. In short, I felt stationary! Senna, who was leading the group, pulled alongside in the Williams, as he did several times later, showing me his fist and telling me to go faster.

'I am awakening memories that I had hoped to have erased from my mind: Charlie and I were the last ones to look Ayrton in the eye. The Brazilian was furious and he was more than right: his Williams was going too slowly and the tyres would lose pressure and temperature. Whiting remained silent and did not ask me to go faster. He was aware that the Vectra didn't have enough power and, in the meantime, on the dashboard all the warning lights had come on … On the downhill braking of *Rivazza* I had to brake early and smoothly, so the speed was

… ridiculous. After three laps, despite all my precautions, I went wide and by going over the kerb that marked the track, I ended up on the grass and then with two wheels on the sand. At that point I got worried and involved Charlie: "Look, the brakes are gone! I run one more lap and then come back into the pits because I can't do anymore: it's dangerous. How would it look if the safety car went off the track?" Whiting reported the problem to the race directors, but they would not listen to reason: we had to stay on the track. The order was peremptory. I continued, but I was going slower and slower. It became embarrassing: nothing personal with the Vectra, but that car should not have been in front of the F1 group! At the end of lap four, we were finally given the order to return to the pit lane, since the race could start again. I parked the Opel in the pit lane and switched off the engine. It never started again. The car was dead. And when, two laps later, there was Ayrton's accident, they immediately stopped the race with the red flag.

Senna was seen in the TV footage gesticulating several times because the pace of the safety car was too slow …
You've all seen that, but now I'll tell you what I experienced: for years I regretted the accident. I thought the Williams's tyres had lost a lot of pressure and the car had bounced on the *Tamburello* bumps and had maybe broken something before it went off the track. The accident, however, happened at the beginning of the third lap after the restart, i.e. the seventh of the race, and the thing was not clear to me: by then the tyres should have returned to the right pressure and temperature, to ensure good grip. To put my mind at rest, after the race I called Gianni Morbidelli, the driver from Pesaro who had been in the race with Footwork: 'Don't worry,' Gianni told me, 'we managed *Tamburello* right from the start and the bumps didn't create a big problem in controlling the car.' The Pesaro driver's words partly reassured me.

In reality, Max carried the inner torment for years. And to make matters worse, there was the publication of an interview in *The Times*: 'Statements were attributed to me that I had never made to the journalist. I later learned that a cut and paste had been made of a conversation I had had with another English reporter. I never understood how my words ended up in the Sunday edition of *The Times* with so many omissions that changed the meaning of what my story was. I hoped that there would be

Angelelli leads the safety car in the 1994 San Marino GP: the driver from Bologna was driving an Opel Vectra that was not suitable for leading the F1 group after the accident at the start.

Angelelli after his victory at the 24 Hours of Daytona: the driver had been unfairly criticised by those who had deemed him unfit to lead the safety car at Imola.

no reaction, but instead, I had to defend myself. I was sued by Williams's lawyers. And I had the feeling it was an attempt to divert attention from what had happened to a hypothetical misconduct of the safety car. According to the Anglo-Saxons, the safety car had been too slow and had caused a loss of tyre pressure, which made the Williams go off the track.'

Even at the trial, strong doubts emerged about the safety car driver ...
They didn't know I was a professional driver. I held the track record at Imola in F3. I had been Italian champion in the feeder series that bred drivers who then went directly to F1. I could not be blamed for anything, considering the problems I'd had with the Vectra. I can assure you that in such a difficult situation I had extracted 100 per cent of the potential from the car. Firstly, I had tried to preserve the braking system and then to maintain the pace allowed by the car. However, I had to submit a series of briefs to clarify my position, but I avoided going through the legal process and the hearings, because eventually it turned out that the track and tyre pressure had nothing to do with the accident. But, in the meantime, just how long have I been vexed? I am left with the doubt that, had there been a 'Mr Nobody' in my place, with no experience of racing cars, the theory of those who blamed the driver of the safety car would perhaps have passed the courtroom.

For Angelelli, as in other situations characterising the Senna case, incredible coincidences and twists of fate emerge.

'Senna's track engineer, David Brown, later looked after my car when I drove for Cadillac,' he says. 'And JJ Lehto became the team-mate I shared the car with. Shall we also talk about Pedro Lamy? I then became the Portuguese's manager for 20 years. Isn't all this simply incredible?'

But, after time had passed, did you ever get a chance to talk to David Brown about your grievances?
No, never. It is a subject we have never discussed. Thirty years have passed, I may not remember all the details of that cursed day, but I do remember the deep emotions and the scars it left on me. Seeing the strongest driver in history flanking you and making a fist to tell you to go faster made me feel tiny: I wanted to disappear, never to have been born. For me it was terrible: it's as though from the cockpit of his Williams he was talking to me, so clear was the message he was sending me. I left the

racetrack feeling almost guilty. It was terrible. Morbidelli's words were comforting, but they did not put my conscience at peace.

After three decades, the deep wounds of the soul have slowly healed. 'I continued my racing career, keeping inside what I felt when I thought about Ayrton. I never wanted to talk to anyone about it. In America only a few people knew that I had driven the safety car in the San Marino GP. After the film on Senna came out, however, I was asked about nothing else but what had happened at Imola. For 30 years I was in the shadows and now the subject has come up again, proving the greatness of a champion who will never end up in oblivion. He was simply the greatest.'

CHAPTER 16

THE DOCTOR RECOUNTS THE RESCUE: THERE WAS NO HOPE

'IT IS the doctor's job to prolong life and not to prolong the act of death.'

Baron Thomas Jeeves Horder, physician to the British royals until the mid-20th century, was able to dig a deep furrow in what, to many, might seem a thin, almost intangible line. Even at heads or tails, it can happen that the coin bounces on the ground and begins to whirl around, prolonging that short but spasmodic wait. This way or that way: life or death. Domenico Salcito, now 80 years old, was deputy head of the medical service at the Imola circuit in 1994 and among the team of doctors who, with great promptness, intervened at *Tamburello* after Ayrton Senna's Williams went off the track on lap seven. It was on that very occasion that Salcito and his colleagues saw a coin spinning madly. Heads or tails? Time was the great enemy, although it seemed that time itself had stopped at 14:17.

In the distance echoed annoyingly the sound of the trumpets of the fans, who still had not understood what had happened. Those who had seen Magic slamming into the wall were plunged into an eerie silence. The rescuers arrived quickly, each one from their own stations. Some on foot, running. Others with vehicles. Like industrious ants with a task to perform, the doctors gathered around the wreckage of the FW16: each one knew what to do. There was no need for many words, but for action.

'There was a call over the radio from the race direction centre,' recounts Domenico Salcito. 'It was Giuseppe Piana, head of the medical service at Imola: "Accident at *Tamburello*!" I was in the medical car parked at the *Variante Bassa* escape route. In the front seat was Mario Casoni, a very experienced driver, and at his side was Dr Sid Watkins, the FIA medical director. In the back seats were myself and a good resuscitator from Ravenna hospital, Federico Baccarini. When we arrived at *Tamburello* we parked the medical car next to the Williams. Senna was motionless in the cockpit of his wrecked car. On the spot was the doctor on duty at that corner, Giuseppe Pezzi, who had arrived on foot: we found him kneeling on the right side of the Williams, busy trying to remove Ayrton's helmet.

'The race directors, meanwhile, had shown the red flag, which led to the race being interrupted. Once out of the medical car, I initially took charge of the rescue operation. The first thing to do was to remove the helmet: Baccarini straddled the bonnet of the Williams, while I knelt on the left side of the single-seater. I couldn't undo the helmet and so I used scissors to cut the chinstrap. The operation was anything but simple, there was a lot of blood and I couldn't see very well, in fact I ran the risk of causing more damage. When we managed to pull off the yellow and green helmet, we were confronted with a chilling picture ... At first I acted automatically, as a doctor aware of the importance of quick decisions is supposed to do. At that moment I felt no emotion: the state of mind with which I had been specially forged to go into the operating theatre prevailed in me. At the *Ospedale Maggiore* in Bologna, I was a senior surgeon and treated the traumatology of large vessels, following road accidents.'

In the meantime, Dr Piana and some people from the race management had rushed to the scene ...
I couldn't tell who they were, because my whole attention was all focused on Senna. I knew immediately it was a serious situation, because I saw the same blood dripping under the helmet that had prevented my colleague Pezzi from undoing the strap.

You said the picture was dramatic: once the helmet had been taken off, what did you see?
Ayrton was unconscious and had no reaction. So I took a big responsibility without thinking too much about it: I was aware that it was not possible to follow the intervention protocol drawn up in the various FIA study sessions with Sid Watkins. The protocol said that a driver who was in

no condition to respond had to be harnessed in a structure called a KED [Kendrick Extrication Device] to avoid injury to the spinal column, an operation that had to be carried out after immobilising the neck with a collar. Extraction with the KED was a complicated procedure, so I told my colleagues that we would get Senna out of the Williams with our arms.

You took quite a risk, going outside the procedures codified by the international federation ...
There was no time to waste. But in the rush of the moment we were about to make a mistake, or at least a bad impression: we started to pull him out when I realised that we had not unfastened the seatbelts yet! After releasing them, and positioning one doctor on each side, we lifted him by the straps of his suit and then from under his legs. Finally, we laid him on the ground.

Senna was helpless, a puppet in your hands. RAI, the Italian state television, was broadcasting the San Marino GP live: they had to cover a race and not the agony of a champion. Giancarlo Tomassetti, the director, had the human sensitivity not to frame those crude moments, respecting the painful uncertainty about Ayrton's condition, which to you, on the other hand, seemed immediately and dramatically clear ...
What had I seen? The unconscious driver, his face swollen, blood pouring out of his nose and mouth, but I had also glimpsed something that chilled me: there were small particles of grey matter all around. And this immediately prompted me to accelerate every procedure.

Usually a traumatised driver is lifted by the doctors, loaded into the ambulance and transferred to the racetrack's medical centre, before then being transported to the nearest trauma centre by helicopter ...
No one, in accordance with procedure, could have decided on the immediate transfer of the injured man directly to hospital. And, in fact, the day before, Roland Ratzenberger had been taken by ambulance to the medical centre. This was not the case with Senna, because we had already been informed by Giovanni Gordini, the doctor in charge of 118 [the Italian emergency service], that the *Bologna Soccorso* helicopter was in the air, and not parked at the side of the medical centre, as it should have been. If Dr Watkins had known about the helicopter in the air, he would

certainly have had something to say about it, but in those moments I met Piana's eyes and it was decided by mutual agreement to let the aircraft land on the circuit.

But didn't you notice Ayrton's injured right eye?
I didn't actually see him until the next day. At the moment of rescue, Ayrton was a mask of blood: his face was all swollen, like that of a boxer at the end of a very hard fight. I held his helmet in my hand for almost an hour and noticed how bad it looked, but I only realised what might have happened when they showed me some photos and details afterwards. The next day, Piana and I went to the mortuary together: on two stretchers, side by side, were Ayrton and Roland. Ratzenberger had a sharp face, typical of someone who had had serious internal bleeding and, in fact, we later learned that the Austrian driver had died of a ruptured aorta, while Ayrton's face was practically unrecognisable, much worse than I had seen it the day before.

When the 118 helicopter left the track were you aware that Ayrton was still alive? Was there a heartbeat?
This is a question I have always been asked. And to this question I have always answered in the same way: Senna did not die on the track. The lack of brain activity I could suspect, but I could not verify it, while the heart activity was present and was detected with the pressure gauge. There was never any uncertainty about that. On the final outcome I might have already had some clue, but on the fact that I left him alive I never had any doubt.

At the editorial office of Autosprint *we thought at first that the steering column had been cut by one of you rescuers, after Gabriele Tarquini pointed out the anomaly of the steering wheel outside the car ...*
I came to the editorial office at Conti Editore to see the pictures taken by Angelo Orsi: my wish was to perform the epicrisis of what I had seen, and the shots reflected what I had experienced. It's something I've always done out of habit, even after major surgery: it's the best way to realise if you've done everything right or if there were mistakes to correct. I was about to say goodbye when you asked me: 'How did you cut the steering column?' If you remember, I had no doubts in my answer: 'We doctors didn't even see the steering wheel.' In fact, while we were about to make

fools of ourselves for not having unbuckled the seatbelts, it occurred to me, as if in a flashback, that the steering wheel wasn't there, because otherwise, in order to extract Ayrton, we would have had to remove the wheel from the column first ... but it wasn't there. At that point you showed me a picture with the steering wheel and a piece of the column on the asphalt, the electric cables still connected.

So Dr Pezzi, the first rescuer to reach the crashed Williams, did not cut the column?
No, not at all. Not least because in our equipment we don't have the tools to perform that kind of operation. If necessary, the CEA 'Lions', the fire-fighting specialists, who have pneumatic shears, would have had to intervene. Only some time later did it emerge what had happened to the column.

Who was Ayrton Senna to Domenico Salcito?
I followed Ayrton very closely from the beginning and I was a fan. I always held him in high esteem, as a man and as a driver. I had great admiration for him, because I saw him not only as a champion, but also as a serious professional. I remember that in collective tests Senna was the first one on the track in the morning, as soon as the green light came on in the pit lane. Unlike many others, he would do an 'installation lap' and return to the garage to give the McLaren and Honda engineers a chance to download the telemetry data. He would exchange his information with the track engineer over the radio and wait for them to give him the go-ahead to return to the track without ever getting out of the car. No complaints, but maximum concentration because then he would start driving and never stop, well aware of how important that preparatory work would be on race weekends.

While you were rescuing him, you didn't have time to think that you were intervening on your idol. Was there no emotion?
No, I was the operating professional. I happened to look up and see Angelo Orsi taking pictures, which is why I then came to the editorial office. The emotional part emerged later.

After Senna's accident, there was the second start: but how could you go back to the Variante Bassa station to see the F1 cars line up for the start?

I spoke to Mario Casoni about this very thing recently: the medical car driver, before making the second start, came to me and said: 'Let's do our best now, but be aware that I won't be coming here again!' And he never came back ...

What is it like to experience the start of an F1 Grand Prix from the back of the grid with the medical car?
I had actually got used to it, but it is a strange feeling to explain. Our car was positioned behind the single-seaters and when the lights went out all you could see was a mass of moving wheels. Before the start, there is a moment of silence, almost unreal, which gives a thrilling sense of anticipation, then the noise of the engines rises and becomes deafening. An explosion. And shortly afterwards the sound disappears, just as the cars disappear.

Do you know what the feeling is? It's as if you are standing still in the medical car, while in reality you are cruising at about 200km/h, as you don't start from a standstill like F1 cars. In those moments there is a lot of tension, a lot of adrenaline, and you keep your eyes wide open, because anything can happen in the group in front. But we had gained experience over time. On Thursdays we would do tests to get familiar with the car, which was not always the same: in 1994 we had an Alfa Romeo 164 3-litre. In the only Italian GP held at Imola, in 1980, we had used a Ferrari Berlinetta, driven by none other than F1 world champion Phil Hill.

In this regard, there was a diplomatic incident that was reported by Dr Watkins in his book. Sid was not really in Piana's league. The head of the medical service at Imola couldn't stand Watkins: in his role as inspector, the Englishman asked for doctors to be stationed everywhere along the circuit. I remember that he also wanted a rescuer at the *Tosa* exit, and so Piana, seeing what he had already arranged changed, became very agitated.

And what happened?
While we were inspecting the track with the car, Piana was ranting and raving at Watkins. Giuseppe was convinced that Sid didn't understand Italian and was going at it hard, knowing moreover that the driver of the car was American. But he did not know that Phil Hill, having raced with Ferrari, understood Italian perfectly. And the US champion could not

resist telling the whole scene publicly, which Watkins later transcribed in his book *Life at the Limit*.

The 1994 weekend began with Rubens Barrichello's flight over the nets of Variante Bassa...
And we were just opposite. All we had to do was cross the track. The Brazilian driver got off lightly, but the accident was impressive in its dynamics. Ayrton was one of the first to rush to the medical centre to see how his friend was doing. And I must say that Senna had also been one of the first and few to visit the medical centre when it first opened. He was a very sensitive person. And he was very alarmed about Rubens.

In an already shaken emotional climate, Roland's accident then occurred...
On the track, an accident can always happen. Unfortunately there was also a technical explanation. Ratzenberger had hit a kerb and broken the front wing, but had not returned to the pits to do the checks. The profile came off and ended up under the front wheels, so the Austrian crashed without being able to control the car.

A death on the circuit is something I had never experienced before, and I must say it was traumatic for everyone. We were not prepared for such a mournful event. Of course, we all knew that 'motorsport is dangerous', but when it happens you cannot remain indifferent. The accident happened at the *Villeneuve* bend: I arrived with the medical car while Paolo Lega was already at work. Roland was quickly extracted and taken to the medical centre, before being transferred by helicopter to the *Ospedale Maggiore*. His condition was indeed serious, but what injury exactly he might have suffered was not obvious, although we suspected: internal bleeding.

The whole procedure was so fast that we did not have time to look at him. Everyone at the medical centre was present: Watkins, Piana and me. Roland had to be transferred quickly. The clinical picture was very critical: a patient collapsed from at least a ruptured spleen. Senna came to inquire worriedly: he looked and did not speak. He was speechless. He was stunned.

We know that, before returning to the Williams pit, he cried between two piles of tyres.

Then came the accursed Sunday: the crash at Tamburello, *the Williams torn apart and Ayrton lifeless …*
As doctors, we acted mechanically, although we were already shaken by Saturday's tragedy. But the world collapsed on us the moment the 118 helicopter left the track. We knew we had sent Ayrton to the *Ospedale Maggiore*, but even though no one had breathed a word, we were certain it would end there.

Surely, everyone's desire was to run far away and, instead, the race directors planned a second start. The show must go on, as the English say. How did you manage to get back in the car?
After the emotion came the anger; we were not ready to go straight back into the medical car. On Saturday, after Ratzenberger's accident,

Doctor Salcito precedes Senna's stretcher as the Brazilian champion is carried to the helicopter that has landed on the track.

qualifying had resumed in the same way, but there was hope that an operation could save his life. It was not the same for Senna. And I swear it was very difficult to do that second start again. I wept secretly. What more could have happened at Imola on that improbable weekend? Don't forget that we had already experienced the crash of the first start. Fate had not stopped yet …

Thirty years later, what has that weekend left within you?
So much bitterness and the certainty of having tried everything that could be done. I kept Senna's brain scan for years: I kept it from 1994 until 2010, out of affection for Ayrton, and I kept it jealously, but then, having moved houses and no longer being in a condominium, I began to fear the arrival of thieves, who later actually broke in despite the burglar alarms. So I destroyed it: I never wanted that CT to end up in the hands of thieves.

And it was the right decision.

CHAPTER 17

THE HOVERING MEDICAL HELICOPTER WAS BREAKING NORMAL PROCEDURES

'We have to learn the rules well, in order to break them in the right way.'

The Dalai Lama's thoughts can sum up Giovanni Gordini's idea in a few words. The 70-year-old doctor from Emilia, now director of the resuscitation unit and the emergency and traumatology department of the *Ospedale Maggiore* in Bologna, was in charge of the 118 emergency service in the city of Bologna in 1994. In short, he was one of the doctors on duty at Imola during that San Marino GP full of strange coincidences. For 30 years a forbidden subject was only murmured in hushed whispers, because no one ever spoke about it in clear terms: the helicopter that landed on the Enzo and Dino Ferrari track after Ayrton Senna's accident was already hovering over the racetrack before the start of the GP.

According to the strict safety procedures implemented by the FIA, the aircraft should have been parked in the lay-by next to the medical centre. Instead, the *Bologna Soccorso* helicopter was already up in the air, contravening all regulations. Why?

'The answer is simple,' says Gordini. 'The day before there had been Roland Ratzenberger's accident, and before that, on Friday, we'd had to transfer Rubens Barrichello to the Bellaria hospital in Bologna, after his accident with the Jordan at *Variante Bassa*, during free practice. Rubens had escaped without serious injury and, after diagnostic checks, he was immediately discharged. We didn't expect another crash at the weekend, but fearing it might happen, we were on the alert.'

Inside the circuit area there was also another helicopter that Sagis, the management company of the Enzo and Dino Ferrari circuit, had requested to comply with the safety regulations of the FIA: 'We had it moved from the medical centre's apron on the Saturday after Roland's accident,' continues Gordini, 'because our side-entry helicopter allowed the doctors to continue working even during the flight, while the one at the racetrack, once the traumatised man was on board, could only ensure his transportation. Ratzenberger was dying, but he was still alive when we transferred him to the *Ospedale Maggiore*, and with the use of our aircraft we could better manage the clinical emergency, even though we had little hope.'

So, on the day of the GP, the helicopter with pilot Antonio Vaccari on board was already up in the air when the collision of JJ Lehto's Benetton with Pedro Lamy's Lotus occurred at the start. A wheel that had come off one of the single-seaters had ended up in the grandstand and had hit a spectator. 'I left the race direction monitor room and took the Vespa [scooter] we used for internal movements, to go and see what had happened: the spectator had suffered a head injury and was immediately taken to Bologna, where a brain scan showed the presence of an extradural haematoma. He was immediately operated on in neurosurgery at the Bellaria hospital, and his condition then improved rapidly. Unfortunately, shortly after the accident at the start, after the race had resumed, Mauro Sacchetti, the medical coordinator of the 118 emergency service, said in a dry tone over the radio: 'Senna – *Tamburello*.' The emotional reaction to that message associating Ayrton with a critical point on the track was distressing, especially because it immediately brought to mind what had happened the day before with Ratzenberger. That's why I immediately took my Vespa again and rushed to the site.'

In the field, medical coordination was headed by Giuseppe Piana and Sid Watkins, a neurosurgeon and FIA doctor at the time.
We knew each other well and understood each other in an instant; we immediately grasped that it was better to take Ayrton away immediately. We decided by gesture to land the rescue craft that was in the air. 'Send the helicopter immediately,' I said to Sacchetti, who discussed the matter

with the race director in the monitor room. There was little to negotiate, as the request was between the necessary and the obvious. In my opinion, it would have been impossible to say no to the helicopter and start instead the usual procedure with an ambulance sent to the track. No one could have imagined that the aircraft would need to land immediately to take Ayrton to the destination hospital.

I went through *Tamburello*, entered one of the marshals' stations and abandoned the scooter, which I did not retrieve until the next day. I crossed the track and arrived at the site. I remember seeing Alessandro Misley, an anaesthetist. The medical team was already at work: I heard Ayrton breathing on his own and saw that he had not been intubated yet. Senna was still alive. We exchanged half-sentences with Watkins and then went to the helicopter, which was not far away: as soon as he was on board we gave Senna the temporary mini-tracheotomy that is practised in flight and is useful for maintaining lung ventilation during transportation.

Dr Gordini has seen it all in his career, and regarding Senna's rescue he adds: 'It was madness to think that the fastest man in the world, involved in a racing accident and in a context where safety had to be at the highest level, could not be offered the same rescue treatment that is guaranteed to any person who has a road accident near Imola.

'To comply with "standard" track rescue procedures, we would have had to load Ayrton into an ambulance and take him to the medical centre, going around the circuit. But since the medical centre's facilities were not adequate for such a grave patient, then we would have had to arrange for him to be transported by helicopter to the nearest trauma centre, which is the one at the *Ospedale Maggiore* in Bologna. Therefore, I think, logic prevailed over rules.'

You performed an innovative rescue operation that was unprecedented in racing ...
Yes, but we were working outside the procedures. In the years following 1994, we also considered the idea of possibly proceeding with the ambulance in the opposite direction to the track, without completing the full lap, because starting from *Tamburello*, for example, it would be much quicker to get to the medical centre [that way]. After the 1994 experience, we also did some reconnaissance on the track to see where

else the helicopter could land in case of need, but fortunately there has been no further need.

The collaboration of the racetrack with the 118 rescue service was positive ...
The emergency system was in our control: there was an agreement that we renewed every year between the Municipality of Imola, Sagis and *Bologna Soccorso*, also defining the costs of the service. I can say that a large part of the trauma centre's IT computer brain was financed with the revenue that came from the Imola racetrack to the local health unit. An effective collaboration was created: the right decision, derived from the Imola experience, was that the traumatised person would be treated by the team of the local hospital, the *Ospedale Maggiore* in Bologna.

The flight to the Ospedale Maggiore *was short: from Imola it took only a few minutes ...*
When we landed, Senna had a cardiac arrest from which he quickly recovered. Then we arrived in the emergency room, where he was intubated and then taken to neuroradiology to perform a brain CT [Computed Tomography] scan. During the helicopter transport I had called Dr Maria Teresa Fiandri, at the time head of the reanimation and 118 department of the *Ospedale Maggiore*, so that she would immediately assemble the medical team and be ready for our arrival.

Then, an incredible and probably unrepeatable media pressure erupted, considering that, at the time, we did not have social media anticipating any rescue action on famous people. I remember that, when we landed, many journalists were already standing outside what we called the 'green branch': a small alleyway to be travelled in an ambulance, at the end of which was the same gate that had not opened up the day before, when Ratzenberger was brought in [the gate had been blocked on that occasion].

Ayrton's condition seemed very serious from the start ...
After the CT scan, we took him to the intensive care unit on the 11th floor of the hospital. By then, the situation was critical and we had confirmation from the electroencephalogram (EEG): it was flat. Senna's brain did not show any cortical electrical activity anymore. The brain scan showed a large bleeding with multiple lacerations in the right frontal lobe, complicated by the fracture of the basicranium. Receiving little blood due

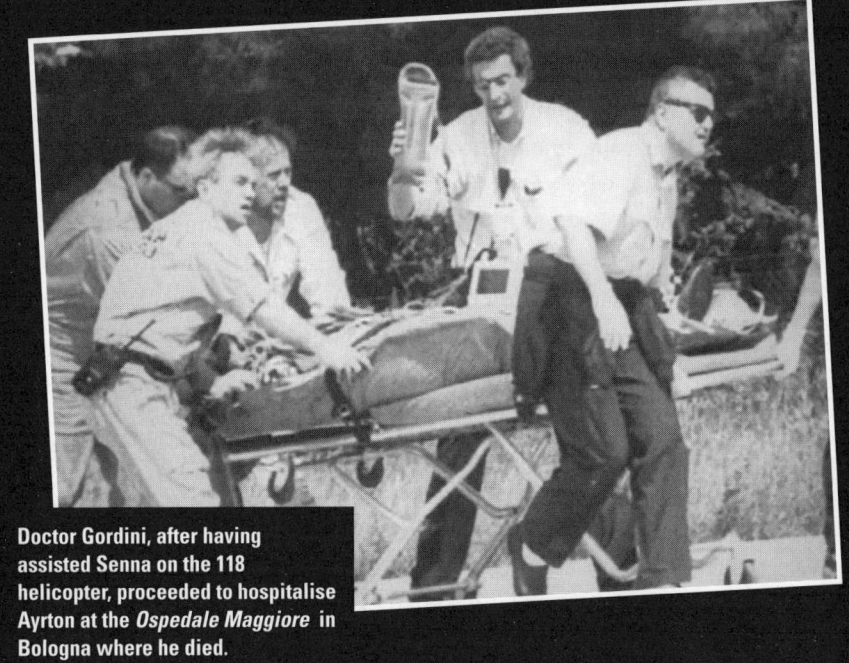

Doctor Gordini, after having assisted Senna on the 118 helicopter, proceeded to hospitalise Ayrton at the *Ospedale Maggiore* in Bologna where he died.

to post-traumatic oedema and pressure on the vessels, Senna's brain had shut down and the EEG showed electrical silence.

Death occurred at 6.40pm and it was Dr Maria Teresa Fiandri's turn to find the words to make the announcement at a press conference in front of the many people present at the hospital. Ayrton was transferred to the mortuary in Via Irnerio, Bologna, at around 9pm.

On a human level, what was the psychological impact of that experience?
As long as you are working and focused on what you are doing, none. Even when you take care of patients who emotionally involve you a lot, like children, the psychological impact is minimal as long as you are busy assisting them. But then, as soon as you take a break ... you feel all your psychological involvement! And it was amplified by the media impact. The first person who really made me understand Senna's drama was Berger. Gerhard had been hospitalised with us in 1989 and I had taken him to the *Maggiore* after an accident with Ferrari at *Tamburello*. He had stayed in hospital for only one night. I met him again on the 11th floor of the *Ospedale Maggiore*: he had left that place as a healthy man and now he had returned to the same room to see his friend in a coma. That was a very hard ordeal for him, but also for me, because I shared with him deep feelings, which are difficult to explain in words.

The Austrian overcame the reticence of drivers, who usually do not want to visit their colleagues in hospital. It was a severe test and certainly dramatic for him, who saw a friend die. A significant occurrence. I couldn't talk to him much, he had few words: he remained silent and sorrowful on the sidelines. He understood what was going to happen. I also remember that Ayrton's physiotherapist, Josef Leberer, and his manager Julian Jakobi also arrived, as well as Dr Sid Watkins.

Then another helicopter arrived, with Dr Franco Servadei, a neurosurgeon specialising in cranio-spinal traumatology, but Senna's condition was so serious that any intervention would have been futile. The Maggiore *turned into a media hub; Senna's death became the hottest news story in the world.*
I remember returning to the hospital, after a short ride home, whilst a live broadcast of *La Domenica Sportiva* ['The Sports Sunday', a long-running Italian TV show] on RAI was starting.

What remains of that atrocious weekend in your mind?
Racing is dangerous, I've always known that. I've always had a passion for motors, every now and then I used to follow rallies with Carlo Cavicchi, editor of *Autosprint*; but who could have ever imagined two deaths in one weekend? We tried to save Roland on Saturday and Ayrton on Sunday, but there was nothing we could do for either of them. However, that damned weekend in 1994 showed the world how an emergency system must work in such cases.

And back to the Dalai Lama's quote: 'We have to learn the rules well, in order to break them in the right way.'

The hovering medical helicopter was breaking normal procedures

IT WAS MADNESS TO THINK THAT THE FASTEST MAN IN THE WORLD COULD NOT BE GIVEN THE SAME FIRST AID TREATMENT THAT IS AFFORDED TO ANY OTHER PERSON.

CHAPTER 18

WHY DID THE 'KILLER UNIBALL' STRIKE LIKE A BLADE?

'WHEN MY body is ashes, my name will be legend.'

Jim Morrison, charismatic leader and frontman of The Doors, the American rock band that characterised music in the 1960s, seemed to anticipate Ayrton Senna's drama at the San Marino GP.

Imola was the third race of the 1994 season, and had to be the turning point in the world championship for him, after two pole positions and two retirements. Zero points in the standings, against Michael Schumacher's 20. The Brazilian absolutely wanted to stop the German of Benetton, otherwise the rising F1 star might have obscured the image of Magic, the three-time world champion who had chosen Williams to continue his ascent into the Olympus of motor racing heroes.

He did not have time to cherish his dream because, on 1 May at the Enzo and Dino Ferrari, Ayrton went from chronicle to legend, metaphorically scattering his ashes over F1. The cursed weekend demanded its epilogue: Rubens Barrichello's crash on Friday, Roland Ratzenberger's death on Saturday and the injured spectators after the first start on Sunday had not been enough. Macabre fate also claimed the life of the greatest. A tragedy experienced live on television by millions of fans around the world. It seemed like the end of F1. Instead, it represented a new beginning that gave the Circus and motorsport in general new rules and new safety criteria. A seed of hope sprouted right on the ashes of the champion.

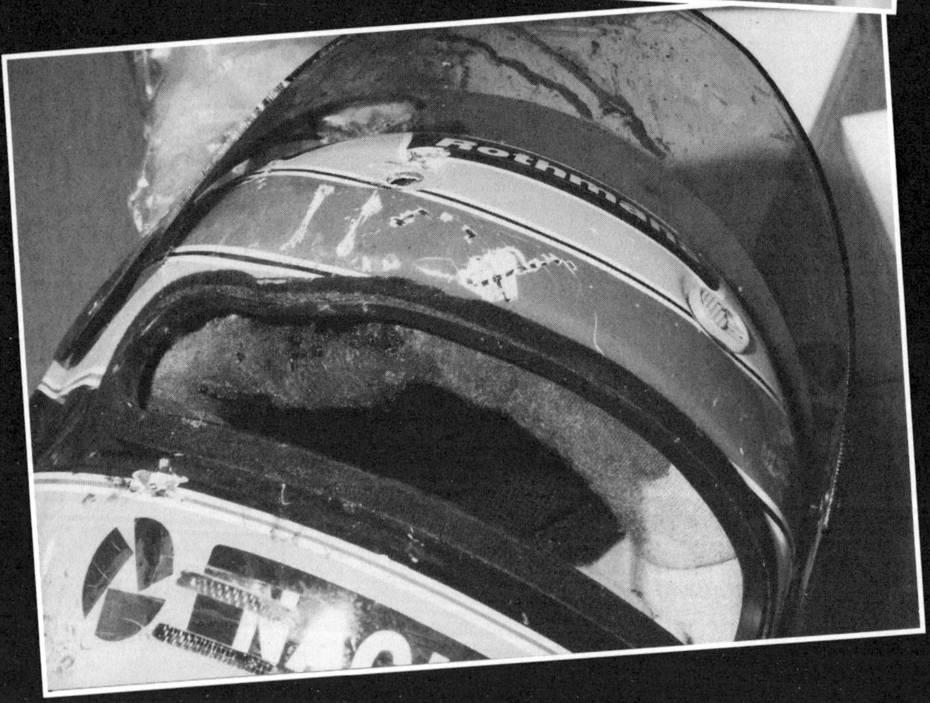

Senna's Williams FW16 stopped on the track after the terrible impact with the *Tamburello* wall. The crude image of the helmet shows how the killer uniball got stuck between the shell and the rubber gasket.

Why did the 'killer uniball' strike like a blade?

Three decades have passed and certain questions, which might have seemed unanswerable at the time, have been answered. The pain of loss that millions of fans in every corner of the globe experienced has given way to remembrance, to memory. We know that memory is positive, it tends to recall the good left behind, while conscience shakes the 'bag' of memories and stirs up states of mind that, from time to time, bring to the surface things we would have liked to erase from our existence. Not only material errors, but also behaviour. And, at the time, Imola did not reveal the whole truth.

Thirty years later, certainly there are consciences that have not found peace yet, although on 13 April 2007, the *Cassazione* [the Italian Supreme Court], closed the Senna case with a statute of limitations for Patrick Head, the Williams technical director (the only one remaining among the suspects), but also reaffirmed the manner and responsibility of the accident. The exit from the track on lap seven of the San Marino GP was caused by the failure of the steering column.

Full stop.

There is no longer any point in discussing this, while we must add that Ayrton died because he was stabbed by the uniball of the right front suspension. An incredible and, probably, unrepeatable circumstance.

When his Williams, irreparably out of control, crashed into the wall on the outside of the *Tamburello* corner, at a speed of no less than 210km/h, what happened was that the right front wheel became compressed between the track guard and the bodywork of the FW16-02. One of the two uniballs, the joints that connected the suspension's lower triangle to the chassis, opened up, turning the metal bushing into a dangerous blade: a sharp 'knife'. The wheel, no longer restrained by the arms, was left free to move (today's single-seaters have retention cables precisely to avoid this risk) and rose, rotating towards the Williams's cockpit.

In 1994 there was no 'halo', the metal safety cage which now protects the cockpit of open-wheel cars, which would have deflected that uncontrolled blunt instrument far away. Senna remained in the open, defenceless. He was not hit by the wheel, but he was pierced by that sharp 'sword', still attached to the wheel hub carrier.

Ayrton's helmet was breached at the only weak point, between the shell and the rubber gasket that sealed the gap under the visor, just above the right eye. A tragic fatality: had the uniball hit a little higher up, nothing would have happened, because Senna did not suffer any damage other than very serious head injuries. Most likely, he would have returned to the Williams pit and uttered harsh words with the team management, but he would have come out unharmed. Alive. Instead, his time had come.

A horrible fate befell the Brazilian: again, for the second time in two days, a driver became a helpless passenger in an uncontrolled car. Unthinkable. Unbelievable. Unacceptable.

The blade thrust into his head, sinking to the base of his skull. From that moment on, it was darkness for Ayrton. As the wreckage of the car stopped in the middle of the track, returning to the cone of vision of the only camera filming from the *Villeneuve* corner, the wheel continued its trajectory, pulling behind it the murderous arm that ended its course far away, after having devastated the brain of the otherwise uninjured driver.

The rescuers, who were very prompt, were faced with an extremely serious clinical picture: there was a heartbeat, but no vital reaction or sign of brain activity. The epilogue would be consummated at the *Ospedale Maggiore* in Bologna: there was no hope. Senna's soul was still attached to the body of that great fighter who continued to fight.

Imola was supposed to be the redemption race, and instead, it represented the end. Why? The empathy between the team and Ayrton had never been ignited. The Brazilian felt like an outsider in it: he never felt accepted. Didcot's team won regardless of its drivers. Adrian Newey had designed the closed cockpit of the FW16 as if a 'jockey' like Alain Prost, the driver of the year before, had still to fit in the car. Beco complained about this on his debut at Estoril with the old FW15D: 'They pay me as the best driver in F1, but they don't put me in a position to give my best. It's madness,' he said to his friend Angelo Orsi, as already mentioned.

Patrick Head and Adrian Newey cared about the performance of the car, not the comfort of the driver. Senna had to use a smaller steering wheel than the one he had used at McLaren, because otherwise the knuckles of his hands would rub against the carbon cover of the chassis, causing him annoying bruises, even though he wore fireproof gloves. Ayrton was certainly a stickler. A resolute character: he was as demanding of himself as he was of others, but Williams did not like being told what to do. And the Brazilian, on the other hand, never gave up, never tried to lower the tension.

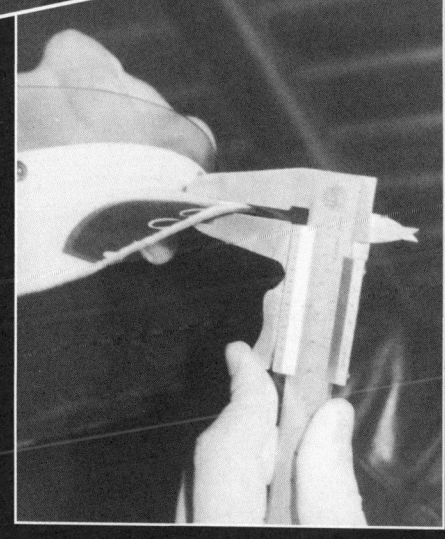

Images that make a certain impression: top, the suspension uniball that, torn from the chassis, transformed into the blade that killed Senna. Above, the thickness of the Williams FW16 chassis and, to the side, the minimum measurement of the bodywork cut for the Imola race.

Constructor : Williams Chassis number : FW16-02 ID Number : 17FCDC2D90
Date : 16/02/94 Place : Didcot
Present : B.O'Rourke; C.Whiting

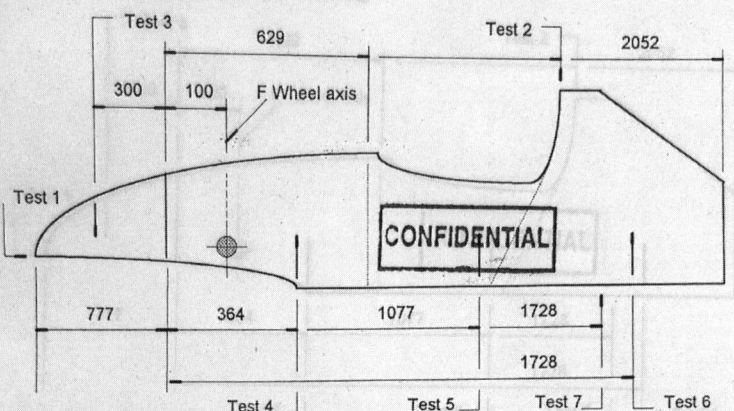

Test 1 :	An impact test against a solid barrier at 11 metres/sec with a total mass of 780kg
Impact speed	: m/s Deformation mm
Deceleration	: Peak g Mean g Dummy g
Nose fixings	: Nose weight kg
Chassis weight	: 40.5kg First chassis : 39.7kg Difference +2.0%
Chassis condition	: Same condition as reference chassis (FW16-01)
Comments	:

Test 2 :	A 72.08kN load applied at a compound angle to the top of the main roll structure
Load kN Displacement mm	
Comments :	

Test 3 :	A 30.00kN load applied to the the nose side 40cm in front the pedals and held for 30 secs
Load kN Displacement mm	
Comments :	

Test 4 :	A 25.00kN or 20.00kN load applied in 3 mins to the footwell side and held for 30 secs
Load 20.00kN Displacement 3.5mm (3.5mm) Difference 100% Deformation 0.1mm	
Comments : Test successful.	

Test 5 :	A 25.00kN or 20.00kN load applied in 3 mins in the seat belt area and held for 30 secs
Load 20.00kN Displacement 4.9mm (4.8mm) Difference 102% Deformation 0.1mm	
Comments : Test successful.	

Test 6 :	A 25.00kN or 20.00kN load applied in 3 mins to the fuel tank side and held for 30 secs
Load 20.00kN Displacement 3.3mm (3.6mm) Difference 92% Deformation 0.0mm	
Comments : Test successful.	

Test 7 :	A 12.50kN or 10.00kN load applied in 3 mins to the fuel tank floor and held for 30 secs
Load 10.00kN Displacement 5.8mm (5.9mm) Difference 98% Deformation 0.1mm	
Comments : Test successful.	

The FIA homologation document for the FW16-02 chassis used by Senna at Imola: it had passed its last crash test on 16 February 1994, after which it should not have undergone any modifications without new certification.

It was not an easy matter for Senna to get his hands on the car as he wanted it to be, because the single-seater had been homologated by the FIA after passing crash tests: the FW16-02 chassis, the one Ayrton used up to Imola, had been declared compliant on 16 February 1994 with an ID number: 17FCD2D90. It weighed 800g more than the FW16-01 that had undergone the crash tests.

Charlie Whiting, the FIA technical delegate, had explained that: 'Each team makes several chassis similar to the one originally authorised. And each chassis has to have similar characteristics to the original one. In the event of a significant modification, the chassis has to undergo new tests and be homologated again according to Article 15 paragraph 4.9 of the 1994 FIA technical regulations. It is my job to determine when a modification is to be considered significant.'

The highly regarded British Federal Commissioner, who passed away in 2019, and who in time also became F1's safety officer and race director, told investigators: 'The FW16 chassis was homologated in February, and that was the only approval given to Williams during the 1994 season. I was never informed by the Williams team, nor did I personally see, any modifications to the chassis in the steering wheel area.'

Images of the car that Williams had provided for Senna at the San Marino GP showed, however, without any doubt, that the area had been modified in three places: firstly, carbon skins had been removed with a gouge near the steering wheel, to prevent his knuckles rubbing on the cockpit; secondly, the upper part of the cockpit had been cut off and replaced by bodywork that reproduced the approved external shapes to offer the driver more space; thirdly, the steering column had been lowered by adopting a three-part tube, with a reduction in diameter from 25.1mm to 18mm in the central part.

According to the rules, a square-shaped template of 250mm per side had to pass inside the chassis with the driver on board, in compliance with Article 13.3, which imposed a minimum space defined by the rules. Williams, during the trial, claimed that the column had already been modified before the Brazilian GP, because Senna demanded to be able to fit the larger steering wheel.

However, photographs taken at Aida, the second GP of the season, showed that the bodywork of the FW16-02 chassis had not been opened at the top yet, just some carbon parts had been removed at the most, to create those niches that allowed the Brazilian driver's hands to move more freely.

We consulted the closing files of the San Marino GP and the verification sheets are impeccable but, according to the testimonies collected, doubt remains that at Imola, just as happened in September at the Italian GP, none of the technical commissioners checked that the Williams conformed with the need for the template to be put through the cockpit.

It is safe to assume that the lowered column was designed between the Japanese race and Imola, after repeated complaints from the driver. I tried to find out more about this directly from Patrick Head, Didcot's technical director at the time, and he emailed me back saying that he was not aware of any modifications to the chassis. But after seeing the pictures I sent him, he commented that the work done was not in the Williams style, because it was rough machining compared to the standards of the world champion team, but that no structural parts of the bodywork had been removed. In the end, Patrick advised me to address my questions to Adrian Newey, who was in charge of the chassis.

Head was only aware of the work on the steering column, but was not involved in the design or the realisation of the project, which, in turn, Newey had entrusted to engineers Fisher and Young. The English genius, on that occasion, had devoted himself to understanding why the FW16 was aerodynamically difficult to drive and tune, despite the two pole positions Senna had earned: a man capable of driving beyond any problems. In fact, it was only after his findings during the tests at Nogaro, and then in the wind tunnel, that the new bodywork took shape, which would have allowed Ayrton to start winning regularly, probably as early as the GP following Imola. Adrian, the project leader, as much as Patrick, had not devoted any attention to the new steering column, believing it more important to deal with aerodynamic instability.

The dramatic result of this situation was that Senna raced at the Enzo and Dino Ferrari with a car that, at certain speeds, and in particular at *Tamburello*, could stall, suddenly and dangerously losing downforce. The Williams with the 'short sidepods' would only arrive later: some time was still needed, but the driver was not willing to wait.

In the meantime, to assuage Ayrton's constant complaints, the steering column was lowered and the modification had serious design errors. That column, according to investigations carried out at the University of

Bologna, could not withstand the mechanical stresses of long driving: it was bound to break and it did.

It was the result of a chilling sequence of events, all the more so as the bodywork of Senna's Williams, after the crash against the *Tamburello* wall, opened up with a gash that started from the carbon gouge around the steering wheel grip and reached the other side of the cockpit, passing through the floor. The right front wheel, the one with the killer-uniball, in the compression of the chassis against the concrete wall, had acted as a lever, causing that nasty tear in the chassis. With today's knowledge of composite materials, one has to wonder whether the lower torsional strength of the bodywork could also have contributed to the stress on the column.

The court found no culprits for Magic's death, but their conclusions leave a shadow of suspicion.

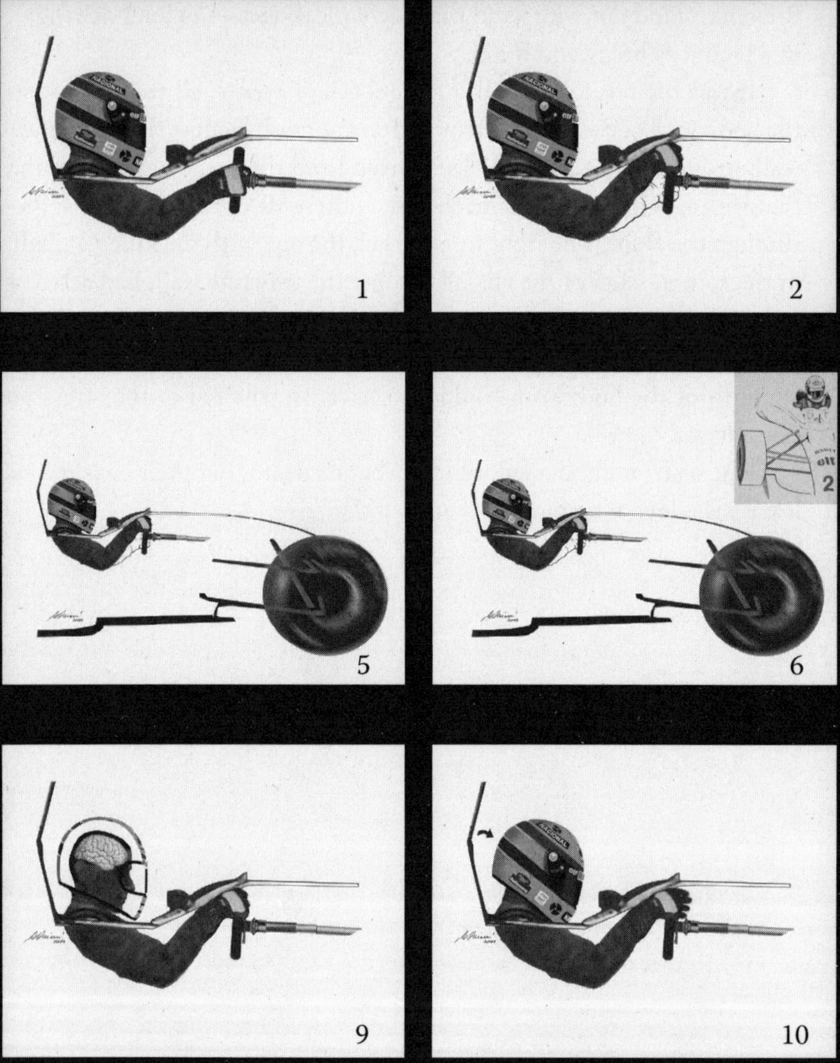

Nicola Acciarri's sequence reconstructs moment by moment what happened on Senna's Williams FW16, from the breaking of the steering column to the moment in which the uniball pierced the Brazilian champion's head: fate played a cruel role.

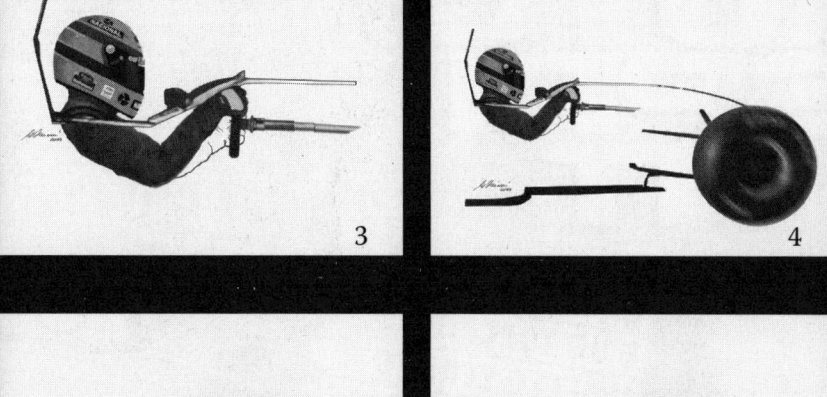

AUTOSPRINT

SETTIMANALE 19
Anno XXXIV - 10-16 maggio 1994
Sped. in abb. postale - Pubbl. inf. 50%
L. 4.000

SPECIALE SENNA
UN DOPPIO POSTER E UN TOCCANTE INSERTO SCRITTO CON LE SUE PAROLE

AYRTON SENNA
Una vita vissuta sempre in pole position

QUESTO PIANTONE DELLO STERZO ERA PER TERRA MA NESSUNO LO HA SEGATO S'E' ROTTO PRIMA O DOPO L'URTO?

IL SOSPETTO

CHAPTER 19

TARQUINI'S INTUITION KICK-STARTS THE INVESTIGATION INTO THE STEERING COLUMN

'INSTINCT MAKES us realise at once what intelligence makes us realise in time.'

Roberto Gervaso, in his summation, has fully grasped the value of Gabriele Tarquini's insight. In 1994 Tarquini was Alfa Romeo's official driver in the British Touring Car Championship (BTCC) which he won with the 155. '*Il Cinghio*' (the Boar), as Gabriele was nicknamed, because of his competitive temperament, had already ended his experience in F1 with little satisfaction to match his talent, due to uncompetitive single-seaters. However, he had found his way in covered-wheel racing, where he had become one of the top performers. He holds the record of the oldest driver to win an FIA world title, which he took away from Juan Manuel Fangio, who became F1 world champion in 1957 with the Maserati 250 F at 46 years and 41 days. In 2009, at the age of 47, Tarquini won the World Touring Car Championship (WTCC) with the Seat Leon TDI and, in 2018, at the age of 56, he won the FIA World Cup in the World Touring Cup Racing with the Hyundai i30 N TCR.

This is to give value to a 'stainless' champion who had the intuition to discover, in a photograph published in *Autosprint*, the steering column outside the Williams cockpit, while doctors were rescuing Ayrton lying on the tarmac. 'The account of such a tragic event,' explains Tarquini, 'involved many people: you recounted it, and I experienced it in another way and from another country. Fact is, there are still people who, so many years later, want to talk about it, because there was only one Ayrton.'

What was your relationship with him?
I met Senna as a boy in his karting days, when he did a race in San Marino, in 1977. He had been in Italy for about a year and was racing karts, but he couldn't participate in all the races on the calendar, because they had to have international validity, otherwise he wasn't entitled to race with a Brazilian licence. And since he was permanently in Italy, being based in Rozzano, at Angelo Parrilla's Dap team, he had a great desire to get out on the track. I had seen him taking laps in Parma during free practice a few months earlier, as he had not been admitted to the race, and then I met him at San Marino on a street circuit. I remember he won easily: he had this strange way of driving. I had a fairly heavy vehicle and I used both hands on the wheel, while he had learnt to drive the kart with just one hand, because the other was always on the carburettor, to grease the mixture at every braking point. It was something that practically nobody did at the time, or at least it was done once a lap and only on the longest straight: you put one hand in front of the carburettor to grease the mixture and let in more petrol than air. It was a way to protect an engine that was low on oil. With this operation you performed a wash of petrol and oil that safeguarded it. Ayrton did this at every corner, and you couldn't help but be impressed. There were many fast guys, but he immediately stood out.

What was he like?
He was a fairly shy guy, he didn't fit in with us Italians. He didn't stand out, except for the way he drove. He was 16 or 17 years old and had a girlfriend who followed him: some said he was already married, creating an additional halo of curiosity, but that was just paddock gossip. He was very fast and almost always won, even though he never became world champion, because the title was played out in just one round. I had won a world championship at Axamo in Sweden, but it was all played out on a Sunday. Schumacher also tried to win it, but was beaten by Tonio Liuzzi.

So, being very much on his own, he wasn't a driver you were hanging out with...
I don't think I ever spoke with Senna during my karting days. Then he moved to Britain and I found him again in F1. In the paddock, like a good smart-arse, he took care of relationships. He knew that, even though I was racing in a non-competitive car like Coloni or AGS, I was important to him, because I had to move away when he lapped me. Was that the reason for his behaviour? I don't know, because when I did something good he would come and congratulate me, and in general he kept good relations with everyone.

During my time in F1 I never exchanged a word with Gerhard Berger. With Alain Prost I may have said hello a couple of times. Nigel Mansell, who was my idol, *I* was the one who wanted to meet him. Ayrton, on the other hand, took care of personal relationships: I might have given him a hand in his fight with Prost. When I saw him coming in the mirrors, maybe unconsciously, I had a different relationship with Senna than with the others. I must admit, thinking back today, that his way of doing things worked: I'm not saying that I got out of the way when I saw him coming, but I didn't get in his way. At the time, lapping in F1 was not regulated like it is now, when you have to give way; the blue flags were waved, but nobody moved and there were cases of lapped drivers blocking the race leader for three or four laps. At Monte Carlo you could lose many seconds. So Senna was good at this.

We also spent some holidays together: I remember that in Port Douglas, Australia, he joined the group of Italians, but he did not bond with us very much, perhaps we were too boorish. We played football and insulted each other heavily. Because of a disputed ball with Riccardo Patrese we ended up arguing and Ayrton decided to leave. He preferred to stay on the sidelines.

Nelson Piquet started rumours that he was gay: the Carioca *(person from Rio de Janeiro) was very heavy-handed with his compatriot, perhaps because he was jealous?*
Rumours circulated in the paddock and these things were told without any foundation. I honestly never had the perception that he might be gay. Some people said he was seeing his masseur, but to me it just seemed like envy, because Senna was very successful with women. I remember that once, in Australia, the beautiful model Elle McPherson arrived, and we

all competed to get her autograph. Then Ayrton popped up and took her away, leaving us in the lurch. There was envy, because he was the F1 champion and also a handsome guy: he was charming and women ran after him.

Is Senna the greatest driver in F1 history?
For me, the greatest is Michael Schumacher, but Ayrton was the emblem of F1, the character everyone knew. Let's not forget that he was the one who invented the signed postcards for fans. He was a person with superior intelligence, who knew how to exploit the media, the journalists. When people were no longer talking about him, he was able to bring up faith and God. And transcendence was part of his character. He had belief in it.

Let's come back to 1994: you were racing the Alfa Romeo 155 in the BTCC, so where were you on 1 May?
At Snetterton for what was a bank holiday: in Britain, if a national holiday happens at the weekend, the race is moved to Monday. We had practice on Saturday and were racing on Monday, so on Sunday I had arranged to watch the San Marino GP with a satellite dish I had mounted on the motorhome. I had recently left the Circus but I still wanted to follow everything, because I still felt like an F1 driver. So I had arranged a meeting with Ninni Russo, the Alfa Romeo sports director, to watch the race. We couldn't get a satellite signal but, fortunately, the race was also broadcast by the BBC. Free practice was not being broadcast on British TV, but we were eager for information. The weekend had started dramatically with Barrichello's accident on Friday and the death of Roland Ratzenberger on Saturday. There was, obviously, more media attention than usual.

On Sunday I followed Ayrton's tragedy live, but the English did not investigate Senna's death as much as in Italy, at least not immediately: the accident did not have the clamour it had aroused in Italy. Not even for a second did I think that his exit at *Tamburello* was due to Senna's Williams going deliberately off the track or the cold tyres. It was all bullshit, because with Coloni and AGS I was already taking that corner at full speed on the first lap. For an F1 car that's not a real corner, and that's what all the colleagues I've spoken to over the years thought, too. Assumptions were made by those who had never driven an F1 car, otherwise certain things, which to me were simply absurd, would never have been said.

Gabriele Tarquini now manages Hyundai's TCR programme. The former F1 driver won the BTCC in 1994 with the Alfa 155 and at Snetterton he won the Monday race with a black bonnet in memory of Ayrton and Roland.

On Sunday evening I called Nicola Larini, who was a friend of mine: nobody remembers him, but he got on the podium with Ferrari and came second at Imola. We both agreed that there was something wrong with that accident.

But in the UK you were not able to gather any more information to dispel your doubts...
In the meantime, Giorgio Pianta, head of Alfa Romeo sporting activities, had phoned us: he wanted us to race the next day in mourning. We had a black band on the bonnet with the names of Ayrton and Roland and their dates of birth and death. I won the race on Monday and went straight back to Italy that night. On Tuesday morning I got up very early because I wanted to know more about what had happened to Senna. I'm from Giulianova and *Autosprint* in my town only came out on Wednesdays, so I went all the way to Pescara to buy the weekly, because after such an unprecedented Sunday it seemed F1 was over.

I began to leaf through the magazine with the greed of someone who had not experienced all the in-depth coverage that Italian TV had devoted to the tragedy. I lingered, then, over the photographs, and my eye fell on the image where Ayrton's feet could be glimpsed while he was being rescued by the doctors and, not far away, was the steering wheel with a column trunk outside the cockpit, with an electric wire attached to it. I was immediately alerted, because the column should not have been outside the car. I knew that, in order to pull a driver out of the cockpit, it was necessary to remove the steering wheel with the specific clip on the column. A very easy operation, but I thought that maybe emergency surgery was needed on Ayrton and they had cut some piece to extract him. But why cut if the rescuers knew that the steering wheel was removable?

The excruciating doubt had to be answered...
I called the editorial office of *Autosprint* and spoke to Diego Forti, the F1 correspondent of my time, explaining my doubt. Forti put me in touch with you, Franco, who was following the case. I remember that you did not immediately understand which newspaper photograph I was referring to, because you had not noticed that detail yet. I described the picture and the situation to you. It had to be clarified whether someone had cut the column. So you questioned the doctors who had intervened

in Senna's rescue and it became clear that no one had used tools such as shears or anything else.

Tarquini's intuition led *Autosprint* to come out the following Tuesday with the picture of the column indicated by Gabriele, and the headline: 'The Suspect'. Thus the enquiry of the weekly edited by Carlo Cavicchi began, and, in parallel, also the investigation by the police that later led to the trial. 'They've tried to sell us many stories,' insists Tarquini, 'but it was clear from the start that Senna could not have lost the Williams at *Tamburello* without a mechanical problem. I talked about it many times with Michele Alboreto, who was the most pissed off of all: the thing that annoyed me most was the team's attempt to defend itself against a very aggressive judiciary which wanted to find out the truth. And the case spread worldwide, with enormous media pressure.'

After three decades, Gabriele still gets heated, thinking about Ayrton's demise: 'I think Williams may have suspected from the start what had happened, but without the in-car camera images of the moment of impact, there was no proof. A lot of nonsense was heard in the trial: of all the things that horrified me afterwards, the one that unnerved me the most was the video of David Coulthard, in which he claimed that it was normal to see the column of a single-seater move several centimetres. The Scot was the team's up and coming prospect and, thinking back, maybe I would have recorded that footage too if I had been promised [the chance] to drive a Williams in F1 in return. I would have done it, but only if I wasn't aware of how that footage would be used, and the reliance on it.

'I recall that Alboreto himself suggested to Public Prosecutor Maurizio Passerini that he should ask Coulthard to swear to his opinion in the video, so that it could be used in court proceedings. Michele and I were convinced that David would clarify the point in court, because otherwise he would have declared something that, in the eyes of all the drivers who had seen the footage, seemed highly surprising. Coulthard, however, reaffirmed his experience set out in the film. Alboreto strongly disagreed with Coulthard's opinion. Even today, when I see Coulthard commenting on GPs on television, I turn away: it reminds me of the low point of the trial.'

CHAPTER 20

DESIGN ERRORS EMERGE AND NEWEY SUFFERS

'A MAN of genius does not make mistakes: his mistakes are the antechamber to discovery.'

James Joyce, the Irish writer and playwright, prophesied at the beginning of the 20th century what would become the drama of Adrian Newey. The English designer, born in 1958, who has a degree in aerospace engineering from Southampton University, is an extraordinary character. The most successful engineer in F1, he has won world championships with Williams, McLaren and Red Bull. He is shy, very shy. He is an introvert who expresses his genius through the single-seaters he conceives and designs, not on the computer, but on a drafting machine: maybe after a freehand sketch.

Adrian is an unconventional figure: if he envisages an idea while in the car, he pulls over, picks up his red notebook and draws, not caring if someone in traffic honks because the edge of his car protrudes from the parking lines. He is able to isolate himself to enter his creative world, where ideas have free rein. He passes for an aerodynamicist, but in reality he is the last F1 engineer who knows almost every bolt on his single-seaters. It is only fair to add *almost*, because in Senna's case he was guilty of questionable omissions.

Newey studies the rules and identifies the grey areas in which to search for the performance of his cars: when he finds a foothold he takes the concepts to extremes, to the point of exasperation. When left totally free in his creativity, he can create racecars which are very difficult to drive and fine-tune, and the 1994 Williams FW16 was certainly one of them.

The Senna trial, which ended in 2007 after a long judicial process, did not lead to any conviction, but it did establish that it was the breaking of the steering column that caused the car to leave the track at *Tamburello*. It was a verdict that Adrian never accepted, and nor did Williams, seeking other truths in the laboratory tests that the team conducted in the factory, at Didcot.

Newey did not shirk responsibility, well aware that it was not with an Italian court he had to reckon, but with his own conscience. In his autobiography *How to Build a Car*, the engineer, born in William Shakespeare's home town of Stratford-upon-Avon, revealed his travails.

He knew *Tamburello* was a corner a driver like Senna should have been able to take flat-out, with no problem, so he worried that a design fault might have caused the accident. When he examined the footage he could clearly see the steering wheel had come off and said the obvious conclusion was the steering column had snapped, causing the accident.

Adrian acknowledged that although neither he nor Head had been involved in the design or manufacture of the actual component, they were the 'leaders of the ship' and so had to assume responsibility.

'Put simply, if the steering column snapping was the cause of the accident, it was our fault, since we were responsible for putting in place the systems [by which the team worked],' he wrote in his book.

He said he spent the following months repeatedly watching footage of the accident from different sources and marrying it to data, to try to understand what happened. But then, something made him doubt the idea that the steering column failure had been the main cause of the accident. The FIA provided Williams with on-board footage from Senna's car which showed the rear of the car had stepped out. In his book, Newey said that if steering fails, a car would carry straight on, so the fact the car stepped out suggested there had been a loss of rear grip.

There was a lot of speculation, some even claimed that a tyre had punctured after the FW16 had run over debris that was on the track, and others spoke of the tyres still being cold after the safety car, but in reality no evidence could be found to support the various Williams reconstructions ... Newey, despite everything, remains anchored to his ideas.

In his book, he concluded there were two possible causes of the accident: the steering column failure, or the car suddenly gripping after it came off a bump pointing left, but with the front wheels pointing straight ahead, so the car was then thrown sharply right. He said that when Williams were able to inspect the steering column it had a fatigue crack roughly one third of the way around and had snapped either in the impact or from the pressure Senna exerted as he grappled with the car when the rear stepped out. He noted that the column failed at a point where it had been reduced to 4mm in diameter.

This led to a further question for the accident investigators: 'Would the remaining two-thirds of the column that had not fatigued have had enough strength to transmit the torque required to maintain normal driving?' The answers of those who did the analysis on the steering column left no room for doubt. The metal bears the marks of its history: the tube fitted was unsuitable for its use. It had broken because gross design errors had been made.

Newey said in his book that he had instructed his team to lower the steering wheel by 2mm to stop Senna rubbing his knuckles on the chassis, and when they told him it would then interfere with the FIA cockpit template, he instructed them to reduce the column diameter by 4mm. He did not look at the detailed design himself or have a 'proper checking system' in place to make sure it would be safe.

He reflected that to maintain the strength of such a component, the wall thickness should be increased, but that wasn't done. He also acknowledged that a sharp corner which causes an area of high stress will eventually cause a component to crack and fatigue, and then to fail. 'There were two very bad pieces of engineering in that diameter reduction. Ultimately, Patrick and I were responsible for that,' he wrote.

An honest admission. Human. Of one who suffered and, most probably, still suffers a 'black hole' in his existence, revealing a psychological picture very much affected by Ayrton's tragedy. Newey went on to say that before Imola he had never asked himself whether he wanted to be involved in something where his decisions or mistakes might result in someone's death.

'If you want to continue in motor racing, you have to square that with yourself,' he wrote, adding that F1 teams cannot guarantee mistakes won't happen, despite everyone's best efforts, because they are pushing the boundaries of design in order to be competitive. Decisions made within races, about whether to bring a driver in to check for damage or to let them continue, are also safety-critical and difficult to judge. A team

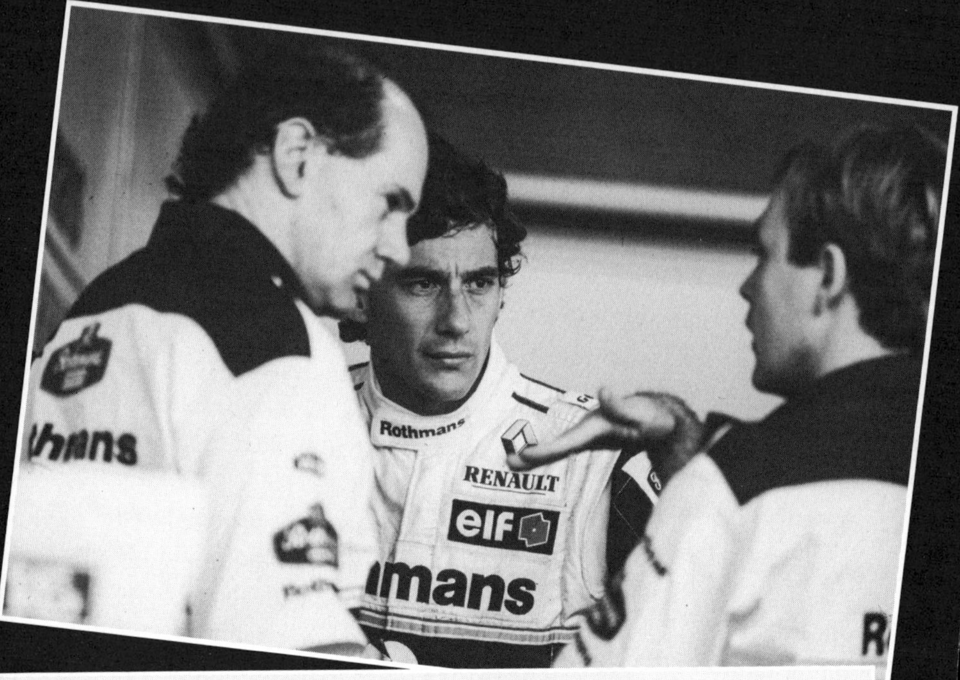

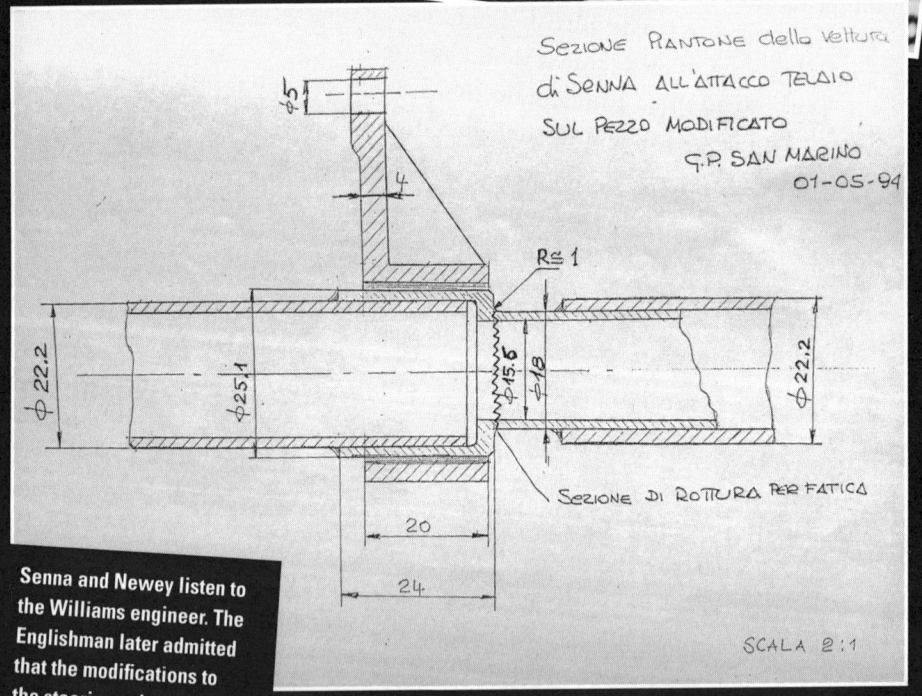

Senna and Newey listen to the Williams engineer. The Englishman later admitted that the modifications to the steering column were inadequate. Above, the drawing with the sections of the three different tubes used.

might be over-cautious and then retire a car for no good reason, or they might be too bullish, causing an accident with unknown consequences.

The English engineer, until the Senna drama, had been quite radical in some of his technical choices; later he did not lose his creative imagination but avoided excesses, especially of the kind he had undertaken at the beginning of his career, when he was a designer at Leyton House.

Newey said in his book that he does feel guilty about Senna's death. 'I was one of the senior officers in a team that designed a car in which a great man was killed.'

He said he and Patrick Head changed their procedures after the accident, introducing a system by which drawings of safety-critical components such as the steering and braking systems, the suspension and key aerodynamic parts, were looked at by an experienced stress engineer who would make sure they were structurally sound.

Williams's defence had claimed that Ayrton's steering column had been modified before the Brazilian GP. From the accounts given by witnesses after the accident, and above all, from the expert reports resulting from the analyses, it was clear that this had not been the case. For years, this was the great mystery to which nobody could give an answer. The modification, however, must have taken place between the Aida GP – where Senna still had a structurally 'closed' cockpit – and the cursed San Marino GP.

Regardless of whether the steering column failure did or didn't cause the crash, Newey said he felt most guilty about the fact he 'screwed up' the aerodynamics of the car during the transition from an active suspension system back to a passive one. He said he produced a car which was too unstable and Senna attempted to do things that the car was therefore not capable of doing.

This is a crucial point in Adrian's analysis: in the tests with Damon Hill at Nogaro it had become clear that the excessively long sidepods of the car stalled the car's aerodynamics, producing sudden and dangerous losses of downforce. And Damon himself later admitted that keeping up with Ayrton at *Tamburello* was far beyond his capabilities and that he did not have the motivation to take certain risks. We are not talking about a rookie, but a driver who became world champion with Williams in 1996.

Newey said that by Imola, he understood what the problems were, but needed more time to work on them and give Senna a better car. The accident denied him that chance.

Senna: The Truth

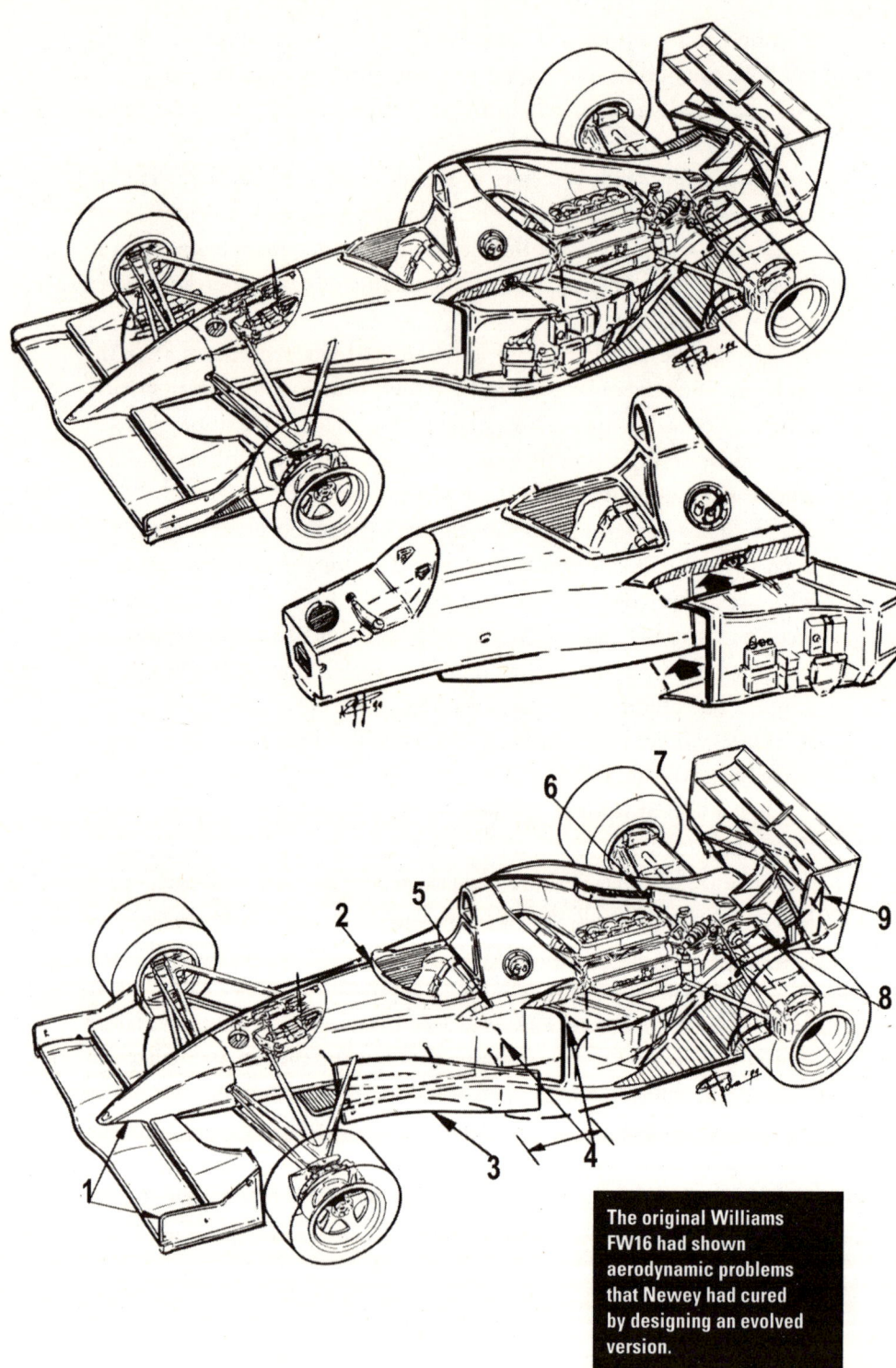

The original Williams FW16 had shown aerodynamic problems that Newey had cured by designing an evolved version.

HE EXPRESSES HIS GENIUS THROUGH THE SINGLE-SEATERS HE IMAGINES AND DESIGNS. NOT ON THE COMPUTER, BUT ON THE DRAWING BOARD.

CHAPTER 21

STEFANINI: THE PILLAR OF AN INVESTIGATION WHICH STARTED WITH A CAR ACCIDENT

'WITHOUT A great solitude, no serious work is possible.'

As much as Pablo Picasso wanted to be on his own to find inspiration for his paintings, so Stefano Stefanini found himself alone on 2 May 1994 with something much bigger than himself that had befallen him. In 1994, he was just a good superintendent of the Bologna Traffic Police, intervening in the most difficult accidents, reconstructing incidents, ascertaining causes and responsibility. This was his daily bread.

He had built himself a mental armour that protected him, even more than the uniform itself, when faced with road victims, often stuck in the sheet metal of crumpled cars, like pieces of waste paper. Experience teaches police officers to distance the emotional aspects from the professional ones so that, after a while, they are able to operate on a sort of autopilot, that allows them to face the horrors of road accidents with the necessary coolness and emotional detachment, so as not to bring home images capable of taking sleep away at night, through spectral nightmares.

Stefano Stefanini, now deputy coordinating commissioner, had been one of the millions of fans who had turned on their television sets on that Sunday to watch the San Marino GP and, like everyone else, had been profoundly affected by the Williams accident, the culmination of a cursed weekend for F1. Not even in his wildest dreams could the policeman have ever imagined that, less than 24 hours later, he would find himself caught up in that tragic story which, over the course of the following few hours, had reached such media prominence as to project it into the dimension of a tragic news story of planetary interest. Everyone was talking about Ayrton's death in every corner of the world, even the remotest. How had the Williams gone off the track? What had caused the Brazilian champion's demise? These were the first questions heard at the opening of every newscast and these very same questions were to be answered by Inspector Stefanini.

'My executive manager, Dr Marcello Gentile, had been called on the morning of 2 May by Dr Francesco Pintor, at the time chief prosecutor of the Bologna Magistrates' Court,' recounts Stefanini, recalling again the ghosts of that investigation. 'I was head of the accidents department of the Bologna Traffic Police, with the rank of superintendent. The Public Prosecutor's Office had assessed the reports of offences and entrusted us with the investigation of the Senna case: at the time I was dealing with about 1,000 road accidents a year, 25 of which had fatal consequences, so I had gained a great deal of experience in the field. However, I knew nothing, or next to nothing, about racing and sporting regulations. Pintor summoned us and said: "I have a big problem to solve and I trust the professionalism of the Traffic Police."'

The big problem was that Imola had become the focal point of the world. The most celebrated F1 champion had died at the *Tamburello* corner and the pressure became immediately overwhelming. Not only the media pressure, but also the political pressure. Everyone wanted quick and certain answers. Italy had to give a demonstration of efficiency in the investigations, because the eyes of the whole world were focused on the facts of Imola. It was enough to make anyone's legs shake, let alone a traffic police inspector with no experience in this type of context.

'I liked F1 as much as all the guys of that generation,' says Stefanini. 'I was born in San Lazzaro di Savena and had attended high school at Alberghetti Institute in Imola, in Viale Dante, opposite the Enzo and Dino Ferrari circuit. Everyone in Imola had a passion for the racetrack and during free practice sessions the roar of the engines in the classroom was so loud that it became difficult to follow the teacher. For me F1 was technology, competition, beautiful women and, above all, noise, chaos and confusion.'

Something profoundly different from the scenario you faced at Imola on 2 May 1994...
For me, the impact of the Senna case was diametrically opposed to my youthful memories of F1. After being assigned to lead the investigation by Maurizio Passerini [public prosecutor in charge of the case], I remember that, upon my arrival at the racetrack, at around 4pm, I felt a very strange sensation: there was a ghostly silence, muffled by the lint of the poplars. And yet, behind the net fences along the river, there were so many people. Mute, distraught. And the concrete escape route was completely covered in flowers, just as the fences had been plastered with drawings, T-shirts and every form of memory of Ayrton.

Why did you go straight to Tamburello?
With Dr Gentile we had to perform some surveying and to do that we had to move the carpet of flowers, while people were watching us. I had a strange feeling: it felt like we were violating something, but we had to do it: we were there *for that*. Of course, it was unusual to investigate an accident at a racetrack: there was no specific method, because you don't obey the rules of the motorway code on the track, but a sporting and technical regulation. Everything was different. If on the one hand I was serene, strengthened by my experience, on the other I was worried, because the vehicles had been removed and, after the accident, the race had resumed, so any tracks had to be detected and associated correctly. We checked the slopes of the track with the uphill curve and the escape route, which was downhill. We performed the surveying with string, chalk, plumb line and spirit level. But the real problem was the location, the regulations, which had nothing to do with the motorway code, and the cars, which were single-seaters, not normal cars.

What was the survey about?
We had to crystallise the data of the event by making it more comprehensible, with the aid of measurements and photographs, reconstructing what had happened in a descriptive manner and using TV images as a supplement. And I must say that I felt great satisfaction when, at the trial, Sagis [the management company of the track] brought its

measurements, made with aerophotogrammetry [advanced technological instrumentation], and I verified that they were practically identical to those I had provided. The first days were particularly complicated, because I was working under terrible media pressure: wherever I went there was regularly a journalist following us. My nightmare was called Roberto Cabrini of TV Globo, I really found him everywhere, like so many others. I wasn't used to working in the spotlight. We had a fantastic collaboration with Dr Passerini and I can assure you that it is not always the case. It is not easy to work in full harmony and synergy with a magistrate, receiving his full trust. I think that was a unique and, I believe, unrepeatable experience. The investigation gradually expanded and, from the initial simple findings of the accident, the prosecutor set up further investigations; in short, there is not a single judicial police document on the case in which my name does not appear alongside that of Passerini. I was also called to attend the first screen-editing of Senna's steering wheel oscillations at Cineca, where Michele Alboreto had been invited to watch the footage of Ayrton's in-car camera, handed over to us by a TV promoter.

The existence of the video had long been denied by Bernie Ecclestone's staff...
The existence of the video was confirmed by Damon Hill during his interrogation. Formula One Management (FOM) had 'played' with words as follows: by saying that there was no video footage of the accident, they were referring to the images of the impact, which, in fact, were never seen. However, it must be emphasised that the analysis of an accident passes through three phases: the antecedent, the climax and the aftermath. For us, that video is to be considered footage of the accident, although what was never seen was the actual collision of the vehicle against the wall.

The investigation was complex, difficult: at least initially it seemed that F1 denied any cooperation in solving the case. And to be pitted one against all may not have been easy...
This fact is rooted deeply in me – I discovered a completely different F1 from what I had imagined. And, honestly, I have to admit that I didn't do it all alone, because I had draftsmen who prepared the plans and collaborators who helped me, but I was the director, the coordinator of the activities, so every problem was reported to me. And I can say that I couldn't sleep at night. I felt a very strong sense of responsibility...

What about your chief, Gentile?
He never completely disengaged himself from the investigation, but materially he had to direct an entire traffic police department: the Senna case was not the only one on his agenda. Magistrate Passerini and I were given no other assignments for at least three months. In May alone I accumulated 178 hours of overtime, a sign that I was devoting myself full-time to this investigation, even though I was busy preparing my wedding.

It has only ever been known as the Senna case, but you also led the investigation into Roland Ratzenberger's death ...
I led both investigations in parallel, but with quite different cooperation from the teams. Simtek immediately made all the telemetry available and there was an immediate opportunity to get objective feedback on what had happened to Roland. From Williams, on the other hand, we did not receive such complete data.

Everyone was pulling the water to their own mill, at a time when there was also great confusion. Especially abroad, it was not easy to understand certain mechanisms of the Italian judicial system.
That's right. One thing I remember well is that Francesco Pinto, Attorney General of the Court of Bologna, opened up with us, saying that the President of the Brazilian Republic had asked that an autopsy not be performed on Ayrton, for the protection of his body and image. But how could a trial be held without an autopsy, to exclude the possibility of an illness or natural causes? Those who wanted immediate answers also demanded that no investigation be carried out!

One wonders how much was going on around the investigation?
I can tell you another tiny detail: it concerns the story of the photos that were taken during the first night: Ayrton's body, like Roland's, remained at the *Medicina Legale* [the institute of Forensic Medicine] in Via Irnerio. A janitor secretly took two photos of Senna's body and rumour has it that the guy then tried to sell them. The would-be buyer of these highly expensive pictures signed a sort of contract with the 'photographer', but then, before proceeding with the purchase, he had the good sense to call the Public Prosecutor's Office, who blocked the publication and denounced the guy. This was not known at the time, but all sorts of things happened in those days.

What was your emotional involvement?
At first I felt anguish, waking up at night and wondering if I had done my job well. In 1994, I found myself leading an event that was climbing towards infinity every day. It was all terribly difficult because we were technically ignorant and the role of the press was also important. If we'd had the sensors on that steering column, we would also have had the bending data, whereas at Williams they were only able to analyse the torque data. Emotionally, I don't mean to say that I was afraid, but I must admit that it was a difficult time. However, we tried to do everything with professionalism and calmness: I remember that the racetrack wanted to resume operations, but we still had hundreds and hundreds of metres of track on which to carry out the measurements.

The racetrack was in danger of dying if it remained closed...
There was a lot of pressure, because the closure of the racetrack was obviously damaging, and not only for economic reasons. On 2 May, when I showed up to make the first inspection there, it was necessary to seize the racetrack: the formal act was simple, but going ahead and sealing all the accesses was more complicated. All the gates were sealed, while the Tower had to remain open because the racetrack staff would continue to work. The investigation began without any useful indications, also because in the first few days all sorts of things could be heard: among many others some said that the yellow marks on the *Tamburello* wall were those of Ayrton's helmet. So I took the helmet from among all that wreckage and went looking for proof of that, but there was none. Also, on the helmet, a small air intake had blown off, leaving the small fixing hole in evidence. It may have actually blown off, or someone had taken it, but the driver did not hit the barriers with his head.

The wreckage of the Williams had been stored in the garage under the Agip grandstand, but was later transferred...
The car and the material that was seized by the staff of the Imola Traffic Police station (helmets, gloves, clothing) were entrusted to Massimo Gambucci, the only one not under investigation among the Sagis executives. When the racetrack was released from seizure, the single-seater was transferred to a room at the Bologna Railway Police school and I was appointed judicial custodian.

The 'shroud' of the Williams FW16 wheel on the Tamburello wall was a tangible sign of the Senna tragedy.

Detail of the findings of the traffic police who began the investigation into Ayrton's death as if it were a normal road accident.

You attended the Italian GP to speak to Frank Williams and Patrick Head ...
Yes, I accompanied Dr Passerini, two judicial auditors and Gentile near the paddock, but I had to park very far from the pit area. It was a long walk, in civilian clothes and with my typewriter in tow ... As I didn't have a pass, it was very difficult to get to the Williams motorhome. Even with my documents and explanations, no one wanted to let me through.

What impression did the two Williams team leaders make on you?
Patrick Head seemed to me a character of a unique coldness. A real block of ice: cold and detached. He didn't seem to understand why we were doing the investigation. Frank, on the contrary, was kind, friendly, helpful. He made himself available. Not that Head didn't, but Williams struck me by how active he was, despite his disability: we stayed together for over an hour and his personal nurse came to attend to him a couple of times. Hats off to him and his incredible inner strength and charisma.

Was the approach different with Head?
Patrick was tense, because he was in the middle of a race weekend. We spoke to him a second time in Bologna, but I did not change my opinion. He seemed to be a very closed person, not easy to talk to although, until the trial, I was never at odds with him. The relationship with the Williams team, on the other hand, was strange: they gave the impression that they wanted to cooperate, but did not understand why we were carrying out the investigation for an offence which, in English law, was not contemplated. We asked for pictures of the accident and they said there were none. We wanted to see the design of the column and were told they could not release it, because it was a trade secret. Then a sketch came out in which we didn't understand much, and which left us brooding on many things, fuelling as many doubts. Let's not talk about the control units: the FIA had authorised Williams to dismantle them. But when they were examined, one electronic control unit (ECU) was empty and the other had been used on a Renault engine test bench, so the data was lost forever. Ayrton's last laps had been downloaded at each pit stop and the data transferred to floppy disks. There was no telemetry of the vehicle control and monitor unit (VCM), the Williams ECU. I only had photos of the lid: it looked intact, but inside I found two broken RAM memories. What strange coincidences occurred. The data on the

floppy disks was handed over to us after an international letter rogatory [court order] against Renault, but at that point it was not data that we had personally taken. I have no reason to say that they were not genuine, but the oddities that emerged were truly incredible.

What do you remember about Adrian Newey?
I was surprised by his detachment, as if it did not interest him at all. I don't know what he felt inside, but he gave that impression.

At first there was talk of a possible problem with the power steering, which was new ...
They'd had problems with the power steering, so much so that in some GPs they had let Damon Hill race without it. At Monte Carlo they said they had raced with a one-piece steering column made from a solid tube.

The body of the FW16 had its chassis partly cut away to allow Senna to mount a larger diameter steering wheel in the cockpit, which closed over fairing at the top.
The sign of weakness started with the 'filings' on the chassis: there was evidence of torsion where the bodywork had cracked. The reason why they had made those interventions on the chassis we only understood thanks to the investigation you carried out in *Autosprint*. Even Gerhard Berger told us that Senna at Imola wanted to talk about safety, both in relation to the characteristics of the cars and those of the circuits.

Analyses carried out on the steering column by two different groups of experts led to a trial truth, but reaching a conclusion was very complex ...
The coldness of some of the drivers affected me a lot. I remember I had the feeling that, if you wanted to race in F1, you had to abide by certain rules, otherwise you were out. Michele Alboreto explained it to us in part, but hearing it in court during a deposition was shocking. My father brought me up with values, and to see drivers who had the world in their hands lowering themselves to the rules of the game made me feel sick: I can't forget Damon Hill's many 'I don't remember', nor the fact that David Coulthard claimed that the steering column of an F1 car could move even centimetres!

Damon would go on to win the 1996 F1 World Championship with Williams, while Coulthard was the driver who won no less than 13

Grands Prix, yet he never won a world championship. Their statements in the courtroom were surprising, but how many spectators remember their testimonies during the Senna trial?

Is it true that there were F1 experts, in the expert panels, who were intrigued by the technical aspects of Adrian Newey's FW16?
There were several episodes: I remember engineer Mauro Forghieri was arguing with his colleague Tommaso Carletti, while looking at the exhausts of the Renault engine. Suddenly he took a calibre out of his breast pocket and measured the diameter of the tubes, judging that the 3.5-litre V10 did not have the power that the French manufacturer declared. I was astonished, understanding clearly that their interest bordered on other aspects, not strictly pertinent to the investigation.

What happened to Ayrton's helmet?
It was destroyed on 10 April 2002 after an out-of-court settlement between Martine Kindt-Cohen, representing Bell, the company that supplied the helmets to Ayrton, and his lawyer, together with lawyers from Williams and the Senna family. They couldn't agree on the ownership of the helmet, so it remained under sequestration until they decided on its destruction, which took place at the incinerator in Via del Frullo in Castenaso. I think it was the best decision.

What about the Williams FW16?
On 14 March 2002 it was handed over to Peter George Goodman in the presence of lawyer Roberto Causo. Someone from Williams came to Bologna with a lorry, onto which the car was loaded and taken away. From that day on, I never heard of it again. Lawyer Goodman was an exceptional person, a true gentleman, a lord. Even after the trial, whenever he came to Imola for the GPs, he would drop by every year to say hello. I remember that, before Hill's interrogation, Goodman asked Damon to sign a replica of his helmet, belonging to a colleague of mine who was his fan. Hill refused, but then signed the visor after Goodman personally went to great lengths to convince him. Here is an aspect that I would like to emphasise: during the investigation activities of the Judicial Police you don't always meet criminals – it can also happen that good relations are established.

On the sidelines of the trial, there was never any mention of the life insurance that Senna or Williams might have taken out to protect the driver. I always thought that, once responsibility emerged, there would be action, but since the driver's family did not file a civil suit, I think that they had obviously reached an agreement.

What was the relationship with Maurizio Passerini, the magistrate who conducted the investigation?
Our relationship with Dr Passerini was beautiful, sincere, he was a great and capable professional. As well as our relationship with you at *Autosprint*, who often inspired us with your insights: we became friends. In the end, I am satisfied with the work that was done, with the utmost commitment.

Did you contribute to finding a truth?
More than anything else, I think we helped to change Formula 1. And that is no small thing ...

Do you have any regrets?
Yes, with regard to my superiors: I never received any formal and explicit appreciation for the work done. I got it from Dr Passerini, but not from my superiors. All I would have needed was a compliment for the work done with the few instruments – analogue instruments – that we had. We had no financial resources. A similar investigation, for an accident, was perhaps performed by the French police at the time of the Lady D [Diana, Princess of Wales] accident. I think the documentation of the Senna case could have been museum or state archive stuff. But I don't think any of it has been preserved, which is a shame.

CHAPTER 22

GAMBUCCI: THE RACE DIRECTOR OF THE IMOLA CIRCUIT

'A RESPONSIBLE warrior is not the one who takes the weight of the world on his shoulders. It is the one who has learned to face the challenges of the moment.'

Paulo Coelho and Massimo Gambucci have never had anything in common and do not know each other, but quite evidently they think alike on certain important things. During the 1994 San Marino GP, the latter was still the deputy race director, i.e. the track official who took orders from Roland Bruynseraede, the FIA test director, and transferred them via radio to the marshals scattered along the 42 positions on the circuit.

At his command was a small army of 206 marshals, 64 pit stewards, 20 technical stewards and 14 in the race direction team. And then there was the coordination with the fire-fighting service, taken care of by Fabio Nobis, and made up of 145 'CEA Lions'. Finally, there was cooperation with Dr Giuseppe Piana, who managed the medical staff of 28 doctors, 45 paramedics and the crews of the two helicopters stationed at the medical centre. A complex organisation that was led from the monitor room in the Enzo and Dino Ferrari race direction centre. A very large room with a number of videos that covered all 5,040m of the track with a Coel closed-circuit system and swivelling cameras to monitor in real time any intervention by the stewards.

Imola was the track where the FIA introduced experimental safety solutions and new intervention procedures, well aware that there was always room for improvement in this field, thanks to advances in technology. Bruynseraede and the federal bodies knew that Massimo Gambucci and his staff, which was considered the best prepared and most efficient in the entire F1 World Championship, were capable of leadership.

Gambucci, a native of Gubbio, might seem gruff, because he is endowed with a temperament averse to showing himself in public, and his shyness leads him to be less than empathetic and rough around the edges, but once you manage to break through that shield of confidentiality, you'll discover an extraordinary person, very helpful and much beloved by his staff. He hasn't been around F1 since the last San Marino GP in 2006, but he currently directs the events that Ferrari organises for its sporting clients, such as the Ferrari Challenge.

It is only fair to explain why Gambucci's role was important at the time of the 1994 F1 GP at Imola: Bruynseraede dictated what had to be done according to the FIA procedures and Massimo had to make those orders operational. Obviously, Roland Bruynseraede could not know all the F1 circuits, so he relied on the local race directors who, on the other hand, knew by heart how to make men and vehicles move in compliance with safety and sporting regulations. Every accident is different and a specific intervention is needed for each off-track. Gambucci's skill had to be that of being able to read what was happening on the track in real time, with such a speed of thought that would allow him to dictate to his collaborators the most correct manoeuvre to clear the track and allow the race to continue.

The preparation for a Grand Prix lasts several months and cannot be improvised; from year to year regulations change, and therefore the single-seaters, which are getting faster and faster, are modified. This also entails an adaptation of the tracks, perhaps adopting new safety guidelines, or modifying escape routes. The Enzo and Dino Ferrari is located on the edge of the Santerno river, in an area rich with several water springs, which is why, regularly, asphalt roughness arises, especially in the *Tamburello* area, adjacent to the watercourse. 'Senna came to visit us at Imola in February,' says Gambucci, 'to see what the asphalt at the circuit was like. The first time he complained about too many bumps and then he came back in March and gave us his OK for the work done. The director of the racetrack, Giorgio Poggi, had invited

Ayrton because he had requested the intervention of a shot-peening machine to level the asphalt, so he wanted the Brazilian to inspect the changes to the surface. We involved the champion in the hope of improving the situation: we needed a reference point and he lent himself very willingly. Poggi wanted everything to be fine: he wasn't just fussy, he was very fussy.'

There was, therefore, a collaborative relationship with the driver considered 'top of the Circus' ...
Although, as a race director, I was on the other side of the barricade, I always found Ayrton very cooperative. I can say that he often gave me suggestions on how to improve the safety of the track: at the exit of *Rivazza*, for example, he asked me to place two concrete slabs on the outside, because the new single-seaters tended to widen the trajectory and ended up with a wheel on the grass. 'If you lengthen the kerb,' he advised me, 'I won't go on the dirt anymore, the car will be more stable, and I won't dirty the track.'

His rivals only realised after a while that there were two extra slabs of concrete. He was a champion who left nothing to chance. Senna was very attentive to tiny details and knew that they could make a difference.

What was the human relationship like?
He was an exquisite person: whenever he came to Imola he would visit a severely disabled boy. He was a racing fan and a supporter of Ayrton, and Senna never failed to visit him as soon as he was here. He was a very human person, who stood out in an F1 world where only a few proved to be the way he was. That was true, however, until he lowered the visor of his helmet: because then he would transform and become very tough. And he wouldn't forgive anyone. I noticed that he suffered a lot from Michael Schumacher's growth with Benetton.

Senna's 1994 season had started with two retirements, while the German had meanwhile collected two victories ...
Senna was uncomfortable in the Williams: he had some carbon removed near the steering wheel to improve his driving position and the upper part of the chassis had also been modified between Friday and Saturday. This was evident from the cockpit windscreen: initially it appeared further

Massimo Gambucci, today is the race director of the Ferrari Challenge, but in 1994 he was the director of the Enzo and Dino Ferrari Racetrack.

Ayrton Senna during the inspection of the track before the San Marino GP with the managers of Sagis.

away from the Rothmans logo on the bodywork, while later it became closer. For me, those modifications looked as though they were made at Imola. Whenever he turned the steering wheel, Ayrton would flay the knuckles of his hands against the chassis, which was fairing. After his complaints, the technicians gouged the bodywork, creating those two 'ears' that were supposed to allow him a better grip on the steering wheel. How crucial the modification was I could never say, but in my view it may have contributed to the disaster. This, however, is only a personal opinion, not backed by any evidence in court.

And, on the Thursday before the race, was it the usual Ayrton?
Yes, from what I can remember I would say so.

Was he not agitated, did he not have premonitions?
I saw him very worried on Saturday, after Ratzenberger's tragedy, while Rubens Barrichello's accident on Friday had not shaken him as much, because he saw that there were no major consequences for the driver. Roland's death, however, affected him greatly. After the red flag, Ayrton took the fire patrol car from the pits and went to see on the spot what had happened. And literally ran away from it …

Did he come to talk to you?
No, he locked himself in the Williams pit and isolated himself. Being a very sensitive person, he suffered the death of a colleague heavily. It was understandable and the impression reported to me by the Williams team was that he did not intend to go back on track. According to Ayrton, stopping the show was the right thing to do, but then they convinced him. I wouldn't know what happened inside the pit. We had already heard rumours in the race direction centre that he did not want to race. But we were all very emotional, there was a very surreal atmosphere at Imola.

Let's talk about Roland…
The Simtek, after breaking the wing that ended up under the wheels, overturned and crashed into the posts holding the net. Roland hit a pole with his head and that caused him a fracture at the base of his skull. Nobody expected such a tragedy. It was immediately clear that something very serious had happened. You are bringing back feelings in me that I

don't wish to relive. If something like that happened again, I would run away. I would take the first plane and leave, far away. Barrichello's Friday crash was impressive in its dynamics, but not in its consequences. The rest of the weekend was terrible.

Even Senna's exit from the track seemed less serious than it turned out to be.
On Sunday Ayrton was immediately assisted by Sid Watkins, the FIA doctor who was on post at *Variante Bassa*. I'm sure that, if it hadn't been for that damned suspension uniball-killer, he would have got out of his Williams unharmed and, swearing about the crash, would have returned very angry to the pits. The accident was abnormal: the driver lost the car at place [track point] three and the single-seater stopped at place four, practically towards the *Villeneuve* corner. The impact against the wall was no worse than others at *Tamburello*. It struck me that he crashed where everyone else usually stopped. Piquet, Berger, Patrese and Alboreto – by the way, Michele also got a suspension arm in one leg once – had already crashed at *Tamburello*, but none with serious consequences. We didn't expect a tragedy to happen there.

Did you have contact with Ayrton on Sunday morning?
No, it was a strange Sunday, there was a lot of tension throughout the racetrack after Roland's death. I felt something bubbling up inside me and I didn't feel like talking. Bruynseraede was also shocked. After the accident at the start between Lehto and Lamy, in which tyres flew into the grandstands, Bruynseraede was on his way back to the monitor room after restarting the race, when he heard the radio announcement: 'Accident to Senna!' His instant reaction was: 'It can't be Ayrton.' He was so incredulous that we delayed the red flag for a moment. Bruynseraede had always been a good race director. We were in good hands with him …

Massimo, where did you witness Senna's off-track from?
From the monitors: on the restart Ayrton had Schumacher very close behind. The Williams had exited the track at a point where both he and Prost had expressed the need of a concrete surface. The FW16 had gone off on a tangent, hovering over the first section of the escape route. At first it had just looked like a bad accident, no more so than others that had happened at *Tamburello*. We didn't realise it was that serious: only Bruynseraede had the immediate impression that something was wrong.

What were the orders?
From the race direction centre I called the *Bologna Soccorso* 118 helicopter, which was already in the air. The one from Sagis was stationary at the medical centre, while the one from *Bologna Soccorso* had planned to follow the first laps of the race in the air. I therefore called Dr Gordini, so that he could land the 118 helicopter on the track; it would arrive the quickest. I won't hide the fact that the decision led me afterwards to some confrontation with Giuseppe Piana, the doctor in charge of the medical service, since, on my own initiative, I had not complied with the procedure, not requesting the intervention of the racetrack helicopter from Sagis. I had no doubt: when I realised that Ayrton was not getting out of the cockpit of the Williams, I activated the most logical solution.

And what were your thoughts?
In those moments you have to act, make decisions. Ayrton might have taken a big blow, but I hoped it was only a slight head injury. I only realised in the days that followed what had really happened. Because for the next eight months I 'slept' with the two crashed cars seized by the judicial authorities [the Simtek and the Williams] in my care. We told the media that we had stored them in pit five, while we had put them in the garage under the Agip grandstand at *Variante Bassa*. The day after the accident a lot of people were looking for even the smallest fragment of the Williams, in the hope of bringing home a small find from Ayrton's car.

It must have been a very strange feeling to spend the nights in the garage hosting those single-seaters that witnessed the death of two F1 drivers: the champion and the latest arrival in the Circus. They were not to be touched by anyone, because they would undergo a technical examination to understand what had happened...
There was an eerie silence, whereas previously the venue had been used as a stewards' base and it was anything but gloomy. I slept with the cars and could not understand what had happened, until Jack Giacobazzi, a racetrack handyman, drew my attention to the uniball, pointing out a horrifying detail near the sealing ring of the right front suspension: on the tip of the detached arm, sharp as a blade, was brain matter residue. At that moment I realised that Ayrton had been pierced by that knife-sharp piece of metal. You know it yourself, Franco, because you took the first photographs.

Why did you call me to help the policemen put the Williams back together?
I sought you out because I always considered you a friend and, above all, because I was sure you would not seek any form of sensationalism. I was certain that you would engage in a serious journalistic investigation aimed at finding the real causes of Ayrton's death.

I found myself wearing a Sagis commissioner's coat in front of Stefano Stefanini, a traffic cop I did not know ...
The reason is simple. I had been authorised to bring in a helper to reassemble Senna's car, possibly putting each piece back where it should have been. We needed someone experienced, someone who knew F1 cars well. Since we were groping in the dark, I thought we needed help, because the experts seemed more interested in seeing what the FW16 looked like, than in finding the cause of the accident. At a certain point it seemed that the responsibility for the tragedy might lie with the track and we had to defend ourselves, so that's why I made that decision: I had to do whatever it took to make things clear. I have removed so many thoughts, I don't even want to recall them. We even learnt how to open the shutter without disturbing the seals of the judiciary and take a look at the column.

I remember one thing that had struck you from the start was that the chassis, which had hit the wall on the right side, had opened to the left with a gash that reached beyond the bottom ...
The bodywork opened as a result of the torsion from the impact against the wall of the right front wheel, which was in the way: at least that's what I think. For me it was a difficult eight months with the car: the Simtek was quickly released, but for the Williams it was a different story. Later Stefanini had the FW16 transferred to Bologna, fortunately. I didn't remove a single piece. I would have become a millionaire if I had, because thousands of people asked me if they could buy one. And the four commissioners who kept me company at night were also exemplary.

The Senna case became world news: what psychological pressure did you have to endure?
At first it was huge, because it seemed that the blame was on the racetrack: we knew we were the weakest link in the chain. I won't hide it: I was very afraid. I didn't even trust the investigators. Luckily, then,

Gambucci: the race director of the Imola circuit

A RESPONSIBLE WARRIOR IS ONE WHO HAS LEARNED TO FACE THE CHALLENGES OF THE MOMENT.

I met Stefano, who was the leader of the investigation. After a while I let myself go with him, because I realised that he was a wonderful person, but the tension was very strong and it was also the first time I had to deal with a magistrate. I didn't have the courage to go to the funeral in Brazil, although Ayrton was a person I knew and respected. His death shocked me, while a whole lot of people went to the funeral just to be seen to be attending. I did not feel up to it. I stayed with the guys watching the car at night, as if it might start to talk. Finally, the car was returned to Williams. I prepared rubbish bags in which I collected even the smallest fragments. The only thing that disappeared was a glove, which has never been found. It disappeared between the site of the accident at *Tamburello* and the paddock. It was the left glove, which was slightly stained with blood.

May I clarify a doubt that held sway for years? In the published pictures you could see a pool of blood on the site where Ayrton had been rescued, but it was not the Brazilian's. It was a blood transfusion bag that was broken by one of the doctors who had intervened. In fact, the doctor who should have intervened first, the one sitting in the fast car at *Tamburello*, had actually just gone to pee behind the wall. The FIA asked me for an account of what our intervention had been and I also had to explain why Dr Pezzi was temporarily not at his place.

How does it feel to come back to it after 30 years?
These are wounds that have never fully healed. Almost everyone was after us. 'Imola, the murderer' were the headlines in some newspapers. I have not forgotten them. I felt guilty for not having done anything. The racetrack was 'mine' and the greatest driver had died there. I knew that from the Monday following the race I would become the director of the racetrack, because Giorgio Poggi was going to retire. It was a planned succession, not determined by events. I knew that we bore no responsibility, but the weight of those days was lacerating. These were feelings I experienced badly. On Monday, Giorgio handed over to me, as planned. Just think, during that weekend, he never went into the race direction centre to follow the various stages from the monitors, he always stayed in the office at the base of the Tower.

Giorgio was always one who kept everything inside. When Prosecutor Passerini asked me not to talk to anyone, since he wanted me as a witness for the prosecution, I complied with the magistrate's instructions, but

Poggi was angry with me, because I did not inform him about it. In fact, I could not tell him anything. Our homes were 40m away from each other. I was forced to ignore him, while beforehand we were always together.

Have you ruined a friendship?
No, I don't think so, but I didn't hang out with him again.

The scars remain.

CHAPTER 23

BENDINELLI: THE SECRET DEAL WITH FRANK WILLIAMS, DISCUSSED IN MUNICH

'NEGOTIATION IS about getting the best out of your opponent.'

Marvin Gaye, a leading American soul and R&B artist, saw this: it is not by fighting a battle that you can win a war, especially if the opponent you're facing does not intend to be an enemy and shoot at you.

Federico Bendinelli, Florentine by birth but Bolognese by adoption, is the 81-year-old president of the *Automobile Club Bologna*. A respected lawyer, he was for years the legal representative of Sagis, i.e. the company that managed the Enzo and Dino Ferrari, Imola's circuit. Bendinelli immediately understood there was only one way to avoid being overwhelmed by the Ayrton Senna tragedy: to talk to Frank Williams and find a non-belligerence agreement in court. Those who followed the hearings in the bunker room of the Imola Magistrates' Court did not have that feeling, as the parties did not spare each other thunderous broadsides through their respective lawyers, until the contours of the painful affair began to unravel, amidst clamorous deception and *omerta*.

Today, Bendinelli has decided to break his silence on a sensitive issue that has remained top secret for 30 years, admitting that there was a handshake with Frank Williams. The English manager feared not only the Italian judiciary, but also the possible compensation claims that could have brought the team to its knees if the Senna family had wanted it and if it had emerged that the team was responsible for the column that broke on the FW16. If there had been negligence, the insurance company would hardly have settled the relatives. And there was talk at the time of an estimated sum of around $50 million. Not peanuts.

Perhaps it was for this reason that a campaign began, targeting the racetrack, the *Tamburello* corner and even Ayrton Senna's driving habits. With the evidence of the telemetry tracks, Magic was totally rehabilitated and, indeed, his extraordinary ability to react practically in real time to the car's troubles, suddenly unsteady at the fastest point of the track, was magnified. At that point even the racetrack went out of the trial and only the steering column remained …

'There was a particular climate,' recounts Bendinelli. 'The affair left indelible marks. There was an atmosphere of tension because Imola was the third race on the calendar and Senna had not scored points in the previous ones. To me and to Poggi, the circuit director, he said: "I have an undriveable car. If I don't win at Imola I risk being out of the World Championship!" Ayrton came to the circuit some 20 days before, to see what the track was like. As there was no longer active suspension, Senna was worried: "I'm in danger of spinning all over the place and I need to keep the Williams with minimum ground clearance." We took him on a complete lap of the track, partly by car and partly on foot, and he particularly lingered at the *Tamburello* corner. Let me take a step back: Imola is a track with a river on one side and a hill on the other, so it is located in an area rich in water sources; it is no coincidence that there is a Mineral Water Park [close to the circuit]. For this reason, every year, as soon as winter was over, a series of maintenance operations were carried out, both on the track and on the grandstands, before the racing season began, in particular, at two or three points of the circuit and, among them, at the *Tamburello* corner, where again, also that year, some roughness of the surface had appeared. At the time, Giorgio Poggi had invited an asphalt technician, an expert in paving, and it was decided to carry out an intervention with a machine capable of bush-hammering, a sort of scraping of the asphalt to make it even and eliminate the undulations. The interventions were completed before Senna came in and were clearly visible, due to the very rough appearance of the asphalt.

'Ayrton, after a careful inspection, had approved a good part of the track, but had asked for further sanding work precisely at the *Tamburello* corner. Therefore, after the Brazilian champion's visit, we had organised another bush-hammering. Senna was unique, he had a care and attention to tiny details that others did not have: he did an excellent supervision job. He feared that the Imola race could become a watershed for his season and, unfortunately, it was much more so than he thought. We had re-done the work and on Friday, at the end of practice, we asked him for his opinion: "It's fine at *Tamburello*," Ayrton told us, "but I would ask you to make a few small changes at a couple of other points on the track, to avoid bouncing."

'So, in violation of the rules that prevented any intervention on the track after the FIA homologation by Roland Bruynseraede, we had intervened during the night. Just small things that were obvious improvements for everyone. On Saturday I went back to Senna for a comment, and he gave his OK. He was jovial and smiling, well aware that maybe Imola could reopen his championship. He seemed very motivated as the track was no longer a problem.'

But haven't you ever thought of seeking a solution that would make the Tamburello *corner less dangerous for drivers?*
Some aspects need to be unfolded here. For the drivers, *Tamburello* is like a straight to be driven in full throttle, from the start to the *Tosa* braking, at speeds well over 300km/h. So what is the problem? That high-speed section is in fact a wide bend and some off-track is possible there, as there have been several in the past, always resolved without serious damage. The worst accident happened to Gerhard Berger, when in 1989 his Ferrari 640 caught fire and the Austrian burnt his hands. Both we and the International Federation knew that a bigger escape route would be needed, and Bernie Ecclestone himself was pushing for an intervention: 'You don't have to cut all the trees down,' Bernie told us, 'just remove the first two rows.' Little did he know, however, how strong the pressure from the Green Party was on the politically left-winged local council. In fact, we had been pushing to lengthen the riverbank for years, but the local administration had never given us the go-ahead, because the Greens in the council were rock-steady and prevented the trees from being removed, despite the fact that they were just poplars that had grown spontaneously.

So there were plans to build a wider escape route at Tamburello?
There was a municipality councillor who interpreted the role in an ideological way, without any form of rationality, with radical attitudes: I took her for a ride around the track, to show her that it would be enough to cut down a few dozen poplars and that twice as many could be replanted somewhere else. She was adamant, because she was against the existence of the racetrack, considering motor racing a detriment to the environment. The idiocies of these characters affected the development and safety of the track. But the most grotesque thing was that, according to the rules in force, no trees at all should have been present on the sides of the Santerno river, because the riverbed had to remain clean in case of flood. So much so that the river authority had authorised us to cut the trees, in the hope that we would bear the relevant costs, a sort of present that would otherwise have been at their expense. In short, we found ourselves in the most classic Italian stalemate: we were violating the very same rules that would have imposed a *Tamburello* with no trees. Being unable to do anything about it, even if we wanted to, is a great regret, and it is certainly aberrant that it came to such a tragic fatality simply because we did not have the strength to enforce rules.

Among the 'colossal baloney' that began to circulate after the two tragedies at Imola was the accusation that the two drivers had been kept alive just in order to let them die outside the racetrack, to prevent the San Marino GP from being blocked by a magistrate ...
It is not true that Ayrton died on the track. Senna died at the *Ospedale Maggiore* in Bologna, a couple of hours after being admitted. Well, of course, the situation was already very compromised, but those who claim that he was transferred to Bologna so that the race could be resumed are telling a falsehood. The same applies to Ratzenberger. Although his condition immediately appeared very serious, Roland died in hospital and not on the track.

No one could think of two deaths in the same GP ...
The truly tragic thing is that, after Rubens Barrichello's accident on Friday, I went to the medical centre to enquire how the Brazilian driver was doing and Dr Piana, in charge of the medical service, replied: 'Rubens has got nothing serious, so much better, we can say we have already paid

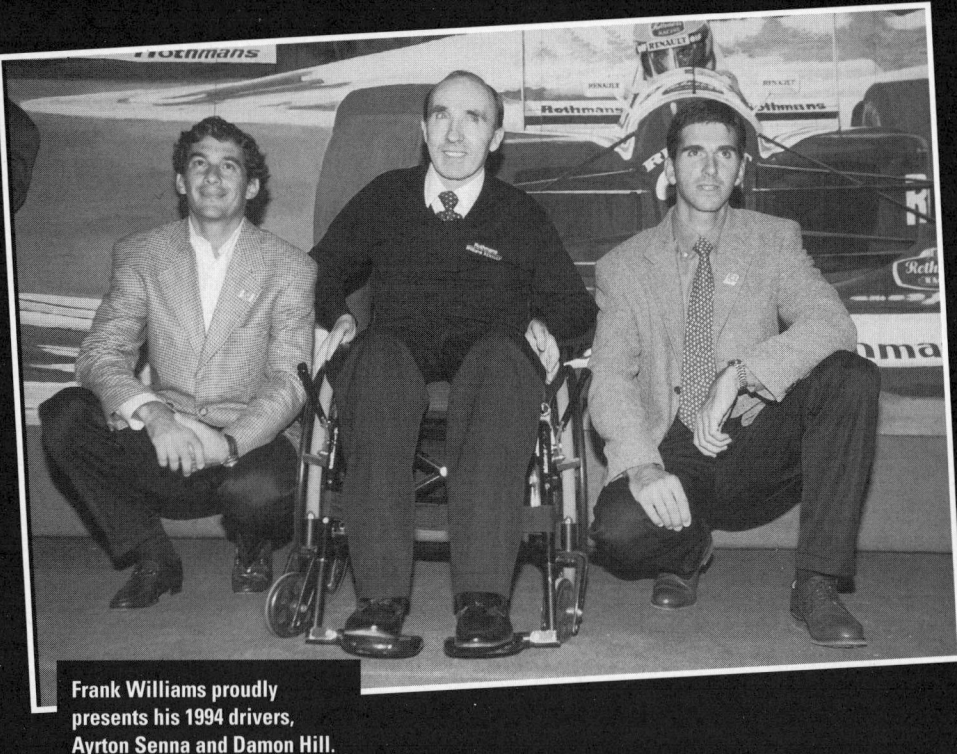

Frank Williams proudly presents his 1994 drivers, Ayrton Senna and Damon Hill.

our toll to fortune for this time.' Superstition, unfortunately, did not help to avert what came next.

What happened after the accident?
The racetrack was seized by the judicial authorities and the activity was completely blocked. A very strong media pressure was unleashed on the Imola track, from which I shunned myself by maintaining a certain tranquillity that came from being a lawyer. I was perfectly aware that I was not risking anything from a judicial point of view: I never thought I had to fear a conviction, but I cannot hide the fact that I was anxious, because Ayrton had gone out at *Tamburello*. My concern was that everything had been properly done in the works, beyond any doubts, and that there was no liability, not even the slightest. I had no judicial fears, but emotional torment over what could have been defined 'moral guilt'.

Did Williams's defence go in that direction?
Yes, but I was calm for two reasons: because of my legal knowledge and because to dispel all doubts, we also did our own investigations, which

ruled out any responsibility. I would like to say that I also appreciated the extreme fairness and human loyalty of Frank Williams, whom I met two weeks after the accident, at the Monaco GP.

Wasn't it the Williams team that tried to blame the track?
Williams's tough stance came later, and I am of the opinion that it started with their legal team and not Frank Williams himself. I had gone to the Principality on a Thursday and, just by coincidence, I had booked into the same hotel as Williams. When I arrived in the lobby I saw Frank, so I went to greet him and said: 'I'm sorry about what happened, have you figured out what it was?' 'We don't know yet,' Williams replied, 'but there was definitely a mechanical failure and the racetrack had nothing to do with it.' This honest admission reassured me in no small measure.

In fact, the Anglo-Saxon world of F1 seemed omertous in not cooperating with the investigators who, at least initially, were groping in the dark ...
Months later – we were in autumn – I went to London to see Bernie Ecclestone, shortly after the expert reports made at Pratica di Mare by the Air Force were filed. It had emerged that the steering column was damaged. I told him the news and he looked at me puzzled: 'Are you really amazed? Look, we knew all along!'

I replied: 'But then why didn't it come out clearly?'

'The reason is simple: at Williams they fear the economic consequences.'

The plan, therefore, was now quite obvious: to try and fight the court action in order to avoid insurance consequences. Ayrton Senna was certainly not a second-rate character, so the risk of tens of millions of dollars in compensation was plausible.

Is it true that you went to Williams's headquarters to talk about the trial?
Yes, because their lawyers had adopted a rather tough defence strategy, so we went to Britain with lawyer Birindelli, a friend of Marco Piccinini – former sports director of Ferrari, president of the Italian Automobile Sports Commission and Minister for the Economy of the Principality of Monaco – who had a great deal of experience in motor racing. We met Frank and his lawyer on the first floor of the factory and asked why they were blaming the track, however unconvincingly. To my understanding it

was more of an action requested by the legal strategy, which had to build a credible defence against the prosecution, than Williams's conviction: they seemed very embarrassed.

In the end, what was the knot to unravel?
They told us fairly clearly that if we did not attack them on the mechanical failure, they would let go of the track. And so we did. I remember that the pool of experts from the Public Prosecutor's Office, who had dealt with the Williams ECU, had done a very disappointing job. At a certain point Prosecutor Passerini came to me and said: 'Lawyer: unleash your guys.' And I replied: 'That's not our job.' It was clear that we did not want to break the agreement with Williams, even though we had high-level professionals on our side, such as Professor Giavotto, director of the Institute of Aerospace Engineering at the Milan Polytechnic.

Among F1's many reluctances to provide information about Ayrton's accident was the initial lack of in-car camera images...
Ecclestone gave me a copy of the VHS tape when I visited him in London. I asked him why there was no footage of the crash and why the video finished earlier. He replied: 'I swear to you on my daughters that the tape is authentic, there was no manipulation.' I was very impressed that Bernie swore with great conviction on his daughters, whom I knew and who were the same age as mine. I believed him.

Senna's death polarised the world's attention: did you come under pressure?
Yes, it was strong, like the effects. The racetrack was under sequestration with the total blockade of activity. And then the trial, which cost us more than a billion lire. A very high burden. That there were consequences due to the fact that the victim was Senna, I can deduce from two facts: first, immediately after Ratzenberger's death, the Simtek people came to me saying that, after what had happened to Roland, they were ready to go home. I had telephoned the public prosecutor on duty, to whom I explained the situation. He replied: 'I saw the accident on TV and I don't see anything preventing them from returning home. If you, lawyer, prepare an application for release, I'll sign it for you.' In short: there was full availability. With Senna's death, however, the climate changed completely. When the investigation opened, I went to the court where I met the chief prosecutor, Francesco Pintor, with whom, after greetings,

we talked about what had happened: 'Objectively speaking, I don't think you have any responsibility,' he explained, 'but the President of Brazil phoned Oscar Luigi Scalfaro [the Italian President of the time], and the President of the Republic called the Attorney General's Office, so ...'

Some threatened that F1 would never race in Italy again if there was a conviction for manslaughter after the Senna case; at risk was not only the San Marino GP at Imola, but also the Italian GP at Monza ...

I was aware of all the rumours and disturbances, and of the British teams' desire to stop coming to race in Italy, but I maintained good relations with both Ecclestone and Max Mosley, who was an excellent person for me. The FIA president was reassuring: 'Do you want to continue with F1 at Imola?'

'Of course,' I answered him.

'Then keep a low profile. When the wind blows, you have to bend down and let the storm pass.'

In this I also found the support of the mayor of Imola, Raffaello De Brasi, one of the best, who immediately after the accident came to see Ecclestone in London with me. The mayor told Bernie: 'What Bendinelli does is also good for me.' And he gave me carte blanche.

So, after a very difficult initial period, a scenario emerged, including a court case, which led to the exoneration of the racetrack.

I did not know Senna in depth, but he was an extraordinary figure for the confidentiality and transparency with which he said certain things. He was a street person, very religious, with a great soul and a strong charisma. Every time I think about this whole thing, I tell myself that maybe we could have done something more. I don't know whether it is more of a regret or a bitter feeling. There is one episode that troubles me: I can't forget that he died in our country. Many times I have thought about it, at night: what more could have been done to avoid that tragedy?

Bendinelli: the secret deal with Frank Williams, discussed in Munich

Procura della Repubblica
presso la
Pretura Circondariale di Bologna

n. 4820/94 RGNR   *Il Pubblico Ministero*

Rilevato che risultano ultimati i rilievi fotoplanimetrici e gli accertamenti di natura tecnica disposti sull'autodromo "Enzo e Dino Ferrari" di Imola in relazione agli incidenti mortali verificatisi in occasione del Gran Premio di S. Marino 1994;

ritenuto pertanto che, allo stato, non sussistono più le esigenze probatorie che determinarono il sequestro dell'autodromo, disposto con decreto 2/5/94;

d i s p o n e

il dissequestro dell'autodromo "Enzo e Dino Ferrari" di Imola e la sua restituzione al Comune di Imola, ente proprietario dell'impianto.

Dispone che il presente provvedimento sia eseguito a cura della Polizia Stradale di Bologna, con facoltà di subdelega.

Si comunichi al Sindaco del Comune di Imola, alla SAGIS s.p.a., alla Polizia Stradale di Bologna ed al Commissariato P.S. di Imola.

Bologna, lì 24/6/1994.

Depositato in Segreteria
Bologna, 24 GIU. 1994
IL COLLABORATORE DI CANCELLERIA
Maurizio Cavaliere

IL P.M.
Dr. Maurizio Passarini

E' copia conforme all'originale
24 GIU. 1994
IL COLLABORATORE DI CANCELLERIA
Maurizio Cavaliere

The document from the Public Prosecutor's Office of Bologna with the request for release from seizure of the Enzo and Dino Ferrari signed on 24 June 1994.

CHAPTER 24

THE MYSTERY OF THE CONTROL UNIT

'A SMALL truth is better than a big lie.'

Galileo Galilei's quote is well suited to the Senna case, which presented many obscure sides that time has never fully clarified. A number of questions, which were the main focus of the court investigation into the accident, have never been answered with certainty.

The easiest way to get to the truth about the accident would have been, of course, to download the data from the electronic control unit (ECU) of Ayrton Senna's Williams FW16. The information contained in the 'black box' could have immediately revealed the cause of the Brazilian champion's crash at *Tamburello*, but when the investigators seized the single-seater, they discovered that the vehicle's control and monitor unit (VCM), mounted inside the right side of the car, just behind the water radiators, was missing.

What might have seemed like a mystery from a criminal novel was immediately cleared up: the VCM unit, serial number 307, had been removed, with the permission of the FIA technical delegate Charlie Whiting, by an electronics engineer from the Didcot team. The engineer had taken responsibility for disassembling it, to the astonishment of the four Italian Automobile Sports Commission (CSAI) technical commissioners present (Giulio Pedroni, Fabrizio Nosco, Alessandro Palmieri and Luca Chinni), who would never have given their permission to remove any part of a car that had crashed and was under judicial investigation.

Whiting's comment on this action was, 'there's no issue', since this action had, in his view, a positive purpose. The Williams technicians were able to download the data from the VCM and could then understand, in his view, what had happened to Ayrton's car, allowing them to immediately decide whether the other FW16, entrusted to Damon Hill, was also running risks before the second start was authorised. All the more so as Patrick Head, Williams's technical director at the time, had radioed one of his collaborators, considered an expert in the matter, immediately after Senna's crash, to find out whether the power steering was on or off. Evidently there was an immediate suspicion that something mechanical had failed, so it was legitimate to look for the first answers in the data stored in the ECU.

The disturbing aspect was that the precious information contained in the 'black box' could not be extracted because, once it had been removed, Steve Wise – head of Williams's electronics and data control department – found that the connectors to the VCM had torn and the sensor on the ECU access door was also damaged. Did they break in the impact of the FW16 against the *Tamburello* wall, or did they break elsewhere, as other unverified malicious rumours suggested? It remains unclear.

The only hope of reading the telemetry diagrams of Senna's fatal last lap was to transfer the ECU to the Didcot factory. The day after the tragedy, the VCM was rushed to Britain and examined at the factory: the cover was removed and Steve Wise recalls: 'It was immediately clear to me that the data could not be extracted, because the battery supporting the RAM memory had broken and was no longer in its original position. Not only that, also other parts of the chips were damaged as a result of the very violent deceleration following the impact.'

In short, the investigation by the public prosecutor Maurizio Passerini began with a major technical limitation, as if incredible astral coincidences wanted to prevent it from arriving at a truth that everyone wanted to know. To this was also added 'someone' who, with a certain shamelessness, suggested that the Imola drama might have been caused by driver error. An insult to Magic that came straight from a Williams consultant and that, fortunately, was later discredited due to its inconsistency, in the absence of evidence of the accusation. However, they were allegations that could have potentially steered the investigation away from the hypothesis of a broken steering column.

The data acquisition system on the FW16 was not limited to Williams's VCM: on the No. 2 car Senna was driving there was also a Magneti Marelli control unit enabled to control the Renault engine. The acquisition system also benefited from a number of channels that transmitted the main chassis data necessary for the perfect functioning of the French 10-cylinder.

Above, the Magneti Marelli control unit that collected not only the data from the Renault engine.

Below is the Williams one marked VCM 307 that was damaged in the impact against the wall.

The Magneti Marelli control unit, marked Aitm 5 no. 049, with Artax software, was picked up on Sunday evening by Renault Sport technicians along with other equipment from the French manufacturer, and taken to Paris. Bernard Michel Duffort, electronic engineer at Renault Sport, explained to the police that, 'As early as Sunday evening the data contained in the ECU had been copied onto a computer. There was also data from Senna's last lap, added to the record of the previous laps, all downloaded.'

In 1994, data acquisition was less sophisticated and advanced than in today's F1. Today's single-seaters have telemetry that allows the values of each sensor to be read in real time via a remote garage that is not located on the track, but in a wing of the teams' ultra-modern factories, where some 50 engineers keep an eye on hundreds of parameters.

Back then, at Imola, each time the Williams crossed the finish line – where a receiver was positioned – the Marelli control unit, which acted as an emitter, was instructed to transmit the data to the pit lane in a time of about three seconds and in a space of about 200–300m. Once the data of the last lap was downloaded, it was no longer recorded in the control unit, leaving space for the information of the next lap.

The Marelli 'black box', therefore, should have contained the precious information from Ayrton's last lap, that damned seventh lap, but engineer Duffort, with some embarrassment, admitted: 'When the ECU arrived at Viry-Châtillon, instead of being read on a Marelli platform, it was used on one of Renault Sport's test benches, so the data it contained was irretrievably lost.'

Why had a serious car manufacturer like Renault put back into the cycle of normal engine manufacture a control unit that may have contained information of substantial use to the investigation of the true cause? Renault and Williams were partners for many successful years and this seems like a surprising decision around such an important issue.

It was necessary to wait for the court to issue an international letter rogatory for the Marelli control unit data to suddenly re-emerge, recorded in two sets of floppy disks (one containing five and the other six), and finally be handed over by Renault Sport to inspector Stefano Stefanini, via Interpol. The six floppy disks contained all the data recorded on Sunday by Senna and Hill's single-seaters and also included the warm-up laps. On the other five discs, however, only the data from Ayrton's single-seater had been extrapolated in Paris. One copy was sent to Williams, so that the team could make its own assessment of the case, while the other was handed over to the investigators.

Thanks to those precious floppies, it was possible to read the telemetry of Senna's last lap, delivering to history a truth that could otherwise have remained hidden.

CHAPTER 25

TELEMETRY EXPLAINED TO ROMBO MAGAZINE BY A FERRARI ENGINEER!

'NOT EVERYTHING that can be counted counts, and not everything that counts can be counted.'

The handwritten note in Albert Einstein's study at Princeton University is an effective incipit to the Theory of Relativity. Man's race towards the innermost knowledge of existence. Numbers as a representation of truth. Numbers were useful in unravelling the Senna case: in order to get out of the 'black holes' of attempted disinformation, the telemetry graphics of the last lap of the Williams FW16 at Imola were indispensable, but it seemed the telemetry did not exist, only for it to emerge after an international letter rogatory was sent by the judicial authority.

After analysing the data, it became clear that the steering column had broken. The telemetry was published by *Rombo*, the weekly magazine edited by Alberto Sabbatini, a competent journalist of long standing, the son of Marcello Sabbatini, the legendary director of *Autosprint* and later also the founder of the competing publication.

The two Bolognese editorial offices were at a stone's throw away from each other: needless to say, they were divided by a strong professional rivalry, but united by great respect. Magic's death at Imola, a few miles away from the two magazines that covered motor racing in Italy, ignited the sacred fire of wanting to understand what had happened to the Brazilian champion.

It was a duty to seek answers to the many questions that remained open.

'The exciting thing about this tragic affair,' recalls Alberto Sabbatini, 'is that *Autosprint* and *Rombo* were based in Bologna. I think the two magazines did a crazy investigation job, taking advantage of the fact that their headquarters were close to the place where everything had happened. We knew all the characters and interlocutors, so an investigation worthy of American novels was launched. A journalistic investigation that could never have taken place if the accident had happened at Silverstone, or at Le Castellet, for example.'

For the record, it is only fair to add that I personally came into possession of the copy of the original telemetry [before Sabbatini], but at *Autosprint* we focused our attention immediately on the broken column, leaving the analysis of the data acquisition for a later date. The scoop on the telemetry was made by *Rombo*.

'I was at Imola on 1 May,' Alberto resumes, 'and the next day I wanted to find out more, so I called a mutual friend, Massimo Gambucci, at the time director of the Imola circuit. Chatting on the phone he said, "Come to Imola in a few days, when the pressure has died down a bit, and I'll show you something." I went to the racetrack and he took me under the grandstand of *Variante Bassa*, where the marshals' garage was based and which was occasionally used for dinners. Ayrton's single-seater had been stored there, after it had been impounded, because they didn't know where to put it. He told me not to touch the car: so I just got closer, to have a good look at it, observing that split around the chassis, but I didn't see the steering wheel. Massimo told me that he also had Senna's helmet and one glove in his care, since the other had never been found.'

How did you get your hands on the telemetry?
Since I was friends with Gambucci, we spoke quite often. Two days after the visit to Imola I called him back and he said: 'I have got something to show you, but I need the utmost discretion. I'll show it to you, but officially I will disavow it. My recommendation: if you publish something, don't quote the source, because there is investigatory secrecy.' I was invited to his house; Massimo lived in Bologna, very close to my place. I entered his living-room and he brought me a big green book, similar to those folders with rings in which we kept our slides.

He told me: 'This is the telemetry block that was delivered to us. I can't understand anything about it, have a look at what you can see and understand. But be aware that I have never shown this to you and won't talk to anyone about it.'

I am recounting this episode now, because 30 years have passed and the investigation secrecy period has expired, but I did not reveal it to anyone else at the time. Back to the meeting with Gambucci, I remember that he told me: 'I'm going to make myself a coffee. Look at everything that may interest you and then we'll talk about it together.' I opened the folder and found a huge packet of graph paper sheets folded in two. I don't know how I managed to locate the one with the right lap, but I guess I remembered the sequence of the accident and the lap number at which it had occurred, so I guess there must have been some reference to it, as I found it quite quickly, and finally had this sheet of paper full of coloured lines spread out in front of me.

What did you see?
I can recall the pinkish graph paper in front of my eyes when I started to look at it. Compared to the telemetry you also had in your hands, Franco, this one had no notes on the side, only item names and acronyms. I realised that the key to the tragedy was all in there and I tried to interpret it, but I could not. So, while I was in Massimo's room – and because he had brought me a drink before going for his coffee – I found some thin paper napkins on the table. I took some of them and spread them open on top of the telemetry. Then, with a pen, I tried to mark the traces that seemed most interesting to me, striving to follow the lines accurately and writing down the lettering, but understanding nothing yet. Then Massimo returned to the room: he knew very well what I had done, because in the meantime I was still busy completing the tracing.

'What are you going to do now?' he asked in amazement.

'I will show these sketches to someone knowledgeable about them, just to see if they understand anything.'

I had put references on the napkins, possibly two or three, to see where the corners were, and then I folded everything. Finally, we tried to study it together, but he understood it less than I did. 'This big folder,' I remember Massimo saying, 'was handed over to me, but I have to take it to the examining magistrate [which he duly did the next day]: see if you can understand anything from what you have collected.'

You had an important document in your hand, but who did you turn to for a competent reading of the data?
The next day I called engineer Claudio Lombardi who was the head of Ferrari's sports team management at the time, and with whom I had an exceptional relationship. We often saw each other for dinner, hence we had established a bond of trust that went beyond the professional sphere. 'Engineer,' I told him, 'I need to talk to you about something very delicate that doesn't concern Ferrari, but I need some advice and a suggestion from you. Can we see each other for dinner?'

Having made the arrangements, we met at the restaurant just outside the Modena Sud motorway exit.

'I'm asking for your advice,' said I, pulling out from a folder an A3 sheet of paper, on which I had glued the napkins.

'What the hell is it?' he replied, very intrigued.

'It's the telemetry of Senna's Williams!'

'But how …?' replied Lombardi, very surprised.

'Please don't ask me how I came into possession of it, but it is clearly just a reproduction.'

So I told him the whole story and invited him to help me interpret the data.

Engineer Lombardi, I imagine, was almost speechless …
'All I understand is that there are some anomalous values,' said the manager of the *Cavallino*, 'but I am not able to get my bearings. I need your help …' Since I had taken note of the codes to which the various coloured lines referred – don't forget I had copied the lines using only a black ink pen – I was able to give him the elements he needed to read those curves. Ferrari possibly had the same Marelli telemetry as Williams. Immediately after starting the analysis, engineer Lombardi was speechless for a few seconds. Then, astonished, he said: 'You can really understand everything here!'

And after guiding me through the interpretation of the tracks he added: 'It's obvious that the steering column got broken!' Lombardi also pointed out a detail to me: on the steering column there was a sensor that indicated the torque applied to the steering wheel: 'If they put a sensor there,' the engineer told me, 'it's because they had something to keep an eye on.' He didn't speak specifically about problems, but about the desire to keep an eye on the type of effort applied by the driver.

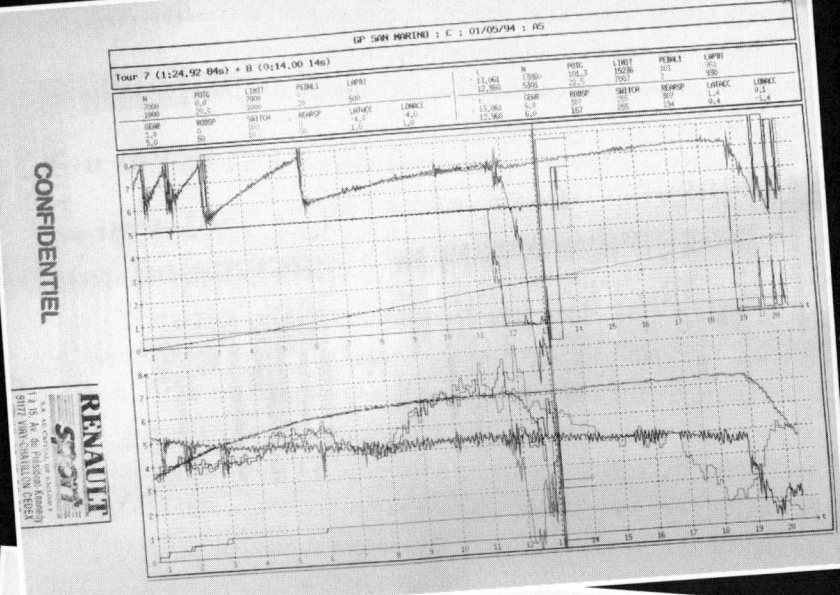

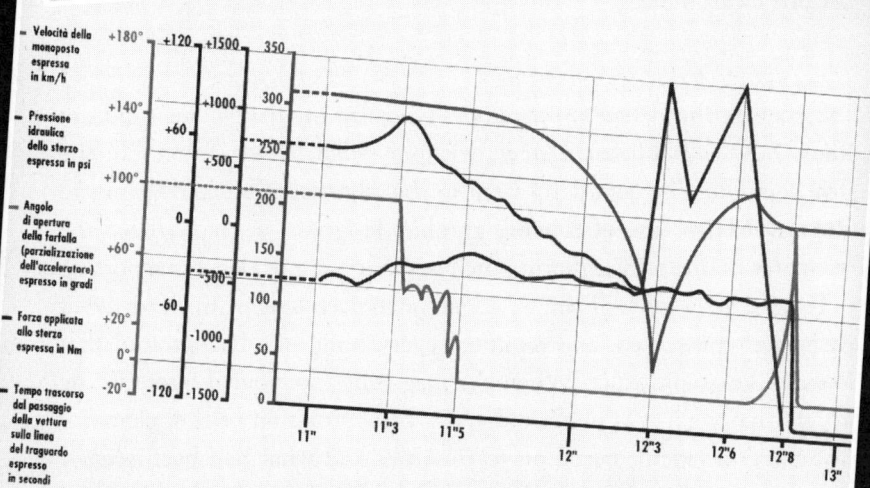

The original telemetry from the floppy disks that Renault had given to investigators.

The graph that Sabbatini had reconstructed by copying the data that he had briefly seen.

'Maybe it was meant to check the function of the power steering, or God only knows what other reason?' I commented at the time.

'They were keeping an eye on the steering angle because Ayrton, perhaps, wanted a different distribution between the steering movement and the force applied,' he speculated.

Following one line at a time he explained to me what the tracks meant, and told me what might have happened. Impressive things emerged, and meanwhile the dynamics of the accident became clear. Of course, it did not certify in black and white that the steering column had broken, but that was the obvious conclusion to be drawn from analysing the data. You could see certain values suddenly rise and then suddenly fall, even before the impact. Lombardi also pointed out to me how the speed value dropped dramatically and then rose again: this was due to the fact that the sensor was reading the grip of the wheels and so, when the single-seater had left the track, Ayrton had braked and the wheels had locked, resulting in a false measurement compared to the real one. We know that the impact speed was 211km/h. In short, the scenario became clear to me.

What did you feel at that moment?
I was aware that I had an incredible scoop on my hands, but I did not know how to publish the news without violating the secrecy of the investigation. The next day I went to the editorial office and thanks to Roberta Massa, one of *Rombo*'s graphic designers, we reproduced the telemetry in fine print, ignoring the lines that mattered less but reporting only the decisive ones. Then we added references, to explain clearly what each one represented, and mounted everything on a background that looked like graph paper. When the magazine came out, I wrote in the article that what was published was a reconstruction of the telemetry of Senna's accident, based on testimonies and what had been seen. I did not quote Gambucci and even less engineer Lombardi. I omitted that the data came from the real telemetry, otherwise the magistrate would have imprisoned me for violation of the investigative secret and, certainly, I would have put Massimo, who had shown it to me, in trouble. Unfortunately, every time we touched on the subject, someone always objected to the reliability of the data we had published, and every time I felt the urge to tell them that I had really seen the original telemetry and it was not an invention.

Telemetry explained to Rombo magazine by a Ferrari engineer!

What was the emotional impact in bringing out a truth from the telemetry?
What struck me deep down was that in those coloured lines you could see the last ten seconds of a person's life. And all the desperate manoeuvres Ayrton tried to do to avoid going off the track and crashing into the wall. There was one passage that particularly moved me: the throttle sensor showed that, at a certain point, Senna reduced the valve opening. This was abnormal, because the F1s drove through the *Tamburello* corner in full throttle, as if it were a straight. He reduced it by 50 per cent at a point where nobody lifted their foot off the accelerator pedal, because he sensed that something was wrong. The car was not turning or following the ideal trajectory: even the forces applied on the steering wheel said so. And after two-tenths of a second he had taken his foot off the gas: it had only taken him two-tenths of a second to realise that something was very wrong, because the throttle dropped to zero.

I shudder to remember that in those lines we could see the moment of terror, or the perception that something serious was happening. We know that those brief moments were the last in the life of a man, of a champion who was trying to cope with a very serious problem.

How does it feel to see the tracks again, the original ones I wanted to show you?
Thirty years have passed. Telemetry was something that sanctioned the transition from a heroic F1 to an F1 in which engineers relied more on numerical data than on the sensations transmitted by the driver. I always saw this, much as I liked computers and technology in general, as something that distorted the driver's job. In this case, the telemetry offers an instant-by-instant snapshot of what the driver did: the track only lasts ten seconds, but in that short space of time the event was reconstructed. I get emotional every time I see it again. Last year I took part in a Rotary meeting where non-racing guests were also present: I have to say that everyone was so moved by my story that even I became teary-eyed and hoarse. It's incredible how, three decades later, this tragedy can still evoke such strong feelings.

Alberto, besides being a good journalist, loves motorsport viscerally: he has raced in karting and has gone as far as competing in GT with demanding cars such as the Lamborghini in the SuperTrofeo ...

'I must add one more thing: I know Adrian Newey well. I'm a friend of his, we did two races together in a Lamborghini, so I became quite familiar with the Red Bull genius,' says Alberto. 'He invited me to his house for the second race and was very kind. And five years ago at Monza, the photographer Mark Sutton was impressed that Newey, seeing me on his way to the garage, came back to chat with me with tea in his hands. "'In all my years in F1," Mark commented to me, "I had never seen Adrian stop in the paddock to meet a journalist: you must have a special relationship with him!"

'This is to say that a sincere bond was established. I never spoke to him about Senna's accident, avoiding the subject. I just asked him a casual blunt question while we were changing in the motorhome, just before the Sunday race: "Adrian," I said, "how did the Senna affair really go?"

'He did not answer immediately, but he started to think. Not looking for a convenient answer. "I think there was not enough grip from the tyres and there were some bumps in the asphalt," was his reply.

'My impression is that Adrian is convinced and firmly believes that the column was not the cause. I didn't get the feeling that he was lying to me while saying this: although he has obviously seen the telemetry tracks, he believes that the accident was caused by a loss of grip in the corner.

'What I wonder is why on earth it took ten years of trial to arrive at a truth that was out there, for all to see: the telemetry data speaks for itself.'

So far we have talked about the Imola accident, but what memories do you have of Ayrton?
I wrote a book on it. I knew a driver with extraordinary abilities. In my days at the *Gazzetta dello Sport* I went to see him, since Pino Allievi didn't want me to follow Ferrari, because I was too critical of Maranello. So I became Ayrton's reference for my newspaper and I established a very good relationship with him right away. I never considered myself as Angelo Orsi, Senna's true friend, but a bond was created.

Andrea Ficarelli first introduced me to him at Brands Hatch in 1984. I had to replace a colleague from *Rombo* and, not following F1 on a regular basis, I had sought out Johnny Cecotto, whom I knew well and had become friends with, after I had written his column when he raced and won in *MotoMondiale*. Johnny, Ayrton's team-mate at Toleman, had a bad accident at Brands Hatch, and I was very touched by what had happened, not least because I had suddenly lost my point of reference – the only person I was relying on to get around in the F1 environment, about which I still knew little, in fact.

And how did you cope?
To make my task easier, Ficarelli thought it best to introduce Senna to me. When I went to see him on Saturday, he was busy with a briefing, so the appointment was moved to Sunday, just before the race. I went to the starting grid imagining that was not the best time to bother the Brazilian, except that Andrea called me, promising to introduce me to Ayrton. We arrived next to the Toleman as he was about to get out of the car, after lining up the single-seater. He still had his helmet on. Ficarelli began the introductions, pointing out that, as well as being a journalist, I had also run a few races in karting. Ayrton was taking off his right glove, before even taking off his helmet, and then stretched his hand out to me. I was struck by the fact that a driver, in the agitated minutes before a race, would take off a glove to shake hands with someone: it seemed to me a formidable sign of great politeness.

At Brands Hatch Senna achieved the second podium of his career with the TG184-Hart...
He ran a beautiful race and I remember going to the press conference of the top three finishers to listen to him. Although I wasn't sitting in the first rows I took note of everything he said, but I also managed to ask him somehow if there was any way we could continue the chat alone, since it was mainly the first two finishers who were talking. So I joined him at the motorhome, where we talked for about ten minutes. Then I didn't go back to an F1 GP until 1987, because I followed motorbikes. Yet, at Christmas, I got his card with Xmas wishes, just like the following year and all the years after. I saw him again in Rio de Janeiro, when he was racing Lotus and I had started following F1 on a permanent basis. I went looking for him in the paddock, hoping to say hello: he recognised me immediately and we started talking. Ayrton had a memory like an elephant. And then he had an extraordinary ability to entertain his interlocutors. There was definitely a bit of cunning: he had the ability to take care of public relations by combining it with a bit of personal opportunism. He knew how to select the journalists to talk to.

You were among the chosen ones, but is there another episode worth remembering?
In 1991 the last F1 race of the year was run in Adelaide. The whole Circus was on holiday for a few days in Port Douglas. The drivers were all at Jelly Beach, a resort on a 5km-long tongue of sand in a U-shape: at the centre was the reception and at either end the bungalows. Senna was at one end. As soon as I arrived, I went to have a look at the pool, where I found Ayrton in full relaxation: firstly he asked me if I knew when there would be the *Autosprint* Golden Helmets Party at the end of the championship and, immediately afterwards, thanks to his elephant-like memory, he asked me how my karting races were going.

'I recently competed in Parma,' I replied, 'where *you* also raced ...'
'And how fast did you shoot?' he replied.
'Well, I can't remember, maybe 51", but I'm not sure.'
'I was doing 46'470"!' he added.

He recalled his best timeprecisely, even though a dozen years had passed. This ability to remember the smallest details was something that always amazed me about him, both as a driver and as a person. Many people claimed that he was obnoxious, arrogant and that he was showing off; in reality he was simply a shy man, who only opened up to those he trusted. And I had the privilege of immediately finding a very good connection with him. He was a perfect interlocutor: only Ayrton and Prost were able to give you a good headline every time they spoke. They knew how to give a cue, because they had the ability to analyse and go in-depth. The Brazilian, in addition, had a certain magnetism, his own way of doing things and a certain – not even too hidden – sadness, given his poor propensity to smile.

You said you were at Imola on 1 May ...
I didn't get a chance to talk to him that weekend. I was the director of *Rombo* and was not operational in the field. The thing I do remember is catching a glimpse of him on Saturday afternoon, while he was having a heated discussion with the mechanics in the pit ... Could it be that they were still working on the column? Ayrton was wearing a checked shirt, the very same one that the journalists from *L'Équipe* photographed, folded up in the briefcase with his personal belongings and pass. I am impressed by those images because they take me back to the last time I saw him

alive. Senna always amazed me with his classic way of dressing, with loose, ill-fitting trousers, very different from the fashion of the moment. He was essential, inconspicuous. Great in his simplicity.

CHAPTER 26

PIOLA: CREATOR OF THE BIG STEERING WHEEL THAT DIDN'T FIT IN THE WILLIAMS

'ART MUST take reality by surprise.'

Françoise Sagan, a French writer, could not have portrayed the image of Giorgio Piola better. He is an F1 icon: he has frequented the paddock for over 50 years and took up the profession of technical draughtsman when he was still a high school student in Genoa. He has got the aesthetic sense of an artist and a unique trait that is now universally recognised. Even though technology has made tools available that make his job easier, fuelling the birth of a generation of skilled 'copyists', Giorgio still draws by hand, to combine the beauty of drawing with the rigour of lines that uncover the single-seater's innermost secrets. He could have been an actor, thanks to his physical prowess and those clear eyes that have enchanted so many female figures, but it is his bird-of-prey look that has made him unique: one glance at new bodywork, or a wing, is just enough for him to immediately grasp novelties and modifications. A click with the camera during the day turns into a drawing at night, in a life cycle that the latest generation of talents would not be able to handle.

Very few hours of sleep and the ability to consume meals with rapid voracity, in order to 'gain time', have made Piola an eccentric character, much feared and respected in the paddock. His drawings – not only the technical ones – speak as much as his judgements: first as a popular TV commentator and as a specialist on YouTube and Instagram. With his edgy character, he couldn't help but become an egocentric: a 'sun' that has illuminated the passion of so many designers who today conceive F1 racing cars, and have become interested in single-seaters thanks to his drawings.

Adrian Newey, the Red Bull genius, is one of them. The Englishman is a shy guy, very reserved; he does not like the attention of journalists and media pressure. It is difficult to intercept him in the paddock, but if he crosses paths with Giorgio, he stops, because he likes that game of guards and thieves, between those who would like to keep the latest winning solution hidden and those who, on the contrary, want to divulge it to the world immediately, giving it its deserved value.

As a young man, the drivers were the peers with whom Giorgio shared an only apparently golden existence: many also became friends and many departed too soon, leaving unhealable wounds in his soul, which forged a certain hardness and roughness in his human relations.

In the 1990s, in addition to being the technical specialist for *Autosprint* and *La Gazzetta dello Sport*, he worked with 13 newspapers around the globe, and had attracted the attention of Dr Boselli, the CEO of Personal, and the owner of Nardi, the two companies which supplied steering wheels to F1 teams. 'He had two brands,' Piola recounts, 'but the factory was the same. He had contacted me because I used to attend all the GPs, and basically he chose me as a collaborator so he would not have to send his own person, with much higher costs. I used to carry all the steering wheel diagrams and we were supplying almost all the teams except Ferrari. Ron Dennis wanted an exclusive supplier, so only McLaren had the Nardi brand, while everyone else used Personal steering wheels. I supplied Toleman, Tyrrell, Williams and other minor teams, but not Ferrari, which I only managed to serve in 1982, because we made special steering wheels for Patrick Tambay, who had back problems. Not only was I the technical manager at the GPs, which allowed me constant talks with the drivers, but I was also responsible for drawing up contracts with the teams. The relationship was easy with everyone, except for Frank Williams and Ron Dennis of McLaren.'

So you found out what the attitudes of the two managers were during a contract renewal. What differences did you notice?
[Piola smiles with relish.] The curious thing I found out was that Frank, with whom I had a more friendly relationship, aimed for a slight mark-up

each time – we're talking about £500 more – to show that the relationship was growing, while Ron demanded the best and most advanced steering wheels. In short, he was aiming for the highest quality.

But what was the magnitude of the contracts?
The amount was ridiculous compared to the figures you hear in F1 today: like £15–20k a year. It was little more than a symbolic sum, while the commitment was to meet the requests of their drivers, which were often diverse and demanding. Keke Rosberg even required a supply of white leather steering wheels for his road-going Mercedes. He wanted two or three of them a year, because they got dirty, while Nigel Mansell demanded in his Williams a steering wheel that was very small in diameter and had a metal armature that was a couple of millimetres thicker than all the others. The reason? For two years in a row at Spa-Francorchamps he had bent the crown with the amount of energy he exerted while driving. Nigel had incredible strength and was the only one who could drive with that tiny steering wheel.

The negotiation with Frank was easy, while with Ron I had to undergo a kind of ritual each time, which was reserved for every McLaren sponsor. At the airport I would punctually find Creighton Brown, the McLaren director, waiting for me in a Mercedes and, during the journey, we would order a breakfast that we would eat together in the factory. At the McLaren Technology Centre there was a dedicated lounge: I remember it was all grey, there wasn't a single white or coloured thing, just furniture in different shades of grey. Then I had to go to the projection room to watch a film about McLaren, as if I had never been to the races. Every year the scenario was identical, repetitive, because you could not get out of the procedure that Ron Dennis wanted. Only at the end of all that would I be escorted to his office. After the repeated world titles won by the Woking team, he could have asked for much larger sums, but from a technical sponsorship he only sought perfection in the quality of materials. He never asked me for an extra pound, but he demanded the exclusivity of the Nardi brand.

Let us come to Ayrton Senna. In 1993 Alain Prost had won the World Championship in the Williams FW15C, which had been 'sewn' onto the Frenchman, who had the physicality of a jockey. Adrian Newey, the technical director, had designed a cockpit that was more closed at the top:

the driver's hands and steering wheel were encased inside the cramped chassis, to the advantage of aerodynamics, while the McLaren single-seater previously driven by Senna was much more open and comfortable for the driver. When Ayrton got into the Williams for the first time at Estoril, he immediately complained about the cockpit: 'Ayrton didn't fit in the cockpit that had been designed for Prost,' recalls Piola, 'but something similar had also happened at McLaren, when Berger had to get into a car that had been designed for Senna. Gerhard, I remember, often complained of leg cramps because his ankles were forced into an unnatural posture. And it was certainly not ideal for someone who had to drive the 300-plus kilometres of a Grand Prix.'

It is clear that the designers of the single-seaters followed concepts inspired by the extremes of the regulations, in order to gain maximum performance advantage from the layout of the car. And the driver, very often, was forced to make sacrifices to stay in the car, as if he were a mere 'accessory'. After the exasperations of the engineers, FIA rules have been introduced over the years to define the minimum measurements of the survival cell, so that even the tallest drivers can have an increasingly comfortable and safe 'office'.

'Ayrton had never felt perfectly comfortable in the Williams FW16,' continues Piola. 'Among all drivers, he was the one who wanted the biggest steering wheel, with a diameter of 280mm and a perfectly round grip that was the thinnest of all. These two characteristics made his crown different from that of the other Williams drivers, who used smaller steering wheels with a more elaborate anatomical shape, in search of the best grip ergonomics. Prost also used a large-diameter steering wheel, and like Ayrton, the Frenchman had come to Didcot from McLaren, which had open cockpits, but Alain used a steering wheel 1cm smaller than his rival's.'

We are only talking about half a centimetre on each side, which may not even seem like a disproportionate measurement, but in reality Personal's engineers were forced to design a specific steering wheel for each driver, and even a few millimetres could make a big difference ...
Senna was a fussy guy and demanded the same steering wheel that he had developed over the years and to which he had become accustomed. It may sound like a triviality, but Ayrton paid almost maniacal attention to every aspect of his single-seater and wanted to know it in detail. Finding the

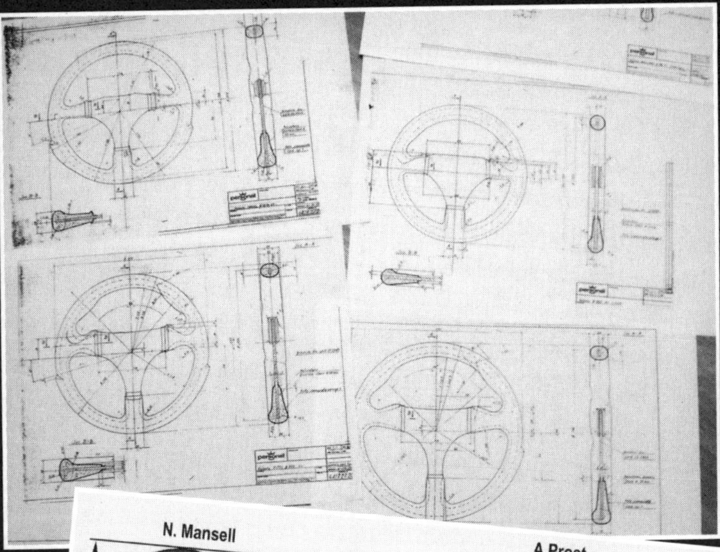

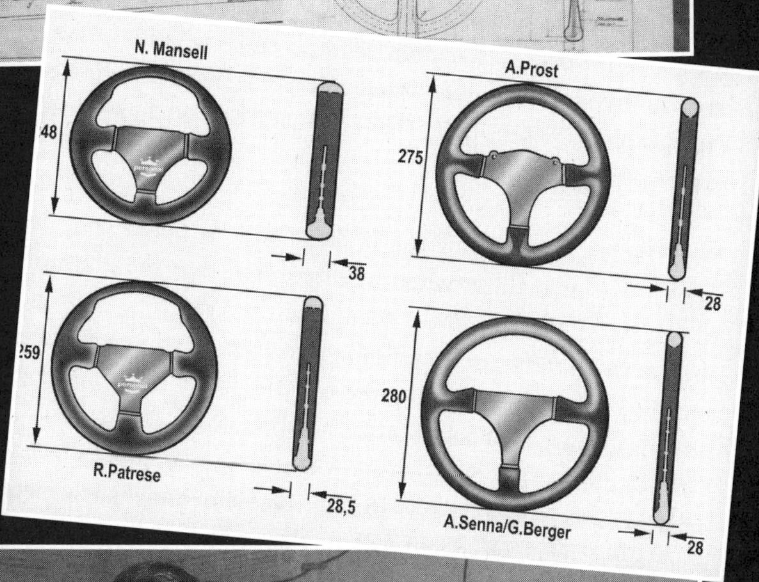

Some models of Personal steering wheels, a company for which the journalist was a consultant, chosen by various F1 drivers.

Giorgio Piola gives an award to a young Ayrton.

best ergonomics in the steering wheel was important: with a large crown, the Brazilian was able to manage the entry into bends by enhancing his sensitivity with calibrated movements, and with more precise steering angles, according to the design of the bend. There were two advantages: clean driving, which translated into less physical effort, and less stress on the front tyres.

Ayrton's steering wheel was very thin, with black leather and white stitching. The grip was small and the diameter large, while Nigel Mansell, to take another example, preferred a very small steering wheel with a chubby grip. The two champions had morphologically different hands: the South American had rather short and tapered fingers, while the hands of the Englishman were larger. Mansell chose solutions more aimed at physical driving, with more brutal and rapid reactions, while Senna, like Prost, exploited a sensitivity that had made him an appreciated aesthete of the steering wheel.

From Piola's account, one can understand how Senna considered it far from a marginal thing when he discovered that the 280mm steering wheel would not fit into the cockpit of the Williams: 'Ayrton was very annoyed with the team,' reveals Giorgio, 'because the cockpit was fairing and the chassis was closed at the top: the knuckles of his fingers were rubbing against the sides of the carbon bodywork, causing him annoying bruises, despite the fact that he was wearing fireproof gloves. On his debut at Estoril with the FW15D the problem immediately emerged, yet engineers Patrick Head and Adrian Newey assured him that on the 1994 single-seater, the FW16, the problems would be solved. But this was not the case, with the tragic effects we later saw ...'

Giorgio, what was your relationship with Ayrton?
Wonderful, at least until the rivalry with Prost exploded. I was very close to Alain, and Senna saw me as the Frenchman's friend, so, as time went on, my relationship with Ayrton became more and more related only to the steering wheel. When he needed something and saw me passing by the pits, he would simply wave his hand to call me. I would go straight to him. He barely greeted me any more, preferring to get straight to the point: it was incredible: as soon as he had explained the changes he wanted to the steering wheel, he had the power to make me feel as if I had suddenly become transparent!

All the people who had anything to do with Ayrton speak of a different person. Evidently there must have been an episode between you that created a rift, causing the relationship to become purely professional. Probably Alain had nothing to do with it …

Well, something had happened at the 1987 Belgian GP. Ayrton in the Lotus was in a tussle with Mansell in the Williams and, on the first lap, he wanted to pass him on the outside at the *Campus* chicane. The cars were paired up and, mid-corner, there was contact that eventually caused both to retire. At Spa-Francorchamps the pits are high above the paddock, and to reach them, you have to climb a flight of steps. I was with Adriano Costa, a correspondent of *Tuttosport*, when we saw a very angry Nigel running up the stairs: 'Adriano,' I said to my colleague, 'let's follow him, look at Nigel: agitated as he is, he will surely go for Senna to make his point.' At the time there was freedom to enter team garages and there weren't all the constraints of today. So we looked into the Lotus garage: in the middle were Ayrton and Peter Warr, the Lotus sports director, while Nigel was approaching, looking furious. Senna sniffed that a bad air was blowing, so he started to back off, while Warr remained impassive, almost as if he wanted to remain just a spectator of what was about to happen, since Nigel was rushing at the Brazilian. Mansell was frightening: he was strong, very strong, much stronger than Ayrton who, walking backwards, trying to find an escape route, had reached the back of the room and, once at the wall, had no way out. The Englishman, with an intimidating gesture, pulled up the zip of his fireproof suit and then, with his big hand, grabbed him by the neck, lifting him slightly off the ground. In reality Nigel had no intention of getting physical, he merely wanted to put fear into him.

The scene may sound serious, but at that juncture I literally burst out laughing. Senna saw me, and that the same evening he phoned Angelo Orsi, my colleague from *Autosprint*, a great friend and confidant of Ayrton, to complain that I had laughed in his face. That's when I lost my relationship with him a bit, but the scene was really funny, like seeing someone slip on a banana peel: at first you laugh and only afterwards you do wonder if the person who fell down was hurt.

Giorgio Piola is an outspoken Ligurian; he never hides what he thinks and, above all, does not consider his words or behaviour just to be pleasant. In the paddock he is famous for the art of his technical drawings, but also for certain 'rough' attitudes. In reality, he is a tough guy with a heart of gold: 'When Ayrton died I was deeply affected by the tragedy. I was so distraught that I never wanted to delve into what actually had happened to him. The best driver had passed away and that was a tragedy I found hard to accept. In spite of everything, I had great respect for him and, beyond certain episodes, the relationship we'd had over the years had been consolidated. Whenever I was asked to draw up rankings, I have always put Senna ahead of Michael Schumacher, even though the German has won more world championships. Ayrton was truly Magic.'

Thirty years after that 1 May, what are your thoughts?
Williams tried to meet Senna's requirements: on either side of the steering wheel they had cut two small portions of the chassis and at Imola Ayrton had seen the changes. When he sat inside the car and discovered that his fingers were still touching the bodywork I think he played devil's advocate and a harsh reaction set in. Whenever Ayrton set his mind to something, he became very determined to get the result. I still remember an episode from his time at McLaren: we were in Brazil and the engineers had already gone to the hotel to relax, as the day was over. Not so for Senna, who had a doubt about the telemetry data: he called the engineers and forced them to return to the track half an hour later. He was the first driver to understand how important telemetry analysis could be in improving the car's performance and, albeit somewhat reluctantly, his engineers discovered that the question posed by the punctilious driver was more than well-founded. He was right. He had silenced them all with facts.

Are you saying he may have demanded further action on the FW16?
At Imola, taken by desperation, I think that the Williams men decided to saw off the column to modify it, intervening on the spot, perhaps without fully informing Patrick Head, technical director, and Adrian Newey, chief designer. This is my idea, totally personal. Knowing the characters and the situation I think it may be plausible, because the modification was done badly, certainly not in Williams's style.

At this point in the chat, the technical designer lets himself go with a secret that he has never revealed to anyone. It's time to talk about a real backstory ... 'That San Marino GP was also the occasion when, for the first time, I went into the Swiss Italian television booth to comment on the race. After the tragic accident, we had an interaction with Nelson Piquet. The Brazilian champion, with his usual picaresque attitude, was capable of desecrating any situation and had always been someone who never had any kind words for Senna. Well, Nelson was the very first one to state that the steering column might have broken. He revealed that he had approached the Williams engineers to find out what had happened and they told him that Ayrton's reaction time to switch from accelerator to brake had been minimal, almost nil. Piquet then explained that, even in a corner taken at 300km/h, if a suspension breaks, the driver has an instant to assess in which direction the car will crash before braking. On the other hand, when Senna realised he had a broken column, he could do nothing more than stick to the brakes, and the speed with which he went from one pedal to the other testified to his awareness that he had no other means of trying to at least slow the car down, by then without any directional control.

But why is this incredible testimony from Piquet only coming out now? Because no one has ever asked me …

Those who do not know Piola may be surprised, astonished even, by an answer that might seem flippant. In reality, Giorgio is incapable of delivering a line and, when he allows emotions to resurface from the treasure chest of his deepest memories – that he himself thought buried within – he endows posterity with an insight into Nelson that puts the *Carioca*'s relationship with his 'hated' compatriot into perspective, and provides further confirmation of what has been sanctioned by the investigations, by the analyses and the trials.

CHAPTER 27

THIS IS WHY PATRESE REFUSED TO GET INTO SENNA'S FW16

'FATE, WHEN it opens one door, closes another. Given certain steps forward, there is no going back.'

The French writer Victor Hugo had clear ideas about comebacks. Certainly more so than Riccardo Patrese, the Paduan driver who won six GPs in his career and, in 1992, was the last Italian to fight for a world championship with Williams. Didcot's team had been his home for five of his 17 years in F1, and, after stormily breaching the contract that bound him to Benetton at the end of 1993, he was looking for a way back to doing what he liked best: racing. Riccardo had never definitively hung up his helmet and the urge to return had been gnawing at him ever since the World Championship had started again and he had remained at home.

'I went to Imola to talk to Frank Williams and Patrick Head. 1993 had finished with a divorce from Benetton and Flavio Briatore, which unfortunately ended badly,' Riccardo says. 'Theoretically I should have competed in the 1994 season as well, but given Briatore's dissatisfaction with me, and since he kept saying that I should retire and that I had become a ball and chain in the team, we had parted company. I had been waiting to choose what to do in the future, as I had not decided to stop with Formula 1 yet. I had had some contacts during the winter, but then the season started without me and, after 17 years in F1 I found myself stranded. I thought this would affect me less and that I could serenely retire, but instead, I felt nostalgic about racing.'

Riccardo, who is now in his 70s and in splendid shape, then came up with an idea that could be a winner: to put himself at Williams's disposal to help Ayrton Senna solve the problems of a hostile FW16. 'My team of reference had always been Williams, where I had been for the last few years and had left a very good impression. They had taken Ayrton and the regulations had imposed a return to passive suspension, because active suspension had been banned. In the first Grand Prix Senna faced big problems with competitiveness, especially in comparison with Michael Schumacher, who won the first two GPs. In Brazil Ayrton retired on lap 55 after a spin after starting from pole, and at Aida he was hit from behind on the first lap. In short, the car was not performing as the team expected and the Imola weekend was just around the corner. I, on the other hand, was suffering from a lack of F1, so in my head I said to myself: "I'm going to see Frank and Patrick to offer myself as a tester," especially as I had been the last Williams driver to test the passive suspension. Damon Hill himself, the driver who raced alongside Ayrton, didn't know about traditional suspension, because he had been taken on as a test driver specifically to develop active suspension. He had done billions of kilometres of testing, but always with the electronic car, so my experience with the traditional car could be useful. I went to Imola on Saturday afternoon, before the last hour of qualifying: I spoke to Frank and Patrick explaining my availability and they seemed very interested.'

Patrick considered you not only a good driver, but also an excellent test driver ...
I think so, otherwise I wouldn't have stayed for five years at Williams. Back then the drivers also had to be able to set up the car, because there were no simulators like today. If I remained at Didcot for a long time it was because they considered me a team man, suitable for a top team. And I was proud to see that they considered me capable of finding solutions to the problems of the FW16.

In the team, they feared that the 1994 car, initially designed for active suspension, had aerodynamic problems, once the regulations had imposed a return to passive ...

Although it was true that painstaking research work was carried out in the wind tunnel, it was also true that the solutions studied in the wind tunnel were truly tested on the track by the driver. Ideas which theoretically should have worked, according to the tunnel tests, often did not achieve the same result on the track, therefore it was always the driver who had the final say in promoting or rejecting a certain modification. I think that we drivers of the time represented an added value, whereas today's simulation systems are so refined that the driver has very few problems to solve. From what I've been told, the current single-seaters arrive at the track with a basic setup that is hardly ever changed, limiting the adjustments to a degree of front wing, whereas once upon a time we were able to turn the car inside out.

Patrick Head was an admirer of Riccardo and his proposal came like cheese on macaroni at a particularly critical moment for the team, so it was immediately welcomed. Patrese recalls: 'Patrick commented: "OK, now let's call Ayrton and see what he thinks – Riccardo could start a useful collaboration to solve the problems of his car." All four of us got together and Senna supported my appointment to his full satisfaction. The chat was over in a few minutes. It was a great opportunity for me: I would be driving a Formula 1 single-seater again, I would have the chance to keep in shape, and since Damon Hill had just arrived in the team and had less charisma than me, I could also have a chance to become Senna's team-mate in 1995, if I helped to solve the problems on his car. When the foursome meeting was over, I left Frank's motorhome and went to the pits to have a look at the cars. Ayrton came with me to discuss the subject: he was very interested in the possibility of speeding up the development of the FW16, and he made me understand how pressing for him was the need to take action on that car.'

For Riccardo, returning to the Williams garage was a bit like coming home, given that the year before, at Benetton, he had been treated as an outsider to the team, all aimed solely at Michael Schumacher: 'I was happy, because I had seen again mechanics who had worked with me and whom I trusted.' The Paduan, after rediscovering the familiar Williams environment, was keen to take a look at the FW16, the single-seater that was putting Magic, the best driver in the Circus, in trouble: 'I couldn't recall how tight the cockpit was: it was still the one I had driven in two

Senna and Patrese almost side by side immediately after the start of the 1992 Monaco GP.

years before. The driver's seat was always very sacrificed, so much so that several years later, when I climbed back into the 1991 FW14 on Minardi Day in 2019, the first thing I said to myself was: "How the hell was I supposed to drive this car? There's not even room to move my hands on the steering wheel!" That was a characteristic of Adrian Newey's cars in those days. I think the most extreme was Ivan Capelli's and Mauricio Gugelmin's Leyton House. The drivers had to adapt: to have aerodynamic advantages in wing efficiency, they had to assume unnatural postures.'

Senna took pole position at Imola in the Friday afternoon session: how did you find Ayrton at the end of qualifying on Saturday?
We were somewhat unsettled because Roland Ratzenberger's fatal accident had just occurred, and when a driver dies nobody is serene, but I found Ayrton very motivated and charged. He was very emotionally

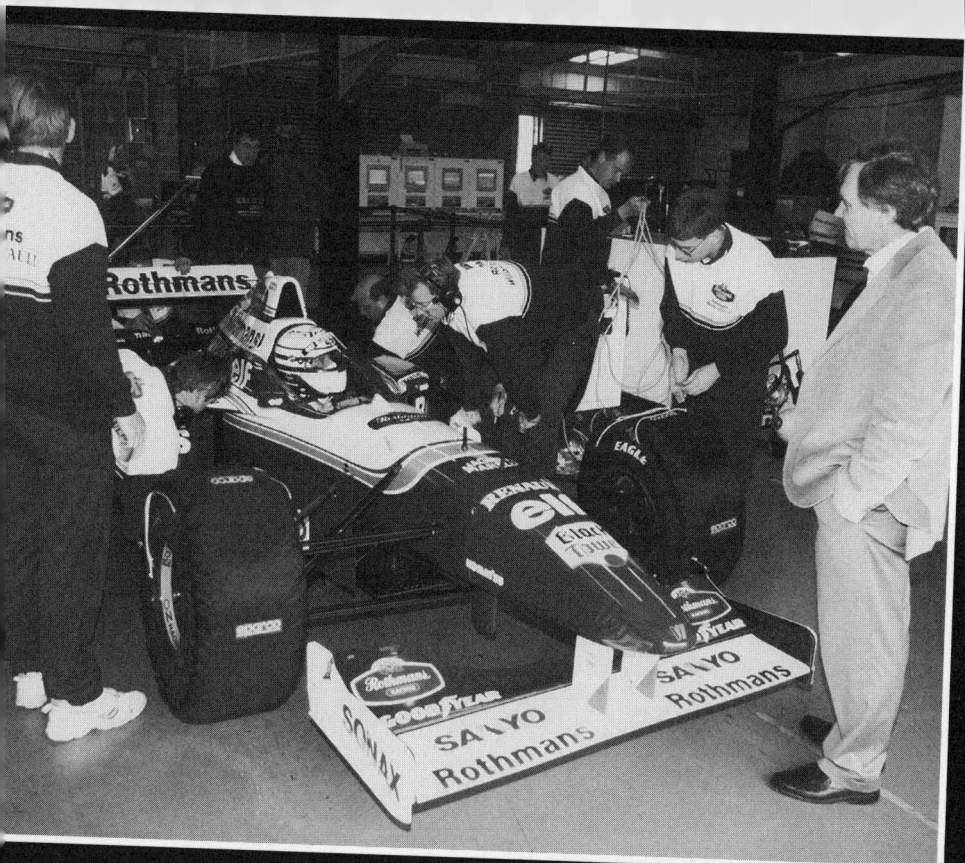

Riccardo Patrese in the 1996 test at Silverstone, where he was invited to drive the Williams of Villeneuve and Hill.

affected by the tragedy, but when we spoke in professional terms about what could be done to improve the FW16 he was very involved, and began to tell me what problems needed to be solved, in the belief that the collaboration that was starting could help him to have a Williams capable of winning races and the World Championship.

Who was Senna for you?
First and foremost a friend, and I consider him one of the greatest drivers motor racing has ever had. He was one of those who could always make a

difference, as well as being one of the very few who would not be swayed by external events that could have caused any upset. It was as if he lived inside a bubble, or in a spaceship where he remained unflappable. Many said, after that 1 May 1994, that he was agitated before the start of the race. I can only say that I knew him for this ability to detach himself from everything else. I have only met two people like that: Ayrton Senna and Michael Schumacher. The only drivers capable of isolating themselves from whatever was going on around them. I, for example, was more conditioned and not always able to be in top psycho-physical form at every GP. Neither he nor Michael felt these variations. They were really impressive.

But how did the friendship come about?
Thanks to the overseas holidays organised by Ercole Colombo: we preferred not to go back to Europe between races and we would all stay together in a resort, in good company, with no professional demands. Even when we were in the Principality of Monaco, it happened that we would go jogging together, to keep us fit, and this way we would chat and cement our friendship.

In short, he was a character with whom you got on well, even if you didn't spare each other on the track ...
I agree, but all drivers can be ... car-crazy, because everyone feels they are the best and wants to win. Rivalry ensues when you put the visor down, but things change when you are outside the professional sphere. No doubt we are different people inside and outside the car.

And on that Sunday, 1 May, what were your thoughts?
I was in front of the TV watching the GP when the accident happened. I was shocked. I couldn't get over it, because just a few hours earlier I had met him in perfect shape. We had made a plan and I was ready to help him. I couldn't accept the idea that he was dead and my reaction was like I was still at Imola.

And what happened?
The pain was so deep that I could not sleep at night. And I also realised that, as a simple test driver, I could suddenly be a replacement for Ayrton. Possibly, I would have to go back to racing immediately because the team,

however affected by the tragedy, had to find another driver to continue the season. Williams at Monaco raced with only one car, but then they were obliged to field the second ...

Did you think about it?
I want to be clear: I wasn't thinking about it ... they just offered it to me! And I can assure you that the 20 days after Ayrton's death were a real ordeal for me. I was enticed by the idea of going back to racing, but the strongest, the best driver had died, in a car that for years I had considered to be the safest. And if the accident had happened to him, it could have happened to me too.

These are all arguments that had never entered my head before that tragedy. Unfortunately, in my career I had lost other team-mates, like Elio in 1986, but while in the past I had tried not to think about it and to get back in the car as soon as possible, so as not to be afraid, in this Senna affair I began to think a lot about what had happened. Perhaps I was psychologically paying for my six-month absence from F1: I had broken out of the mental protection mechanism and, if in the past my passion for racing had taken over, at that time I was overwhelmed by so many thoughts.

You went to the Monaco GP, the race after Imola ...
Frank wanted to talk to me. When he met me in the paddock he told me verbatim: 'We need a driver. We were talking about using you as a tester, but now would you feel up to getting back into the car to be a regular driver?' The immediate response was the instinctive one: 'Yes, I am available!' But at the very moment I spoke, doubts arose. I was reminded of the worst accidents I had had and which, thanks to God and Saint Anthony, I had overcome. I thought that something might have broken in my car too, because it was clear that something had broken in Ayrton's.

When you spoke to Williams and Head did you ask what had happened to Senna, or did they give you an explanation of the accident to reassure you?
No, but after a few days my inner turmoil continued to grow, while everyone was putting me forward as the Williams driver who would drive the FW16 in the Paul Ricard tests. Ercole Colombo called me for confirmation: 'Dear Ercole, I've made a decision now and I'm telling you

first: Riccardo Patrese is definitely retiring from Formula 1. As soon as I get off the phone with you, I will immediately call Frank Williams to let him know. I have made the choice and you can write the news in the *Gazzetta dello Sport*.'

Ercole could not believe what he was hearing: 'But are you sure? You could go back to driving a competitive car; think it over again …'

'No, you have no idea how I have spent these last few days: there are too many thoughts running through my head. If I got into the Williams, I don't think I could be the driver with the same determination that you have known.'

I said goodbye to Colombo and immediately called Frank, who said: 'Hi Riccardo, so will you drive our car?'

'No Frank, I am feeling uneasy about it, I have too many doubts. Do not take me into consideration anymore.'

'But are you sure?' replied Williams. 'Take some more time before you give me the definitive answer.'

'Dear Frank, I am telling you that I am retiring. I will never drive a Formula 1 car again.'

Thirty years later, how do you feel about that choice?
I think, emotionally, I wanted to go back to racing, but objectively I was aware that I would no longer be the driver Williams knew: because getting into the car with my doubts, I would not have been able to give 101 per cent of my potential. It was clear that something had been triggered inside me that had altered my consciousness to the core. A sort of mental brake took shape and I could no longer fight to win: what would have been the point of going back to racing just to participate and not trying to stay ahead? I didn't want to be just an underdog, because, if I got back into the race, I wanted to get a monkey off my back with Briatore, but to do it under those circumstances would have made no sense.

It's all understandable Riccardo, but then you went back to driving a Williams in a test at Silverstone …
I confirm this: I was invited in 1996 to drive the car of Jacques Villeneuve and Damon Hill. I accepted because I took it as a gift, not as a professional opportunity. And I can say I took great satisfaction, because as a retired driver I had been faster than the Benetton! A nice way to show Flavio that

I wasn't finished. But it's one thing to take a ride on a merry-go-round, it would have been quite another to get into Ayrton's car. The Silverstone test was the one where I had the most fun, but it was just a quiet and relaxing game: I decided how many laps to drive, with which tyres and which settings. Racing would have been something else and, thinking about Senna, I wouldn't have been able to do it.

Full stop.

CHAPTER 28

THAT IN-CAR CAMERA FOOTAGE THAT APPEARED WHEN IT SEEMED IT DID NOT EXIST

'ALL THAT is said, but not shown, is lost to the public.'

Alfred Hitchcock, one of the most famous 20th century directors in international cinema and a master of suspense, could not have summed up better an aspect of the Senna tragedy that unleashed a sea of controversy. Was there anyone who had seen the in-car camera images of Ayrton's crash at *Tamburello* during that cursed lap seven of the San Marino GP? The Formula One Constructors' Association's (FOCA's) answer was a peremptory: 'No'.

According to the staff of F1 championship promoter Bernie Ecclestone, there had never been any footage of the accident from the on-board camera mounted on the Williams No. 2. Yet, many in the paddock were ready to bet that on-board footage had been seen. RAI, which in 1994 was the state TV company in charge of the production of the Imola event, had not broadcast anything different from the sequence that was aired live and etched in the collective memory: i.e. the FW16 leading the race that, filmed by camera no. 3 positioned at the *Villeneuve* corner, went off at a tangent at *Tamburello* and crashed into the wall on the outside, before stopping in the middle of the track with the single-seater destroyed and the lifeless driver in it.

The shots were those of the RAI director Giancarlo Tomassetti: the scene had made the whole world's blood run cold, but they were shots taken from far away, not at all helpful in establishing what had actually happened to Ayrton in the out-of-control Williams. It was expected that some answers might come from the 'FOCA TV' which managed the images incoming from the in-car cameras mounted on the single-seaters, since Senna mounted one on the left side of the roll-bar which also partially filmed the cockpit.

The saga of the in-car camera was like a murder mystery. Was it just a misunderstanding played on words, or a deliberate attempt not to let anything out in order to defend a sport that was under attack, with all the eyes of the world on it? The story can be read in diametrically opposed ways and everyone can draw their own conclusions.

At the editorial office of *Autosprint*, on the evening of 1 May, we received a report from Francesco Longanesi Cattani, the former FIA communications manager, that his acquaintances in France had seen on TF1, the transalpine broadcaster which owned the F1 rights, a replay with some images from the in-car camera, crediting the hypothesis that there was a film.

For months, nothing more was heard of it, because the British stubbornly clung to the idea that the crash had not been filmed by an in-car camera, while the investigators were sure that it had been and that finding the images would easily solve the court case.

A year later, on the occasion of the 1995 San Marino GP, clarity began to emerge, when Alan Woollard, director of the FOCA, was interviewed by the public prosecutor Maurizio Passerini: 'I was in the control room of the FOCA,' Wollard had explained, 'and I had in front of me the monitors with the images from the in-car cameras in operation. I was the one who chose which ones to put on air.'

At Imola in 1994, there were 13 single-seaters with a mounted in-car camera, while the FOCA control room only had four channels to use at the same time: 'These four were the images we could broadcast to the host broadcaster,' continued Woollard, 'but RAI at Imola could only receive three. It was then the local TV station that decided whether and which images to broadcast. Senna's in-car camera was running until a few moments before the accident.'

RAI actually did not receive three signals, but only two due to the limited means available. However, Alan made an initial admission by adding: '[Ayrton's camera] was active from the second start, after the safety car came out. I was the one who decided to disconnect it at

Tamburello for two reasons: first of all because Senna was in the lead and there was nobody in front, so you could only see an empty track, then because the signal quality was getting worse. I had decided to free up the channel to switch to Katayama's Tyrrell, as the Japanese driver's images were of great interest to Fuji TV. I don't remember if the in-car camera footage of Senna, which stopped just before the accident, was given to RAI. I was following the race and it may be that RAI asked us if we had taken the accident, and we said no, because we didn't have the images of the moment of impact.'

The existing video preceding the accident was therefore not considered important ...
I recognise that it may seem incomprehensible that, after Senna's death, no one felt the need, from a journalistic point of view, to broadcast what were the last images of Ayrton at the wheel of an F1 car, but I repeat that the quality of the images was not good, so I find nothing strange in the fact that they were never broadcast.

From the story, one would think that the choice to keep everything under wraps was Woollard's.
I don't know whether Eddie Baker was aware of Senna's images, nor whether Bernie Ecclestone was informed. In any case, the decision whether or not to make the latest images available to television stations was not mine to make.

Andrew James, the FOCA technician who was in charge of switching from one in-car camera to another on the director's orders, provided another piece of information: 'I do not believe that the in-car camera images at the time of the accident were provided to RAI. In fact, we generally did not stop the images while they were being supplied to the host station. As a rule, we would first disengage from the broadcaster and only afterwards would the in-car camera be switched. So I commented to Eddie Baker that, all things considered, we were relieved not to have the images of Senna's crash, as they would have been important as a document, but probably very unpleasant in terms of their content.'

The veracity of what had been declared was later verified, because the four in-car cameras in action were recording the time, but not the date. Obviously Bernie Ecclestone was informed about everything by Eddie

The last image taken from Senna's camera car at the entrance to the *Tamburello* curve a few moments before the tragedy.

Baker and, at least initially, the strategy of FOCA was clear: they chose to take a reticent position, which to many seemed even omertous, in order to defend Williams and F1 in general, squaring off in front of an Italian judicial system that had started an accusatory investigation. The British could not understand why, in a world as dangerous as motorsport, a trial would even be instituted after a crash, when under British law at most a civil suit would have started to seek damages.

Equivocating on the fact that there were no images of the impact, FOCA had always maintained that there was no footage of the accident, and only when the prosecutor specifically asked for the VHS recordings to be handed over did the images of Senna's in-car camera emerge, active at least until a few moments before the crash. Although the entire accident was not available, the moments immediately before the collision could have provided useful clues as to what had really happened at *Tamburello*.

Initially, there was also a well-founded suspicion that the video might have been manipulated, but analysis carried out by Cineca, the government agency based in Casalecchio di Reno (Bologna), showed that there was no falsification of the file.

In fact the agency, thanks to its scientific visualisation laboratory, succeeded in creating some very sophisticated multimedia software for the time (enhanced multi sequence viewer), which allowed the synchronised multiple viewing of images and data relating to the dynamics of the Brazilian driver's accident.

Thirty years after the events, it is fair to admit that the frames of the terrible crash never existed, but it is at least curious to note how FOCA's attitude changed when the judicial attention was no longer limited to Williams's responsibilities, but threatened to extend to the whole of F1, its rules, and the homologation of circuits.

In this scenario, I can say that, while the magistrate came into possession of the tape that 'did not exist', I also received an anonymous envelope from Great Britain, delivered to the editorial office of *Autosprint*, which contained the same pictures delivered to the prosecutor.

The attitude seemed to change, but why not cooperate right away?

CHAPTER 29

THE RAI TV DIRECTOR WHO DID NOT TURN THE TRAGEDY INTO A SHOW

'TELEVISION? A metaphor for the death of intimacy.'

Anthony Burgess, one of the greatest British authors of the 20th century, framed the spectacularisation of live TV in a very definite, not to say definitive way. And yet, this aphorism is not an axiom.

Giancarlo Tomassetti, born in 1945, knows this well. Profession: director. The moustachioed man from Ascoli Piceno used his images to narrate the most important sporting events for RAI from 1981, for about 30 years, after having also worked for *Tribuna Politica* and *Telegiornale*. Between the *Giro d'Italia* cycling race, the Football World Cup and the Skiing World Cup, he could not miss Formula 1.

'The debut was in 1982 with the San Marino GP, contested by only 14 single-seaters. With the two Ferraris of Gilles Villeneuve and Didier Pironi fighting for the victory and with the Frenchman who pretended not to see the "slow" sign, imposing himself without respecting the team orders. I remember a furious Gilles who did not want to go on the podium because he felt defrauded. I was very impressed by the sanguine environment of F1,' Giancarlo recalls.

In those days there was no single director: each GP organiser entrusted the national broadcaster with the television coverage of the event, and therefore RAI, which broadcast all races live, took care of both Monza (Italian GP) and Imola (San Marino GP).

'I have directed some 40 GPs and in certain foreign races, such as Monaco or Spa-Francorchamps, we would show up with two or three extra cameras to supplement the international direction.'

So, Giancarlo, you knew F1 and its rituals well...
Of course, but I never had to deal with the death of a driver until Imola 1994, indeed of *two* drivers on the same weekend. I still have the drama of Roland Ratzenberger's accident in my eyes, who ended his race by crashing into the wall on the left of the *Villeneuve* corner, after losing his front wing.

I vividly remember the piece of wing flying off, while another part got stuck under the single-seater, making the Simtek unsteerable. The situation was chilling and, for the first time in my career, I found myself deciding instantly whether to broadcast a gory image or not. I did not broadcast it, at least not live, because then some images were taken from the recordings. I excluded the shot of Roland's blood dripping from his helmet. They were scenes that chilled me: the shot came from the *Tosa* camera. The cameraman had started to tighten the image on Ratzenberger a lot and I had to decide on the spot whether to show the ongoing tragedy or not.

Since 1986, with Elio De Angelis' accident in testing at Paul Ricard, nobody had died in F1 and, therefore, there was no thought that a driver could suffer extreme consequences in an accident, as the single-seaters seemed very safe.

Was there no company policy indicating a procedure to be followed, as there is today?
No, it was a choice left to the director's conscience. I had once before found myself in the situation of having to distinguish between news and spectacle: perhaps you remember Mika Häkkinen, the McLaren driver who in the 1999 Italian GP had been forced to retire while in the lead. The Finn had thrown away his steering wheel and gloves and then taken refuge on the small road next to the track, bursting into a liberating cry, confident that he had found some privacy.

Our cameras had found him in tears and I decided to go on air with that very private scene that had affected the whole world. But Mika hadn't hurt himself...

After Roland's death, what was the climate in the control room?
There was a surreal atmosphere, all the more so because, after the warm-up, we had recorded some chilling statements from Senna, since the Brazilian champion felt a strange air. Somehow he had the perception that something was wrong and that it might fall back on him.

What did you think when Ayrton's Williams went off at a tangent at Tamburello *and disappeared from the frame to crash into the wall and then reappear to the cameras half-destroyed?*
That something serious had happened again. And it was an event that we could not obscure. The only available alternative was to use the helicopter shot, because there was a serious lack of means at Imola [which restricted the director's options]. In F1 not only the track had to be covered, but also the outside, the escape routes. If there was an exit from the track you risked missing it because of the lack of cameras. And the same reasoning applied to skiing, especially downhill skiing: if an athlete fell, it was OK if you found him in the nets, otherwise it meant he had ended up in the woods. And not covering those shots was a director's responsibility. Nothing intentional, but determined by the availability of fewer cameras than necessary; but when something happens, you never know how to justify it.

At the beginning, in 1982, we had 11 cameras and the equipment was barely adequate. When I left F1 there were about 30, four at each corner. From the point of view of coverage, I had serious difficulties with Senna's accident, because I had no coverage at *Tamburello*. There were no fixed cameras from which I could see him, except at a great distance with the first camera at *Tosa*, but the long straight was barely covered.

Was the shortage determined by RAI or by the F1 promoter, Bernie Ecclestone?
The black hole was due to RAI, for the lack of cameras. The production was done by the broadcaster. And I repeat it, in the beginning only the track was covered. This was true for all disciplines and for the most important events: there were just 11–12 cameras. Then, we started to increase the coverage and the personnel available. I can assure you that Imola, the year after Ayrton's crash, was certainly better covered.

Seeing another accident, the day after Roland's death, how did you react?
It was a dramatic moment even in directing, because we are men and we are involved for better or worse in what happens: for a moment you

lose your reflexes and your ability to know how to inform in the right way. Then professionalism takes the place of emotion and you become lucid again, but these are not easy moments. You cannot imagine what happened in the director's office in 2006, when the Italian national team won the World Cup in Berlin: a hell of a mess broke out. The same thing happened, but in the opposite direction, with Senna's accident.

The Brazilian champion was helpless in his Williams. There was no radio communication to reassure anyone about his condition. And the racetrack plunged into a strange silence, waiting for a miracle that would not happen ...
At the beginning the long camera shot assisted me, then the helicopter camera granted me the only extra shot I had. I must say that I was greatly helped by the skill of that cameraman, a very strange guy from Turin, anti-system minded, always in conflict with the company, but with an exceptional professionalism.

I remember the helicopter hovering around the Williams, but during the critical moments it would hide behind the trees near the Santerno river ...
Exactly, that was the game. I had asked him to hover above the car by tightening the frame to the maximum when he could film the cockpit. And that cameraman was the one who told me first that, according to him, Ayrton was dead, because his head was tilted to one side and he had no vital reaction. At that moment we understood the seriousness of the situation.

Obviously we knew nothing about the broken column, nor about the suspension that had pierced the helmet. But the bent head and the motionless helmet had alerted us. At that point, another transmission started: it was no longer the live broadcasting of an F1 GP. I was helped by the director of TGS, Gianfranco De Laurentiis, who was in the newsroom in Rome and took over from the studio. I remember sending a mobile camera along with Ezio Zermiani, the pit reporter, but they wouldn't let him move around much. I won't hide the fact that there was chaos in the director's office until the moment I decided not to show the spectacle of death. And those poplars at the edge of the river favoured my choice, along with the poverty of the shot, due to the fact that I only had the helicopter camera at my disposal.

The helicopter pilot was also very good ...
Of course. My friend understood instantly what he had to do. I had only given him one instruction: 'Make sure you see and not see.' To blur and not to show that motionless helmet. We were somewhere between the news and the spectacle of death. And I didn't want to broadcast death. I behaved just as I had done the day before with Ratzenberger.

You did not go down in TV history as the director of 1 May 1994 at Imola ...
Absolutely not. There were so many sporting events that I crossed paths with. My son was very close to Senna: he had his shirt and that closeness stayed with me, but that remained just one of the 40 GPs I directed. The event is made by the protagonists and not by the directors.

As the images chased each other on the monitors, doubts assailed me. Anyone who is a journalist either breaks the news or makes a show of it, and the line between the two visions is always very thin. Which is the right way? You never know how you will react when faced with a tragic event.

Has anyone in the RAI world ever asked you why you didn't show more?
No, from this point of view I should be congratulated, because no one objected that I had omitted anything from the story, nor that I had turned the tragedy into a spectacle. This was the end result, but the question is: how would I have behaved if I'd had the extra camera? Would I have been able to keep the same line? I do not know.

It is fair indeed this makes you doubt ...
I always had this doubt. On a different occasion, I chose the show, but I don't know if I did the right thing. It was in 1999, when Ronaldo, an Inter football player, broke his knee in the match against Lecce. The control technicians showed me a zoom on Ronaldo's knee and I aired it: I remember that those images made a big impression. But no one had died. Believe me, distinguishing the private from the public is very difficult. You never manage to have a dividing line. And the doubts stay with you.

When a Grand Prix, a sporting event, is transformed into another story, how does the approach to broadcasting change?
Since the Senna tragedy, the approach has changed significantly for me. The directors of that time, who were in the field with a lack of means,

were relieved of a great responsibility: even if they wanted to, they could not show certain things. The story therefore passed through the words of those who were in the paddock, like Ezio Zermiani, and those who commented from the studio. Gianfranco De Laurentiis was on duty in Rome: there was always a commentator ready to intervene if there was any problem, even a technical one. It was a sort of parachute, which for Senna's accident turned out to be essential, because the director took over the reins of the live broadcast, leading it with great professionalism and humanity.

RAI's live broadcast never showed the replay of Ayrton's exit from the track from his in-car camera. At the time a violent controversy broke out over the absence of the images that, for example, TF1 in France had broadcast …
In our live broadcast those images had never been there. I remember that the in-car camera topic was discussed at the Imola trial, and I was asked questions by the judge.

In 1994, FOM had four signals coming in from the in-car camera-mounted single-seaters, but via the helicopter bridge only two were passing through, so the technicians following the images supplied by the promoter could switch the camera from the cockpit of Senna's Williams to another car. Wasn't it strange to log-off from the single-seater going off the track?
Everything was possible. I confirm there were only two signals out of four on the output. I remember this well. I never knew who had done the switching, but the FOM technician who came to the trial did not convince me at all.

The VHS tapes with the images of Senna's in-car camera appeared long after the investigation had begun, while at first, it had even seemed they did not exist. A real treasure hunt began …
I confirm this. A few days after the San Marino GP two *Guardia di Finanza* agents [the Italian financial police officers] came to the RAI headquarters in Saxa Rubra: they asked me to give them all the material that was available. I didn't say no, but I asked if I could inform director De Laurentiis first. I went to see Gianfranco and asked him: 'There are two agents here who want all the images. What shall I do?'

'Try not to comply, and then see what happens …' he laughed.

I made the archives available, but even doing so, I needed to understand what they meant by 'all the images'. In reality they found nothing that interested them.

Did you know Ayrton personally?
Yes, I had filmed a commercial with him in which he was the star. The Toleman TG-184, in which Senna had raced on his Formula 1 debut in 1984, was sponsored by Candy. The payoff of the advert was 'clean driving'. Peppino Fumagalli had been the great industrialist who had launched washing machines in Italy. With the introduction of the household appliance he had paved the way for the emancipation of women, who were no longer forced to stay at home and wash clothes. Fumagalli had invested in F1 to give visibility to his own brand, but also to give vent to his passion for racing, hence the idea of promoting 'clean driving' through an ad with a young up-and-coming driver (whom women liked a lot) could represent the squaring of the circle.

Ayrton was a very helpful and easy-going person: I liked him immediately for his approach, which was both simple and professional. Initially we had to highlight the excesses in the way young people drove cars and mopeds, and Senna would always point out how certain manoeuvres were very dangerous and should not be shown on television. He was a man on the edge between life and death at every turn, yet he seemed to be afraid of all the stupid things you do in a car on a daily basis. He would go crazy when we showed him particularly bad driving behaviour. I was very impressed by what seemed to be his emotional vulnerability. That somewhat special day came back to me after hearing his words at the end of the Sunday morning warm-up, with all those forebodings …

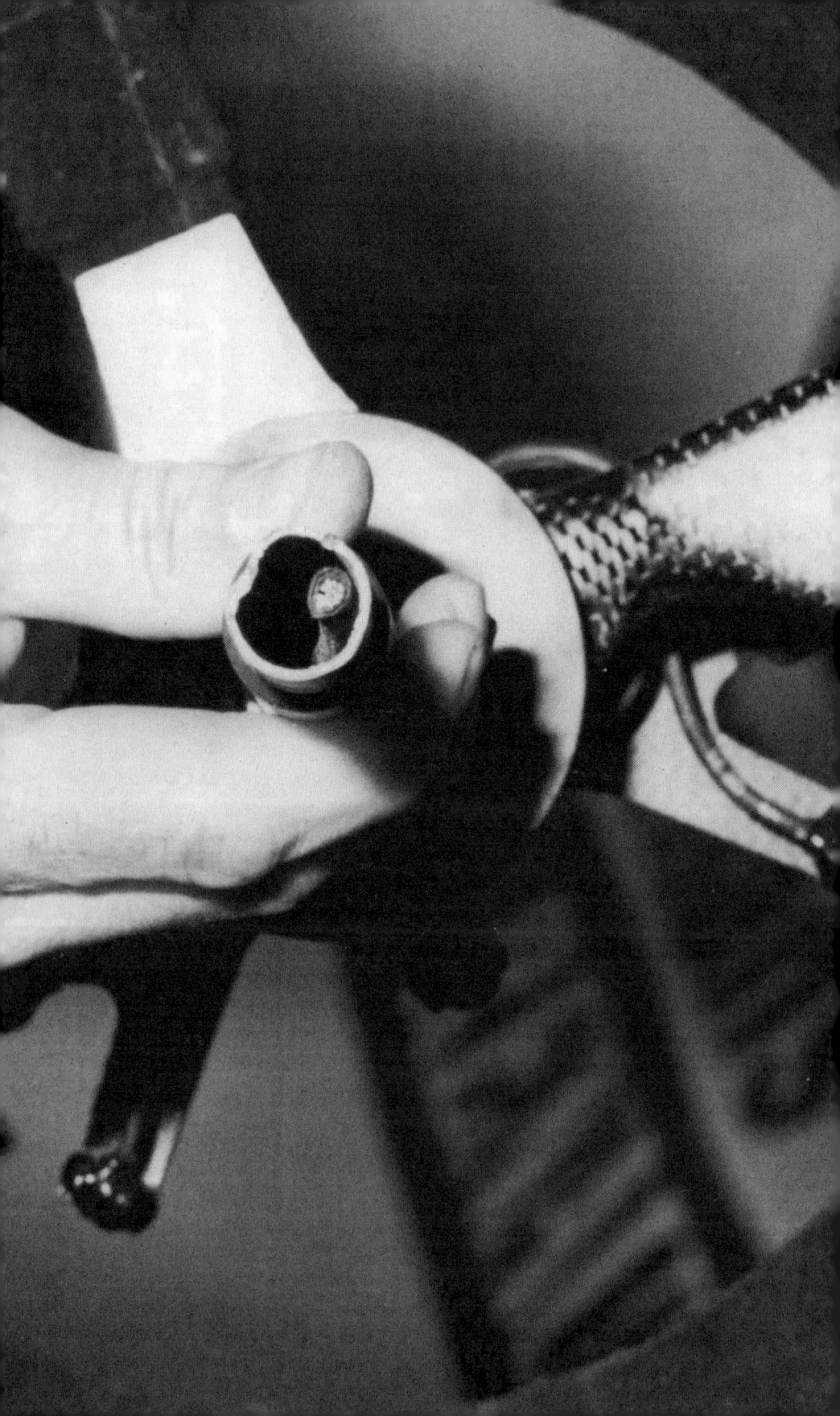

CHAPTER 30

PASSERINI: STUBBORN MAGISTRATE BREAKS HIS SILENCE AFTER 30 YEARS

'CONSCIENCE IS the best judge an honest man can have.'

José de San Martín, Argentine general, patriot and revolutionary, defined as *libertador* for his contribution to the independence of Argentina, Chile and Peru at the beginning of the 19th century, is worth mentioning. Maurizio Passerini, public prosecutor in the Senna trial, now a retired judge, is entirely included in this definition. He is not a colossus, in fact he is rather petite in size, but you can recognise him by two eyes that sparkle with curiosity, attention and intelligence, behind the lenses. He is an anti-personality who, in his long career, has never liked the limelight of the news, preferring to let the judgements do the talking. The work. The facts.

In his book, *How to Build a Car*, Adrian Newey suggested Passerini's reason for bringing manslaughter charges against some Williams executives and circuit administrators (all of whom were acquitted) over the death of Senna might be his desire for 'personal glory and notoriety'. That assessment missed the mark. He may be a genius as an F1 designer, but Newey probably deals better with cars than with men.

I got to know the former public prosecutor only last year, on the occasion of this long chat. We hadn't made eye contact for 30 years, but I always held him in high esteem. A great worker, a prosecutor who never looked anyone in the face. I can say that with full knowledge of the facts.

The work of *Autosprint* on the Senna case, at certain junctures, opened up investigative fronts: from the outside, it might have seemed that there was mutual collaboration, but that was not the case. Not at all. So much so that Maurizio Passerini had no problem in investigating the editor of the weekly, Carlo Cavicchi, and myself, with the accusation of violating the investigative secret for the pictures published in our issue no. 47 (1994). We had shown a world preview of photos of Ayrton's bloody helmet and the suspension bracket that had pierced the Brazilian champion like a blade. The suspicion was that we had 'stolen' the shots from the proceedings and for that we risked a two-year criminal indictment. Carlo and I, at one point, even risked being the only ones convicted. It did not happen because, rightfully, the respective investigations were sometimes running in parallel but totally separate, and we proved that the photos published were not the ones in the folders of the deposited documents.

This preamble is necessary to frame the character of Passerini who, almost 30 years after the events, has agreed to tell his story, breaking his demure reserve.

'I worked mainly from my office, less immersed in the F1 affair. I wasn't even supposed to be the duty magistrate, because there were rotation criteria, but two or three days before the San Marino GP a colleague asked me for a favour to replace him. Even from that point of view, it was rather coincidental that I found myself dealing with this investigation.'

What responsibility did you feel? At first it seemed to be a case like any other, the approach was similar to that of a car accident ...
The immediate difference was very strong media attention. Journalists were coming to ask and enquire: a situation absolutely not comparable to any investigation I had done before and, in general, to any investigation carried out in Bologna.

What has been the impact of it on your career?
It was one of the best and most exciting experiences, for the pleasure of carrying out certain investigations, I got to know some remarkable people, Inspector Stefano Stefanini in the first place and Michele Alboreto, who made a great contribution. And then another peculiarity: there were actually two ongoing investigations. We worked on Ratzenberger's death and Senna's accident in parallel.

Did you come under pressure during the trial preparation period?
Now I have the pleasure of admitting it: of course, there were people who approached me to ask me if it was really necessary to go to trial, because everyone knew that racing was dangerous and maybe going ahead would have jeopardised the future of the GPs in Italy, not only at Imola, but also at Monza ... There was a lot of pressure. I don't want to mention the names, but I can say that various organisations that orbited around motor racing wondered whether it was really necessary to do certain research. I knew how to address such topics and there was never a problem. It may be that, if the investigations had started in the UK, they would have ended up 90 per cent ruling out the possibility of them resulting in a trial. In Italy, the regulation of culpable offences is different from England and therefore it was easy to imagine that, here in Italy, it was more than likely for an investigation to go to trial.

Was it right to go to trial?
According to me, yes, because the causes of the accident were clearly understood.

Without a trial, would the crash have been dismissed as a driver error, losing his single-seater on the asphalt bumps?
It would have been categorised as an accident that could have had multiple causes, and it would have been said that it had not been possible to work out which was the main one, which, in fact, was clearly ascertained later on. Under our criminal law, liability for recklessness, or negligence in the execution of the steering column, had been proved and consequently had been raised. That's why it was inevitable to institute a trial. And I would add that, irrespective of the Italian or Anglo-Saxon legal system, I believe it was a fair, equitable trial: with more care in the modification of the steering column, that accident would not have occurred.

You have often been caught up in controversies: is there anything you would like to clarify?
The only thing that really bothered me was to hear people say, 'You held a trial for Senna and you didn't do it for Ratzenberger': Senna was the champion recognised by everyone, while Roland was the driver in his first year in F1. Apart from the insiders, nobody knew who he was and, therefore, Roland's tragedy passed by in silence and his accident became

a minor thing. To this I have always replied: if it had emerged from the outcome of the investigation that the Austrian's accident had not been the result of chance and it had been possible, therefore, to identify responsibility – as became evident in the case of Ayrton – I would have chosen Ratzenberger's case without the slightest hesitation, providing I'd had the possibility of choosing which trial to follow, which was not the case. The reason is, I am sure, it would not have created that attention that turns a trial into a spectacle, often triggering much controversy.

In Roland's case, it was immediately clear what the cause of the accident was...
Yes, a carbon front wing flap, almost certainly damaged at the *Acque Minerali* corner on the previous lap, broke while the Austrian was doing his qualifying lap: it occurred at the fastest point of the track, where the aerodynamic load exerted the greatest thrust. It was evident right from the start. At this point, I would add a hint of controversy: at the time, I read an interview with Adrian Newey, in which he made it clear that he knew that the investigation was trying to ascertain whether the column had had any responsibility in Senna's accident. For this reason he took it out on the magistrate, i.e. on me, claiming that I would have played on the notoriety of the case to gain publicity. Let me repeat it: had I had the choice, I would have followed Roland's trial.

Much worse things were said at the time, namely that in order to 'extinguish' the process they would transfer and promote you...
What actually happened was that the investigations into the two accidents started in parallel. Rather quickly, the causes of Ratzenberger's accident were clarified, so I asked the investigations department to dismiss the case, because no responsibility could be identified. Since, however, some acts were common to the two events, the whole file passed to the judge for preliminary investigations. The latter took time to decide whether or not to file the case, and because of this, the time frame became longer, giving rise to strange rumours. I even heard people saying that we wanted to bury Senna's trial, but that was nonsense.

More than a cover-up, it seemed that they wanted to transfer the case and put the proceedings in the hands of another magistrate...
This is really a joke, because the trial has its own timeframe, as does the drafting of the expert report. On top of that, there was the extension of

the investigation, a fairly common practice in even slightly complicated cases. Then the rumour of the cover-up spread, as well as that of my removal. In reality, I had already been transferred: in the sense that, when the trial began, I was about to move from the so-called 'Small Tribunal', which deals with crimes within the jurisdiction of the Praetor, to the Public Prosecutor's Office at my request. The agreement with Pintor, head of the 'Small Tribunal' and with Fortuna, head of the Public Prosecutor's Office, was that I would complete the Senna trial. So an abandonment was never in question: I followed the investigation and then the outcome of the trial in the courtroom.

There was also a long controversy over where to hold the trial: whether in Imola, where the accident had occurred, or Bologna, since Ayrton had died at the Ospedale Maggiore …
The issue was debated, but the rules of jurisdiction dictated Imola. What counted was the place where the causes of the accident were determined and in the end the trial was held in Imola and, all things considered, the choice was the right one: that was the natural venue.

Was there any attempt to influence the process?
No, none.

Not even government pressure?
Well, that indeed. The president of Brazil called Oscar Luigi Scalfaro, our president, and the latter contacted Francesco Pintor to find out the timing of the delivery of Senna's body, so that the funeral could be organised in São Paulo. I can't remember the terms, but it seems to me that in two or three days Ayrton's body was made available to his family.

No reaction from the Anglo-Saxon world?
Not at all, and not even by the FIA. There was only astonishment that it could come to a trial for an accident in motorsport, where the risk factor is inherent in the sporting discipline itself. For the British, the threshold of the degree of guilt justifying a criminal trial is certainly higher than ours. They did not understand how there could be criminal proceedings, while they considered civil suits for compensation as possible. I dealt with the lawyer Goodman, who was representing Frank Williams, and I must say that he was a very fair person.

Lawyer Bendinelli, the legal representative of Sagis, the management company of the Enzo and Dino Ferrari, revealed to me that Frank Williams had a compliant attitude from the outset, while Patrick Head, technical director, and Adrian Newey, designer of the FW16, took a tougher approach in their defence. Allegedly, did they feel responsibility for the accident?
I think it is natural: nobody likes to be involved in a public trial. For the prosecution's argument, because of a mistake they had made, a person had died and, in addition, that person was Ayrton Senna, so the trial was immediately world-famous. I put myself in their shoes and I believe that it would have been difficult for anyone to admit guilt during the trial.

The engineers who designed the column modification have never been investigated, only Williams's top technical management: how come?
According to the Williams version, the design of the column was entrusted to Gavin Fisher and Alan Young, two engineers I never knew. In my assessment, the modification of the column was not the choice of a second-row technician, but a decision of the team's top engineers. And, therefore, Patrick Head's responsibility became evident the moment he authorised the steering wheel modification. And it was a rather impromptu modification. The only real curiosity I have left would be to know when and where that intervention was made.

What is the answer to this sacrosanct question?
That changes had already been made after the Brazilian GP, the first race of the 1994 season.

Subsequent images, however, show that the cutting of the upper part of the bodywork was carried out later ...
No doubt about it. After all, the work in some respects was carried out with a sort of craftsmanship, certainly not worthy of Williams's high level of professionalism. I find it hard to believe that this work was done in the quiet peace of the English countryside, at the Didcot site. It is plausible that it was done, instead, just before the San Marino GP. Two or three things emerged that lead one to believe that it was a last-minute modification. Initially, we were given a drawing of the column that was nothing more than a sketch, with no dimensions indicating diameters, thicknesses, lengths or quality of materials. It was only when Williams

Maurizio Passerini, the Public Prosecutor of the Senna trial, now retired.

had the column back in their hands – because in the meantime the FW16 had been impounded for investigating experts to examine – that they gave us a drawing of that part worthy of the world champion team. I wonder why they didn't provide us with that design straight away! The answer is simple: they hadn't made the drawing in time after the last-minute modification. The other strange element concerned the metals, which were different: the quality of the steel in the section used to connect the two cut column segments was different and on average lower than the steel used in the original tube, as was the diameter. And this also gave me pause: if the work had been done normally, they would have used an identical material.

During the trial, what feelings did you have about certain F1 characters who seemed to be playing a part in a play?
The thing that struck me was the deep passion of the drivers. Some of them would have been willing to pay to race and they didn't race just to get paid. I didn't really get to know them well: I remember hearing Gerhard Berger at Mugello, during some tests. The only one I got to know more was Michele Alboreto. When I was young I followed F1 racing and, when Michele was racing with Ferrari in 1985, he almost won the World Championship. The Milanese driver made an important contribution in the investigation to interpret the images we had, to understand certain reactions that Senna had and that could be guessed from the telemetry data. When I got to know Alboreto in person, I realised that he was not only a good driver, but also a great man, willing to give his contribution. One thing I would like to say is that I must apologise to Emanuele Pirro. There was never an opportunity to do so publicly, so it is only right to do it now: at the time I had appointed a panel of consultants. There were engineers (Mauro Forghieri and Tommaso Carletti), technicians from the faculty of the University of Bologna, and also some military personnel from Pratica di Mare, to whom we had turned, so that all the details of the column could be analysed with the scanning electron microscope; among others was engineer Nosetto, who had studied the coplanarity of the track. I also appointed Pirro as a driver who had experience in F1, so that he could give us his assessment of Senna's conduct. Emanuele signed, along with the other consultants, the expert reports that were filed. At the trial, however, when I realised that the heart of the debate would focus on the technical aspect of the column modification, while no one was questioning aspects of the Brazilian driver's driving, I did not call Pirro to testify, thinking I was doing him a favour. I realised later that I had perhaps wronged him instead, because I did not recognise the very valuable contribution he made to the investigation, and for that I wish to apologise to him.

Let us come to the first verdict: did the acquittal of the defendants seem like a 'slap in the face' to the prosecution?
Like all sentences, one tends to read the operative part, which is only about ten lines long, in which one tries to condense the decision: in this case it was an acquittal. What one realised at first reading was that the defendants were not found to have committed the fact, even though the cause of the accident was to be found in the breakage of the column. In short, the breakage was not attributable to Patrick Head and Adrian Newey, because the names of the two engineers, Fisher and Young, had emerged. My reaction was one of enormous disappointment because I, by nature a pessimist, had at least expected Patrick Head to be convicted. But the real disappointment would have been if the causes of the accident had not been clarified. Instead, already in the first instance, the breakdown of the steering column emerged as the cause of the crash. In fact, the most disappointing judgement was the one at the Appeals Court: there were also doubts about the causes of the accident. I am a magistrate, so I feel free to criticise my colleagues at times: that first appeal was done in a somewhat superficial way, reading the papers very summarily and coming to the simplest and least demanding conclusion. Basically the sense was: let's end it there, because things are not clear.

The Corte di Cassazione [Italian Supreme Court] *then annulled the sentence of the Appeals Court and remade the judgement working only on the papers.*
The second appeal came to the following conclusion: faced with the acquittal at the first instance and reaffirmed at the first appeal, if it had been held that the causes of the accident were clear and the responsibility could not be attributed to anyone in particular – therefore neither to Head nor to Newey – the formula would have been to repeat the first instance judgement. Therefore, instead of stating that the offence was time-barred, it made it clear that the accident was caused by the breakage of the column and that the defendant was not convicted simply because time-barred. The offence of manslaughter became time-barred after seven and a half years: the accident occurred on 1 May 1994, and therefore the statute of limitations had expired on 1 December 2001.

Years later, what is your assessment?
There was disappointment in the first instance, a moment of anger at the appeal, realising that the verdict would not hold up in *Cassazione*,

but I knew there would be an appeal, which I did not follow personally. I didn't want the Senna case to become a personal thing: 'Passerini who has it in for Williams'. I collaborated with the people who ordered the appeal, but it was a colleague from the Public Prosecutor's Office who went to the *Corte di Cassazione*. Now let me say that the most important thing was not so much to get a conviction, but to understand how the accident had happened. I remember that I also went to examine the other accidents that had happened in Italy, and I remember Jochen Rindt's at the *Parabolica*, during the qualifying of the 1970 Italian GP. There were pictures showing the Lotus bending to the left before the moment of impact, due to the front left axle breaking, as the brakes were mounted inboard. Although the pictures directed the investigation, they led to nothing. We are all human beings: when I and those who collaborated with me in the investigation, such as Stefano Stefanini, saw that, in spite of the facts, there was an attempt to deny what I considered to be the evidence, we put a little extra effort into the work. In my heart I am sure that at Williams they knew exactly what had happened, but there was a playing of the parts.

Were there forms of 'deception' that, at one point, seemed to be able to influence not so much the trial, but the media orientation?
To speak of deception seems to me a strong word, because in reality the defence was trying to bring evidence to support its thesis, more or less well-founded. Williams claimed that the accident had occurred due to a loss of stability of the car at *Tamburello* as a result of bumps, which in fact were there, but had nothing to do with it. They used an American Adams program. It was one of the first simulation systems that was supposed to show that the reason for Senna's crash was not a broken column, but a loss of grip. The Adams program was created to see how a vehicle would behave by modifying a series of parameters (weight, rather than aileron incidence or tyre inflation pressure). Already the use of this program to find the cause of the accident was improper, anomalous. The Williams consultants presented us with the Adams simulation to prove that we were making a colossal mistake. Engineer Forghieri turned up his nose as soon as he saw the simulation and then, with the trial in progress, we turned to Professor Fanghella in Genoa, who worked on programs to find the causes of accidents. We sent him the Williams material and he, within a couple of weeks, was able to prove in court that the use of the

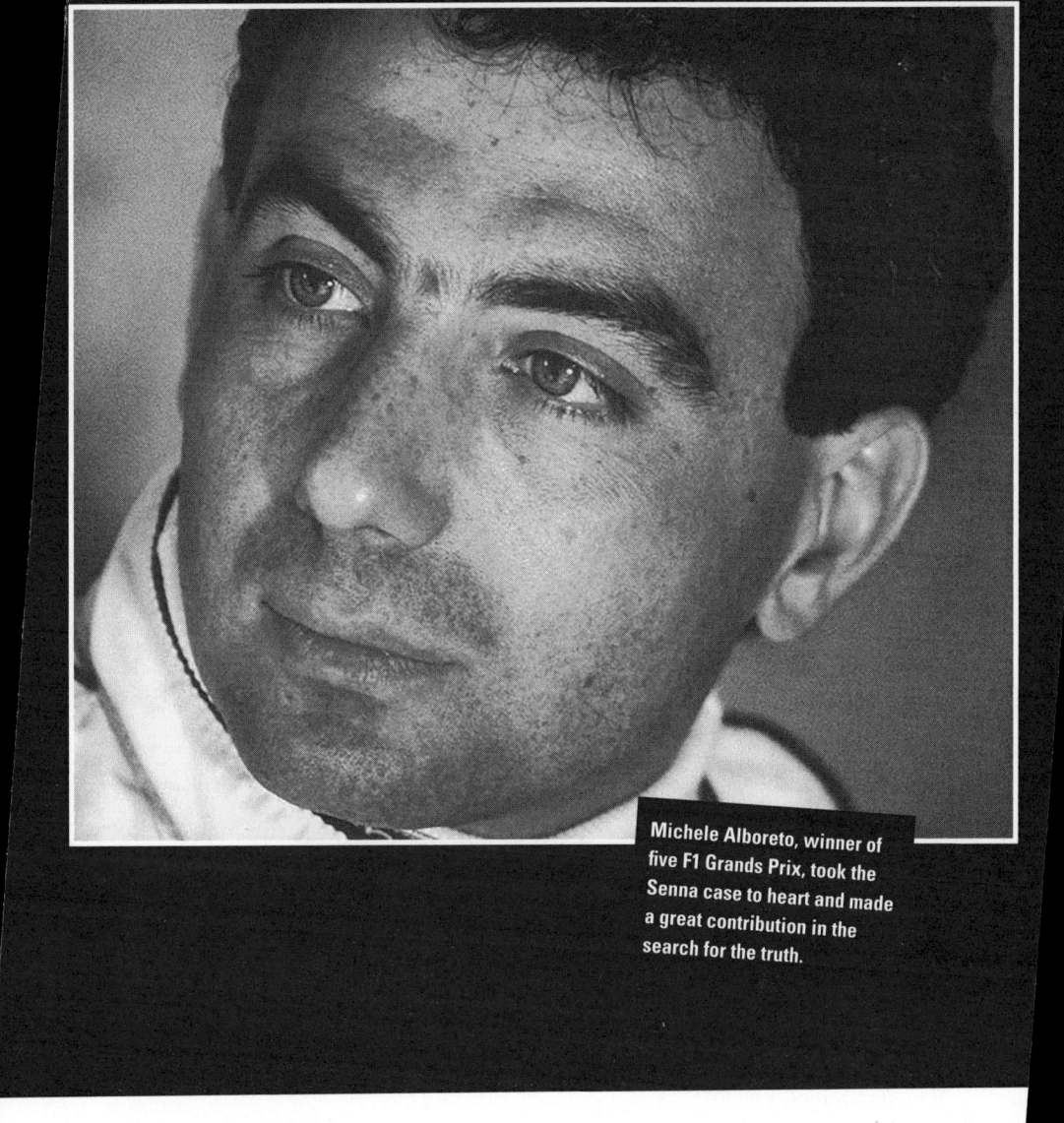

Michele Alboreto, winner of five F1 Grands Prix, took the Senna case to heart and made a great contribution in the search for the truth.

program had been very much forced by the world champion team. The professor ran the Adams program according to Williams's parameters and it emerged that only on the 39th attempt, by dint of changing the data against all the evidence, '… they had managed to get Senna off the road'. But I did not consider this an attempt at misdirection. On the contrary, it was a source of satisfaction, because we managed to dismantle a defensive construction that had puzzled us from the start.

When did the investigation into the column begin?
We started from the photograph in *Autosprint* and then heard from the doctors who had rescued Senna, to remove the doubt that someone had cut the column to extract the driver from the cockpit. The moment we realised that there had been no intervention, we began to ask questions. And the answers came when we had the telemetry. We didn't have all the data downloaded from the car, but we were able to read the tracks which revealed how Ayrton, at a certain point, had only acted on the brake: there was no lateral acceleration, which would be seen if the driver had tried to steer. If we assume, as Williams claimed, that Senna had gone off due to a loss of grip, why had the Brazilian failed to correct his trajectory with the steering? Since there was no lateral acceleration, it became obvious that the steering column had broken.

Not as a magistrate but as a man, how did it feel to discover that it was the tip of the uniball that pierced Senna's skull?
The game of destiny comes into play, because that damned uniball only needed to pass a few centimetres further up, or perhaps over the visor, without finding the only weak point in the [helmet's] gasket, and Ayrton would have escaped without serious consequences. There the enmity of the gods was at stake, because if that accident were repeated ten times, it would hardly be possible for the support torn from the bodywork to follow the same path and become the steel arrow that pierced into Senna's helmet. Obviously, from a legal point of view, all this does not change anything about the cause of the accident and possible liability. It was already clear from the autopsy reports that there had been a frontal crushing due to a blunt instrument that had landed at the base of the skull. Fate played its part.

How does it feel to talk about it 30 years later?
Many trainees, when they are entrusted to a magistrate, out of curiosity like to have a look at his CV, to understand who they will be facing, and it happened that they asked me about the Senna case. After all this time, I still talk about it with great emotion, because it was an investigation into which I put passion and enthusiasm. From a professional point of view, it remains a good memory and I am still happy to talk about it.

But how, in your view, did the modification of the column come about?
I always took it for granted that Senna had put enormous pressure on the team to have a car he could drive the way he wanted. From this point of view, Ayrton must have used all his persuasive powers, but whoever made that steering modification should have done it as God intended. The work should not have been done so poorly, just to please the driver.

CHAPTER 31

THOSE WHO ANALYSED THE STEERING COLUMN NEVER HAD ANY DOUBTS ABOUT THE BREAKAGE

'I WRITE these words in steel, for nothing can be trusted that is not written in metal.'

It took Brandon Sanderson, the American writer of fantasy literature, to give credit to those who did the analysis on Ayrton Senna's steering column. The entire criminal trial focused on one main theme: the accident on lap seven of the San Marino GP had as its main cause the failure of the steering column on the Brazilian champion's Williams FW16. To prove the validity of the thesis, Prosecutor Maurizio Passerini appointed Professor Enrico Lorenzini, dean of the Faculty of Engineering at the University of Bologna, as consultant. The professor arranged for the column to be analysed by two teams of experts belonging to different structures, so that the results could be compared, and there could be no doubt about the outcome.

One part was entrusted to the Air Force's Research and Experimentation Division, based at Pratica di Mare, and the other to the Metallurgy Laboratory of Industrial Chemistry at the University of Bologna. Both organisations had a scanning electron microscope (SEM), the most advanced instrument of the time. The working groups found identical results in their analyses and came to a single conclusion: Senna's steering column gave way before the impact against the *Tamburello* wall, and this was the cause of the car going off the road. Thirty years later, I managed to get in touch with Gian Paolo Cammarota and Angelo Casagrande, the two professors at the University of Bologna who carried out the tests in Bologna. They have remained friends and still see each other from time to time.

Cammarota, born in Milan in 1936, now retired, divides his time between Bologna, Venice and Germany. A slim figure, very reserved, he ponders every single word he says. He has been a pillar of industrial chemistry, while Casagrande, a genuine Bolognese, with a lean but more powerful figure, is still part of the teaching staff in the Faculty of Metallurgy: 'We are discontinuing SEM at the moment: there are much more modern and avant-garde investigation systems now, but the scanning electron microscope gave us certain, indisputable answers on the Senna case.'

Before going into the merits of the metallurgical tests carried out on the column, Gian Paolo Cammarota recounts a curious detail: 'I had seen the accident on television and, when I heard that Senna had died and that his body was to be transferred from the *Ospedale Maggiore* to the Institute of Legal Medicine in Via Irnerio, I had the urge to go and see for myself. I can't explain why, and I certainly couldn't imagine that I would then be called to assess an expert opinion on the column. I did not see Senna's body. I entered the ground floor and found technicians in Williams uniforms: they told me that Ayrton was a great driver, but during that weekend he had changed the tyres more often than usual because he felt vibrations, and he was not satisfied with the set-up when he lined up for the race. The tyres had nothing to do with it; I think it was the steering column that was generating the vibrations, and not the tyres. But I would only realise this months later.'

In the original design of the Williams FW16 a one-piece steering column was planned. Ayrton's repeated grievances with the Didcot team's engineers had led to a three-part modification, to stop the Brazilian champion's knuckles rubbing against the upper part of the bodywork and improve his driving position. It was not an easy exercise, because the regulations dictated that, once the steering wheel was removed, there had to be enough free space in the cockpit section for a 250x250mm template to pass through, in order to comply with the 1994 FIA rules.

'Reducing the diameter of the tube was a major design error,' says Cammarota. 'Originally, a single column was planned, which was then modified into three pieces connected by welding. The chemical analysis and the mechanical characteristics showed the parts were different, they revealed the use of two different materials.'

What checks did you carry out?
We did a surface metallographic analysis, then internal and external roughness tests, and a fractographic examination. Chemical analysis was delegated to Cermet.

The experts' report delivered to the court by Professor Lorenzini states: 'In general terms, it must be said that the three-piece column is indicative of a poorly designed modification, since the thinness of the section right at the point of maximum stress, the abrupt variation of the section with a much too small radius of connection, and the scratches caused by the mechanical drilling and turning operations combine to determine a critical structural situation, with a consequent strong danger of failure under the action of static loads and dynamic fatigue. Accidentally, on the outer and inner surfaces of the fitting, immediately below the fracture surface, evident circumferential tooling marks are detectable, so that the outer and inner surfaces of the column have a surface finish unsuitable for components working under fatigue and under extreme experimental conditions.'

The original steering column consisted of a metal tube 910.2mm long, measured from the connection with the steering box to the steering wheel rim. At a distance of 685.5mm from the lower end (steering box), the steering column was connected to the chassis via an aluminium alloy support with a bushing made of Teflon-type self-lubricating material, so that the remaining 224.7mm was cantilevered.

The modified tube was divided into three parts, with different materials and sections: the first part, made of T45 steel, ran from the steering box to the support and was 685.5mm long, with an external diameter of 22.225mm and a thickness of 0.9mm; the second part, made of EN 14 steel, was 32mm long from the intermediate support, towards the steering wheel, and had an external diameter section of 18mm and a thickness of 1.2mm. This portion of the tube was obtained by hollowing out a solid tube – starting from the solid, as they say in the jargon – and drilled by turning; the third part, 193mm long, was connected to the steering wheel and had the same characteristics as the first. The three parts were connected by welding.

Let us begin to shed some light after so many numbers: could there have been human error when welding?
Cammarota: I exclude that. I showed our pictures to Prof. Herold from the University of Magdeburg, a luminary in the field, and he assured me that the welds were perfect. The problem lay in the reduction of the tube section right at the point where the stress was greatest.

So why did the steering column fail?
Casagrande: It was already damaged before the start of the GP. In a nutshell, there was a previous cleavage [a thin crack, which preludes fracture] prior to the race in which Senna lost his life. The presence of oxide didn't allow us to define when the fatigue phenomenon had started, but it was enough for us to understand what had happened.

Are you telling me that a tube was fitted that was not fit for that specific purpose?
Of course I am! Materials have one great characteristic: they never lie. The mechanisms by which these failures occur and the times of exposure of the material are perfectly in line with what happened. We can try to alter a few things, but metals are a bible.

In Formula 1, only the top available materials are usually chosen: what could have happened?
They had made an unplanned modification. The size of the column and the overhang were such that even with a super-material, at its most, it would have lasted for another race. Then, if not replaced, it would have failed, because it could not take the strain. There is no point in looking for fault in the material: that was an aggravating factor, but given the size and given the consistency of the component, that metal could have withstood very little else.

For how long did you keep the column with you?
Cammarota: Less than a week, then we returned it. Just rt45enough time to do the tests with the SEM: during the analysis, engineer Danesi, representing Williams, was always present. Initially the British team didn't want to hear about fatigue, but we immediately saw the failure and had to assess how much the tube had broken due to fatigue and how much due to tearing. When Didcot accepted the fatigue concept, they claimed that the car would still be drivable even with 50 per cent of the

circumference broken. For sure, it would have been if the Imola circuit had been a straight, but this was not the case! Of course they tried a defensive strategy, but the numbers spoke for themselves.

Returning to Professor Lorenzini's report, we read: '... A process of oligocyclic fatigue was triggered, with the development of cracks originating from machining notches, which, due to the application of repeated stresses a few thousand times, progressively extended and weakened the section, until it failed under the overload resulting from a correction of the trajectory by the pilot. The presence of the streaks was decisive in attributing the fracture to fatigue, and the area affected was about 60 per cent of the fracture section, also taking into account that in some areas there were zones of mixed fracture, i.e. with fatigue streaks and with ductile fracture micro-holes. In conclusion, the fracture occurred due to bending and torsion fatigue.'

A fatigue streak expresses a cycle: in the case of the steering column, we can refer to a left or right turn by the driver, while the micro-hole is the effect of a ductile fracture, i.e. when the material is subjected to an overload. The combined effect produced a condition where more than half of the column section was damaged. This evidence produces goose bumps just reading about it. All the more so as negligence emerged not only in the design of the column, but also in the treatments to which it had been subjected.

Roughness tests were also carried out in the survey ...
Roughness represents the ratio between the base of a groove and the surface: if the value is high, you risk serious trouble. All surfaces in aviation must be polished to a high gloss. No streaks should be seen that can concentrate and become the trigger point for surface alterations to the stress, when the fatigue limit tolerable by the material is exceeded. In our tube, there was partial polishing on the outside that should have been done to a mirror finish, and nothing had been done on the inside at all. The crack, therefore, definitely started on the inside, probably already during testing. There were three sections in the tube: one had fatigue, the middle one had mixed fatigue and ductile fracture, just as would be expected, because the material was too tough. Finally, in the third one, the crash fracture from the impact against the wall was clearly visible.

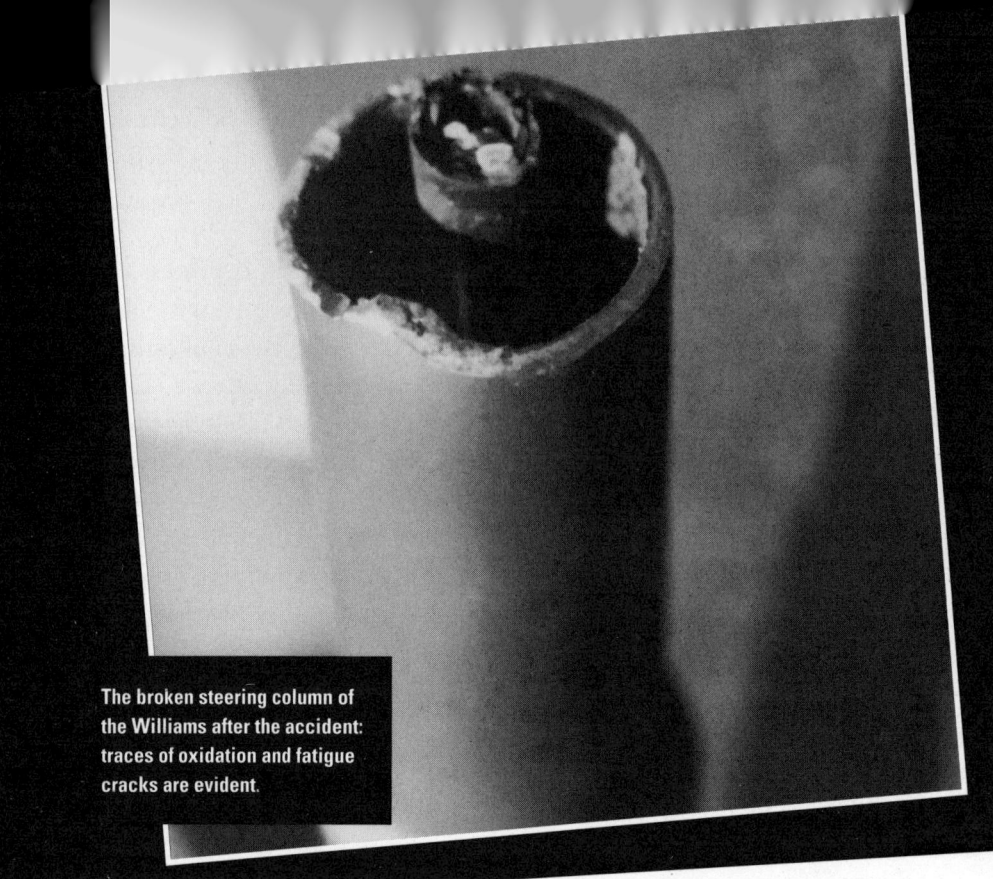

The broken steering column of the Williams after the accident: traces of oxidation and fatigue cracks are evident.

There is a disturbing number that has emerged from the analysis: I speak of the critical intensification factor K1c. What is it?
The unit of measurement that describes a material's resistance to crack growth. The intensification factor, to be clearer, is more simply referred to as fracture resistance. Well, the value Senna's column should have recorded was 96 K1c, but the metal of the actual column would only have resisted up to 86 K1c [according to the tests]. The analysis data, in short, incontrovertibly confirmed the inadequacy of the materials chosen to make Senna's steering column.

The Williams technicians had removed carbon skins and cut part of the cockpit cover. These interventions reduced the stiffness of the bodywork. Could they have contributed to the fractures in the steering column?
It is possible, but in the trial the subject was not touched upon. There may have been an acceleration of the propagation. We would need to know exactly when the crack started.

What surprised you above all, Professor?
That the column was in three parts. It was not normal. Nobody would have thought of a modification like that, and yet a project manager had to be there. I don't think it was Patrick Head or Adrian Newey. But someone had to have designed that modification ...

Cammarota doesn't know, but an answer to his question was given by Adrian Newey, when the chief designer was interviewed by the investigators at the 1994 Italian GP at Monza. In his autobiography, *How to Build a Car*, he repeated his answer, saying he had told the investigators that Gavin Fisher had come up with the concept of the three-part column and the detailed design was by Alan Young. 'However, Patrick Head was aware that a modification had been made to the steering column, but I don't know if Frank Williams was.' However, Newey added that he did not know if Head had examined the drawing of the three-piece column, as it was not Head's specific area of interest.

Newey, still at Monza, also reported another detail that must make us reflect on how Williams acted during that troubled period. He said that after Imola, the team modified their steering columns to a one-piece design, with an increased diameter, because they were concerned the cause of Senna's accident would be traced to the broken column – although Newey still believed it had not been the reason. He told the investigators that with a one-piece column, the Williams would not comply with the FIA template regulation, for space inside the cockpit. The investigators then wondered why the FW16 lined up at Monza had passed the FIA technical checks, and it emerged that the checks in the cockpit had not been carried out with the template required by the regulations. CSAI commissioner Carlo Assennato recounted how on the inspection form, in Article 13.3, an 'OK' had been indicated on the basis of a simple glance, taking it for granted that the technical rule had been respected by Williams. The large number of checks required made it impossible to carry them all out and, in this specific case, it was stated that on that occasion the stewards did not have the necessary template to carry out that particular check.

It is worth reporting this episode, which followed the events at the Enzo and Dino Ferrari, because there is a strong suspicion that there had been similar behaviour at the San Marino GP scrutineering: the technical commissioners at the time still maintain silence on a subject that, for them, remains top secret, as if 30 years have not passed.

After all, the last modifications made to Ayrton's Williams for Imola would only have needed to last for that GP, because Adrian Newey was deliberating the evolution of the FW16, not only in terms of the aerodynamics, and it would probably have been ready for the next Grand Prix, in Monaco.

We are talking about a car that never raced, because Ayrton's tragedy changed the history of F1 forever, imposing modifications decided after Imola: the first of which were introduced in the GP raced in Barcelona at the end of May 1994.

Fate was cruel to Magic, because everything was almost ready to get him out of a car that he felt was hostile, difficult, uncomfortable. In order to extinguish the obstinate remonstrance of the Brazilian, who was making use of all the political weight of being a three-time world champion and his 'temperament', changes were authorised that should not have been. Patrick Head and Adrian Newey discharged these tasks to subordinate figures in the team.

An error of judgement that they will carry with themselves forever.

Those who analysed the steering column never had any doubts about the breakage

NOTHING THAT IS NOT WRITTEN IN METAL CAN BE TRUSTED.

CHAPTER 32

THE DIRECTOR OF *AUTOSPRINT* DID NOT BOW TO PRESSURE

'WORK HAS never killed anyone, it's the pressure that kills people.'

Jerry Lewis did not want to make people laugh this time, but to reflect. With one joke, the American comedian touched on a slippery, difficult subject. How many can bear the weight of their role to the full? And how many, at some point, prefer to turn away and give in to conditioning? A word, a phrase, a figure: can a pebble in the shoe become a boulder capable of overwhelming friendships and ideals? Indeed.

Pressure has often changed the course of a story. Not this time. The big thing is that it took me 30 years to find out what was actually going on behind the *Autosprint* investigation into the Senna case. Despite the fact that I was the journalist on the front line after Gabriele Tarquini's phone call, which had given our suspicions the go-ahead.

How had that piece of column ended up outside the cockpit of the Williams? Who had cut it? Or had it broken off?

Carlo Cavicchi, who was the editor-in-chief of *Autosprint*, one of the most authoritative voices not only in racing, but more generally in the automotive world, did not hesitate for a moment to come out with 'The Suspect' as the cover headline with which a drumbeat campaign began, aimed at finding answers to the questions that all F1 fans were asking themselves in those days. A clear stance, but at the same time a lone ideological stand.

Bolognese, born in 1947, he began his career by following his passion for rallies: he had raced and written about them, becoming one of the most authoritative 'dusters' before agreeing to direct what was considered the bible of racing: *Autosprint*, a specialised weekly that sold around 150,000 copies per issue. A true publishing success, a golden goose that had no equal in the world, even though it was only written in Italian.

On the Senna case, Cavicchi had no doubts. And he pursued a clear editorial line, repeating for months a call-out on the cover with a photo of the steering column and a warning: 'We want the truth'. It was an act of courage, because the vast majority of other media took cover, waiting for possible trial truths. F1 was producing its antibodies and had raised its defences. It manifested a willingness to cooperate with the investigators, but did everything possible to prevent a truth – known in the Circus – from emerging.

'Motorsport is dangerous', is the motto printed on F1's paddock passes. That's why, especially in the Anglo-Saxon world, which is the heart of F1, they could not understand why those guys in Italy would not give up and accept that a driver, even the greatest, like Magic, could die in a race. It was inevitable, therefore, that powerful dissuasive actions would start, which reached the publisher but did not intimidate the editor, so much so that the editorial staff never perceived that there were lawsuits with claims for billions of lire in damages at stake.

Did Ayrton's death on 1 May 1994 at Imola have a worldwide echo?
Well, the scale of what was happening was measurable by the impressive viewing figures: 11 million viewers for Michele Santoro's programme *Il Rosso e il Nero*, in the week after the tragedy. In the history of F1, Senna's fatal accident was the first one to be broadcast worldwide, because the 1982 Gilles Villeneuve tragedy had been documented by images in which almost nothing had been seen. The Brazilian champion was considered the greatest driver, and his death created a worldwide wave of emotion, so there was no media that did not talk about it and give its own interpretation of what had happened. In Italy the echo was enormous, there was also some nasty speculation that went on for a long time. We mustn't forget that Senna is a myth recognised by everyone nowadays, but back then the world was very much split: there were more ... opponents – if you'll allow me to say so – than supporters. Ayrton was a very divisive character. At the time there was a clan of 'nice guys', among whom were Nelson Piquet, Ezio Zermiani, to which was added Alain Prost, who was adept at having almost the entire press on his side. The transalpine

champion was very good at dealing with journalists: he was very political and 'French', even in the good sense of the word. Senna, on the other hand, split the group in two: there were his friends and those he disliked, to whom he made no concessions. It should come as no surprise, therefore, that after the Imola accident two factions built up: guilt-mongers and defenders.

A real campaign had started against Senna: some even called him a drug addict and some claimed that he had gone off the track because the tyres had cooled during the safety car's stay on the track and he had taken unnecessary risks. There were also those who ventured that he had lost control of the Williams on track bumps. It was even claimed that it was normal for the steering wheel to 'dance', as it appeared for a moment on the in-car camera. The ambiguous stances of Damon Hill and David Coulthard raised crazy doubts. It was a very hard period to live through, because taking sides meant taking a difficult position, which many people did not understand. When we came out with the suspicion of the broken column, a front-page blurb popped up in a major sports daily.

The newspaper was La Gazzetta dello Sport ...
It was an unsigned article pointing out the incompetence of a director who did not know the world of F1 and claimed absurd theses. I had erased it from my memory, because it was very insulting to me, although my name was never mentioned. It was an unpleasant attack and it hurt me a lot, but since neither the journalists nor the magazine concerned were mentioned in that article, I could not even reply.

It was a cowardly anonymous stance.
Yes, and also particularly violent. But that too is part of the story I had forgotten and which you are now reminding me of, but that was the climate in which I experienced that very harsh moment.

How did the idea of taking a clear, raw and hard stance come about?
You know very well, it all started with a phone call from Gabriele Tarquini, who pointed out to us that piece of column outside the Williams. I called Dr Salcito, who had been a neighbour of mine for years in San Lazzaro di Savena and whom I knew well. I asked him who, among the rescuers, had sawed off the column to extract Senna from the cockpit. 'No one,' Domenico answered me, 'because we were just ER doctors and had no

tools to saw.' The idea behind that question was that one of the doctors had placed the steering wheel on the ground to intervene on the injured driver, but Tarquini seemed extremely adamant and calm when he stated that the column had broken. Gabriele is someone I held in high esteem then and still do, I found him very convincing. At that point I made a decision: *Autosprint* wanted to know what had happened. It was right to do so from a journalistic point of view. We didn't exist just to report what people wanted to be told: we were a specialised weekly magazine looking for answers. We had the shots of Angelo Orsi, Ayrton's big friend, who had personally taken those photographs: he had been the first photographer to arrive at the accident. It's incredible how strange life is!

We had a document in our hands and came out with the cover 'The Suspect'. From that moment there was an extremely violent reaction to that hypothesis. I am of the opinion that everything started because the F1 world did not want to be watched from the outside. I remember the phone calls from Luca di Montezemolo, Ferrari's president at the time, who called me to say: 'Honestly Carlo, what are you doing? With this campaign you are irritating them. It's not that F1 doesn't want to solve the problem, on the contrary, internally they must already have found out what happened, but they don't understand why people from the outside want to investigate.'

The message was clear, but you did not back down ...
On a similar note, I can say that another very unpleasant situation had also arisen. I was not immediately made aware of this directly, but my publisher, Parrini, kept telling me every time I met him to let it go. He never forced me to stop the investigation, but in his polite manner – he was a very decent person – and with a certain shyness, he feared the consequences of the pressure others had put on him. I don't know if 'lawsuits' is the right word, but Conti Editore had received several: one from Max Mosley, president of the FIA, who had been a very good friend of *Autosprint* until the Senna case. I'd always had a good personal relationship with Max, but as a genuine Anglo-Saxon he took a hard stance against us, and he wasn't the only one, so much so that Parrini told me that there were claims for damages of over five billion lire. I don't know if the other complaints had come from Williams or Patrick Head: I never saw them, because they arrived in his hands, but it is clear that the matter had become very heavy. My wife could not sleep at night

after I had privately told her a little of what was happening, and consider I had not explained the whole thing to her. But to go on was a matter of dignity for the magazine. The magazine was published by a small group of people who were very close in all they did, and in our opinion it was right to go on. For many months, we reprinted the picture of the column on the cover with a reminder: 'We want the truth!'

Together with Alberto Antonini, I personally followed the various stages of the investigation and I want to thank you for only revealing these details to me 30 years later. I am grateful to you, Carlo, because you left us free to carry out our work as reporters, without any conditioning that could, in some way, have affected the research. Knowing that there were claims for billions of lire at stake, which could probably have blown up the publishing house, would probably have affected our investigation in a negative way.

The trial eventually reached the statute of limitations for the defendants in the last instance, so, when all was said and done, there were no guilty parties, but it did sanction one clear point: Ayrton's accident was caused by the failure of the steering column.

And that is exactly what we wanted. I'd like to say that we were not fighting a war against Williams. In racing you always look for maximum performance, and Senna was a person with a very strong character, demanding, and he *demanded* certain changes because he couldn't drive the single-seater as he wanted, and most likely, the team tried to do what they could to please him. As was particularly the case on the race track, they worked in a hurry, some may have made mistakes in total good faith, just to try and give Ayrton what he wanted. The driver complained about the position in the cockpit and the fact that he couldn't use his larger diameter steering wheel. I'm sure at Williams they tried to meet his insistent demands.

What they could not understand at Didcot was why a magazine wanted to find the cause of a tragedy at all costs. A misfortune had happened, which is part of the risks involved in motorsport, and I think they were very torn inside too, but to deny the evidence they came out with all sorts of things. We went ahead with the investigation, but how long was the publisher going to cover us, given that the claims had reached billions? They were probably figures shot to put a lot of pressure on us.

Parrini was exemplary, because newspapers do not always protect you to the end: he was terrified, but I still have great admiration for the way he behaved, because he never imposed anything on me. He managed to be very delicate on a matter that could have had devastating effects on the publishing house. We just wanted to understand what had happened. In our opinion, the accident had been caused by a broken steering column, and if that wasn't the truth, someone should have explained to us what had happened.

On a human level, I was very annoyed by the accusations that were made against Senna, as a man. I remember that an attempt was made to discredit him on a personal level, and this gave me all the more reasons to get mad, but not in the real sense, because that wouldn't be the right word, but it certainly gave me reasons that prompted me to go ahead with the magazine campaign.

It's unbelievable: if you talk to young people today, they all know why Senna went off the track at *Tamburello*, while back then they treated us like we were Martians. We were isolated and nobody followed our line. Nobody! In the absence of in-car camera images, we tried to recover a replay clip that had gone live in France, on TF1. I was ready to fly to Paris when we were told that they could not deliver the tape to us, otherwise they would lose the F1 rights for the following year ... Franco, you followed the whole case with great care and attention, I followed it more from the heart and ... nose. I've tried to erase some things from that period, because it was very hard for me: in some cases, in order to look forward it's better to remove, but I don't want to be a martyr. I can say that I was hurt when I heard about the Florentine photographer who entered the morgue to take some photos. I won't mention the offers that came in, at the time, to buy the pictures that Angelo [Orsi] had taken [at the scene of the accident]: they came from all over the world. I even went so far as to deny that we were in possession of those photos. I asked myself: 'What should I do? Do I have to make money for my magazine and my publisher, or do I have to follow what I feel is right?'

We destroyed the most gruesome slides on the Sunday night itself, when Orsi returned to the newsroom ...
I don't recall how many there were, because I never saw them. It was enough that you told me they were gruesome pictures and I didn't want to look at them. The whole world hunted for those pictures: tabloid

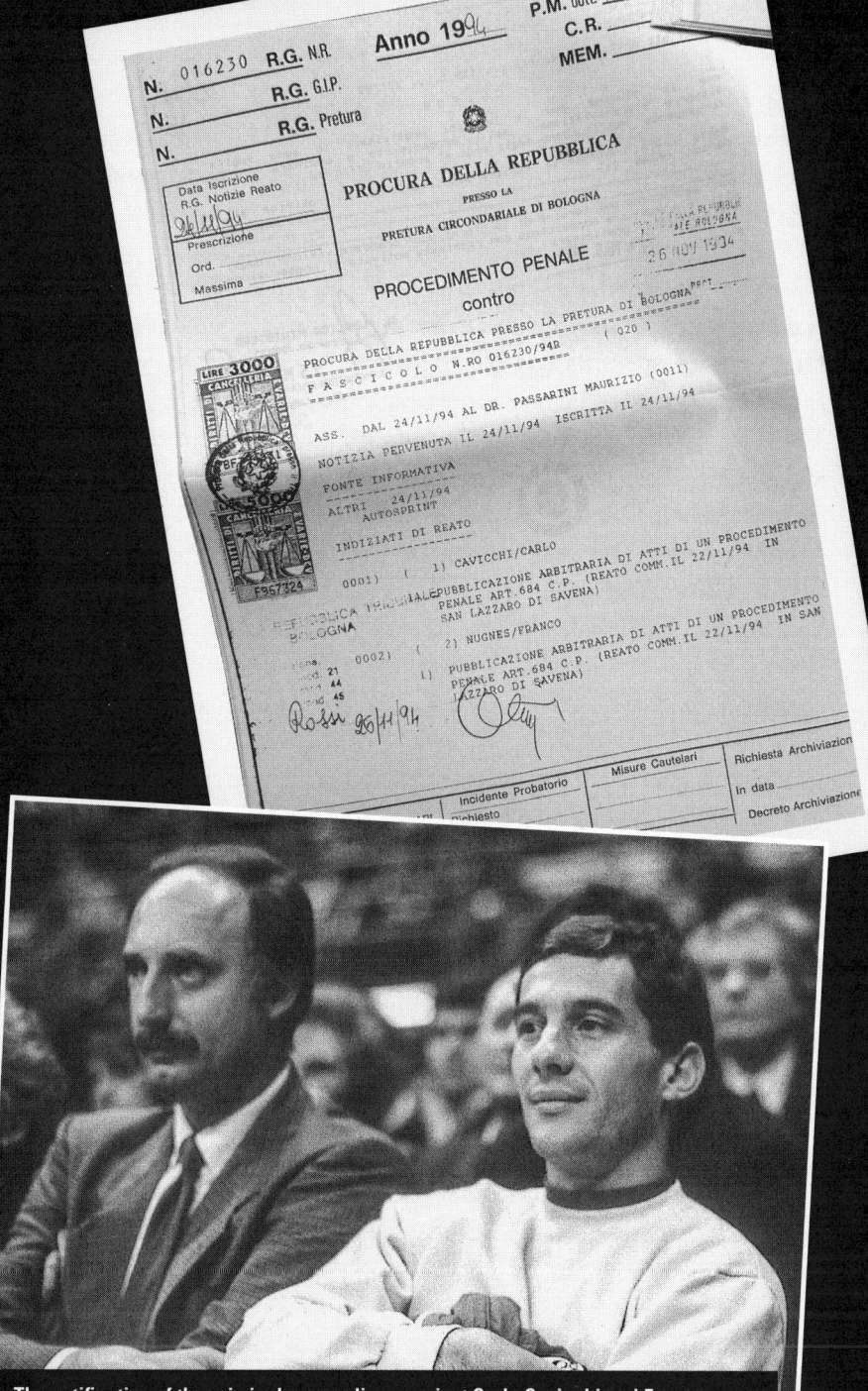

The notification of the criminal proceedings against Carlo Cavicchi and Franco Nugnes for the suspected violation of the secrecy of the investigation: the two were acquitted.

Carlo Cavicchi and Ayrton Senna attend a basketball game of Virtus Bologna together in the city of Bologna.

newspapers went wild looking for them. It was not entirely fair to our publisher, because that would have been big money he could have earned. From this point of view we listened to a moral imperative that outweighed the material aspect.

It must be said, for the sake of the record, that no one criticised us for the decision to destroy the few shots of Ayrton's devastated face ...
Hey, we used to print a newspaper about racing and not about blood. I care a lot about that. We made the decision together and not me alone. You were there too. I will thank Tarquini all my life for the lucidity and serenity with which he enlightened us. Gabriele was already an established, credible driver, and his amazement at the image of the steering column, his confidence in claiming that it had broken, gave me a lot of self-assurance. And self-assurance is something that comes from the gut ...

Ayrton's death was the epilogue to a terrible Imola weekend for F1 and the racing world. How did you experience it?
It brings back memories of an episode, another piece of the jigsaw puzzle that I had erased. On Friday I was in the Renault Italia hospitality area, on the second floor of the pit lane, right on the corner, above the pit lane entrance, and while I was watching the cars at *Variante Bassa* Rubens Barrichello had his bad accident with the Jordan. Next to me was Chiara Luciani, a colleague who, after being at *Autosprint*, had moved to Milan, and another colleague who had nothing to do with cars and whom I didn't know. They had waved the red flag to rescue Rubens, exactly while Roland Ratzenberger, in his Simtek, was returning to the pits. At once the guy next to Chiara commented loudly: 'Oh, at least this one's not taking any risks, his mum won't be anxious!' In his eyes it looked like Roland was going slowly compared to the others. This struck me very much, because the very next day we witnessed the tragedy of the Austrian driver.

Those are phrases that should never be said in the world of racing, firstly because accidents can happen to anyone, as we have unfortunately seen, and secondly because drivers should not be divided into good and bad without due consideration of the reason why one goes faster than another: perhaps because of the car he drives. On Saturday, I came home very shaken by that sentence about Roland that was still bouncing around in my head, and on Sunday, while we were watching the GP in the editorial office, we heard the 118 helicopter pass overhead, so much so that we immediately sent Marisa Imbrogno to the *Ospedale Maggiore*, even though we were aware that there wasn't much hope. And finally there was a magazine to issue, after the most terrible weekend in F1 history.

We also had to reprint a portion of the 'pre-cooked' part of that number 18 issue of Autosprint, *because in it there was a cartoon by* Matitaccia, *Giorgio Serra, who was being ironic about Senna and it would have been in very bad taste to come out with satire in a tragic situation ...*

I remember that, when I decided to print a black cover, without pictures, to honour Ayrton, many in the editorial staff turned up their noses. I know that was not the case with you or Angelo Orsi. While I can say a part of the group was extremely united in carrying out our campaign, not everyone thought in the same way. I saw sceptical faces and looks said more than words.

Who was Ayrton Senna?

He was a phenomenal driver, but also a person who had a wonderful relationship with me. I never used the word friend, because we were 13 years apart, and that's a lot when you're young. He was friends with Angelo Orsi and Keith Sutton, but he was extremely friendly with me. I hung out with him many times, I even took him to see a Virtus Bologna basketball game. Together, we wrote *Senna Vero* [*The Genuine Senna*], his book-interview. Ayrton was very outspoken, someone who did not like half-measures. Today we would say someone who 'always knows how to give you a headline', with an extraordinary capacity for synthesis, and for this I admired him, because he was never ambiguous. Not everyone can do that ...

Did the esteem for you arise because you were the editor of one of the most influential magazines or did it develop over time?

It developed over time. Ayrton arrived at *Autosprint* brought to me by Andrea Ficarelli: he was carrying a small suitcase that gave him a very professional air and only after a long time did I discover that it was not his but Andrea's, although there really was his stuff inside. I was impressed and the editorial staff liked him immediately: a good relationship was born with the group, which was enthusiastic, and the same was true for Senna, we always behaved correctly with him.

What feature struck you the most about the Brazilian?
The lucid ability to criticise even himself. While working on the book, Ayrton reminded me of the time Alboreto had braked in front of him on the straight at Zeltweg, because he himself had done it to him before, at Hockenheim. Michele deliberately skipped revenge at Hungaroring, because it was too slow a track, and gave the Brazilian a run for his money in Austria, so much so that he slammed the nose of his Lotus. Senna told me personally that he was in the habit of staying on the track after taking pole position and I remember him saying: 'Alboreto was right, that is something you shouldn't do!' And even about the episode in which Nigel Mansell, after being bumped on the track at Spa-Francorchamps, had grabbed him in the pits, lifting him by the lapels and saying: 'Next time I'll really throttle you,' he admitted to me that Nigel was right. And I must say that this aspect of him impressed me, because even in a book-interview like *Senna Vero*, he had the ability to admit his mistakes. That's not a gift that can be given to everyone. That's why I found him out of the ordinary: his analysis was always above average. He would have become a great leader of the FIA or a president of Brazil or whatever – in any case he would have played an important role in society, because of this ability to synthesise even the most complex issues. That's not for everyone. His phrase about Nigel that I like to repeat to the point of boredom is: 'Mansell is the only driver you can see in both mirrors when he's tailing you.' It's beautiful because, in just one touch, it describes a whole situation. A character like that can only be fascinating.

The myth of Senna does not die out, while the memory of other champions fades with the passing of time. What explains this?
Women had a crazy fascination with him. The female public was all for Ayrton. Even now I meet not only ladies, but also very young women who are attracted to Senna's figure. And I think this aspect counts a lot. They liked him even then, but his death consecrated to eternity the driver who was considered the strongest of all. I won't go into the merits of these rankings, which I wouldn't know how to draw up, but even his end was like a drawing to enter into legend. And let's not forget his intimate relationship with God.

Did you ever have any doubt about his genuine attitude, or did he also play around with it?
Ah, that's a good question. To me he was very genuine, but he probably did play around sometimes. But I can assure you he wasn't playing with faith. It was something he felt deep inside. Although, when he married Lilian Vasconcellos, he had a civil wedding. Much as he had also invited a priest to the ceremony. He was not wearing a tie, she was just in a suit and trousers, and apart from some relatives, there were only a few people there. It is curious that Ayrton chose the civil ceremony, while he was so religious.

Perhaps the deeper spiritual aspect only emerged later…
Perhaps. In 1981 he was little more than a kid. He was so young…

CHAPTER 33

WILLIAMS'S DEFENCE: STIRANO, DIDCOT'S ITALIAN

'I BELIEVE that the only sure things in this world are coincidences.'

Leonardo Sciascia, a Sicilian writer, traced Giorgio Stirano's role in the Senna case with a brushstroke of words. He ended up being involved somewhat by chance. Or rather by '*Causo*', as will become clearer a few lines below. He did the job as representative of the Williams defence in Italy in a very conscientious and professional manner.

Giorgio Stirano is a Piedmontese engineer now 74 years old. I knew him on the race tracks as an F1 designer of Osella and Forti, but also as a Formula Alfa Boxer designer, and the 'father' of the Alba, a prototype that conquered the 1983 and 1984 junior world championship in Group C, with drivers Carlo Facetti and Martino Finotto. He has always been accustomed to making do with what he had available, because he has always had to deal with teams struggling with limited funds and budget constraints.

'I wrote an autobiography,' says Stirano, 'in which I portray myself as a wandering figure in Formula 1: I was back and forth from the Circus. In my appearances in the F1 world, I never met Ayrton Senna. But although I never saw him in person, I can say, however, that I know the last ten seconds of his life perfectly well. The last seconds of his existence, the ones relating to the data acquisition, which formed a part of the investigation into his death, I analysed and studied them over and over again. I was a supporter of Ayrton. For someone like me who lived for racing, he represented the top: he was the three-time world champion driver, in the world champion car. It was the perfect match: Williams had won the year before with Alain Prost and Senna was yearning to join that team. On 1 May 1994 I was watching the San Marino GP on television, comfortably seated in my armchair, and immediately after the crash I thought: "Now he'll get up and out of the car." Instead, he never moved again, and his end came as a shock to everyone. It was unimaginable that a driver could die at the *Tamburello* corner at Imola. This is how my story with Senna began.'

At this point, it is necessary to explain how a character totally unrelated to this tragic affair ended up in it ...
It was 24 May 1994 when the garage where both Senna's Williams and Ratzenberger's Simtek were kept was prompted to be opened. I was at Imola, because I had been summoned by Roberto Causo: the Roman lawyer was an international sports commissioner and an influential man at CSAI, the Italian Automobile Sports Commission. At that time, Causo was representing, to an extent, all the parties involved in the investigation, and he couldn't certainly take on all of them. He was also representing Simtek: Roberto sought me out for that reason.

Engineer Stirano was supposed to assess Roland's single-seater, the other victim of that accursed weekend of 1 May: the causes of the Austrian driver's tragic end were clear from the outset, so the matter could have been resolved quickly, but ...
On site I met Patrick Head, who had just arrived from England and knew absolutely nothing about Italian legal procedures.

'Hello Giorgio, do you know Patrick?' said Causo as soon as we entered the garage.

'Yes,' I replied, 'although in a superficial way, as can happen in an F1 pit lane. He was always at the front of the grid, while I was usually at the back and, therefore, we were usually far away from each other.'

In his gruff voice Head had promptly replied: 'Of course, Giorgio, I know him.'

'Patrick,' Causo continued, 'you don't know the Italian procedures, but be aware that there is one that provides for the representation of the technical party on top of the legal party, so you'd better have a technical reference on site. Your call ...'

After a moment's reflection Head replied: 'I understand. If you think it's important, Stirano will be my technical reference in Italy. That's fine with me.'

It was an opportunistic situation on Head's side, the result of a completely chance meeting, not intended at all. Giorgio Stirano was supposed to become Simtek's consultant, and instead, completely by surprise, he found himself to be Williams's man in Italy. An unpredictable and unforeseen change of role, which increased the pressure exponentially on the dangling man from Turin, who was ill-prepared to enter into an affair that kept the attention of the world's press burning. How had Ayrton died? Was Williams responsible? What had happened at the *Tamburello* corner?

'Causo is an old fox,' Giorgio adds. 'He was aware that a competent figure would be needed on site. I took the job somewhat in the dark. Up to that point I had just read what was written in the newspapers. I was immediately informed that the ECUs of Ayrton's FW16 had been returned the same evening of the race to Williams and Renault, to see if there was any data that could give an explanation for what had happened. I started to look into that, so much so that I personally handed the Renault ECU back to the investigators. It was clear that there would be a further liaison between Williams and the investigators to provide more information, if requested. It should be added, though, that at the time there was no suspect, but only a start to the investigation: it was a due practice as there had been two deaths.'

In the garage under the Agip grandstand was also Mauro Forghieri, who had been appointed as an expert witness by the court. The engineer from Modena was a big deal: a genius who had designed Ferrari racing cars, among others, for over 20 years. He knew about chassis, aerodynamics, engines and even gearboxes: he knew every bolt, every secret of his cars.

'We went into the garage together where the two single-seaters were stored,' continues Stirano. 'I was a little in awe of this illustrious F1 personality, even though I had known him for some time, that is, since I had worked at Osella and attended FISA meetings. We inspected the two carcasses with care. After this inspection I received no more news. Then, there was a long silence, although I kept in touch with Williams by correspondence. So I learned that Mauro had filed his expert report for the prosecution. At a certain point everyone seemed to have disappeared and I knew nothing more until I got a phone call at the beginning of February 1997. It was a Friday evening: "Is that engineer Giorgio Stirano?" said a female voice.

'"Yes, that's me," I replied.

'I am lawyer Edda Gandossi, Oreste Dominioni's assistant, I am looking for you because we know that you started liaising with the court at the beginning of the Senna case, while we have just taken over the representation of both Frank Williams and Patrick Head in the trial. We have to go to London for an initial meeting, would you like to come with us?"

'"If you need me," I replied, "I will be there. Exactly when do you plan to go to Britain?"

'"Tomorrow morning on the 8am flight from Linate, we've got a ticket for you too," Gandossi added.

'I had to laugh, but I realised they had called at the last minute because they had lost time in appointing lawyers, and since the preliminary hearing was scheduled for ten days later, there was no time to lose.'

The meeting took place in a small room in a hotel adjacent to Heathrow airport, as was customary with F1 team managers when they had to discuss important matters with Bernie Ecclestone, the father and master of the Circus.
Present at the meeting were Gandossi, Dominioni, who didn't speak a word of English, and myself. For Williams there were Frank, Patrick and the team's lawyer, Peter Goodman. I was astonished not to see Adrian Newey. Head explained to me a few days later that the chief designer had left the team and gone to McLaren, '... because he had asked me for a salary worthy of a top driver and I couldn't pay an engineer like an F1 champion. For that reason we let him go and Adrian chose to go to Woking. Having left the team, he will have to care for his own independent defence.'

There were, therefore, two defensive lines. Not the ideal situation ...
I had the clear perception that Newey had taken a very aloof position, because only Williams was mentioned in the investigation and not Adrian. At least, that was the feeling at the time.

After the pleasantries, Frank Williams's position on the team was discussed with Dominioni, and the lawyer took my position on the defence team for granted. Frank, on the other hand, asked for a break, because he wanted to speak directly with me, alone, to ask me personally if I would accept the position. Which of course I did, and I greatly appreciated his fairness, which never failed in our mutual relations. Thus began my total involvement with the team, with Head and rest of the team at Grove, where Williams had opened their new headquarters. I was a figure from outside Williams, my job was to get an idea of what had happened and to coordinate with the various consultants, most of whom were Italian.

What had really happened [to the car] was the question many would have liked to ask Head, but no one dared to speak up, because he was much feared within the team. The calculations engineer, with whom I went to the Ministry of Air Defence, had once been asked: 'How is it going with Patrick?'

'Well,' he replied, 'he hasn't yelled at me yet.'

Dickie Stanford, who had become general manager, added: 'When I have to ask him something, I stand in the doorway of his office, always in a position from which I can easily escape.'

In short, it was clear that Head was not an easy character, beyond the gruff air he carried with that massive physique. However, I had become their strategic advisor and needed to understand how I should behave. So I began to interface with the Williams team to build up an opinion that I would then report to Patrick. Everything always went smoothly with me! Obviously Head took all his time to discuss the issues that I submitted to him, but he always gave me his opinion.

At Williams they were convinced that the steering column had broken in the collision with the Tamburello *wall and Didcot's team engineers spent no time looking for other answers to the many questions about the causes of the accident that had blown the Senna case wide open ...*

A couple of months after the accident, Patrick called me and asked me to join him at Didcot. After welcoming me, he took me to the Williams workshop and showed me a bench where the front end of the FW16 had been rebuilt and mounted on rigid blocks. In the telemetry traces two strange signals had emerged, two peaks of hydraulic pressure, so they had wanted to reproduce the conditions of the accident in the laboratory, to carefully study the behaviour of the steering column. The technicians had transferred to the steering arms the same impulses they had detected in the data acquisition. There were about 4 degrees of planarity between the asphalt and the run-off track where the car had gone off the track at *Tamburello*, so the FW16 took off and then landed on the right side twice before crashing into the wall. Senna's car that year was fitted with hydrodrive for the first time and, therefore, was monitored by various sensors, useful in directing the engineers' development work. In addition to trying to understand the significance of the impact, we observed that, with the steering wheel correctly mounted, we could see the two famous peaks. The presence of those two signals in the telemetry graphs proved that the steering wheel was attached because, when we removed the steering wheel and repeated the experiment, the signal on the monitor became flat. That test convinced me: the column didn't break. That was the key element, the reason why I defended Williams by believing what I was saying. It was not a question of money or even prestige, rather an objective fact. In my opinion, until the impact against the wall, the column was attached, which is why afterwards, in the courtroom of the Imola Magistrates' Court, a sea of arguments and controversy arose with those who did not think alike.

Discussions and controversies took place not only during the trial, but also in the media. Giorgio Stirano argued persuasively – and now I understand why – for a thesis that was the exact opposite of what had blatantly emerged from the journalist's investigation I had conducted for *Autosprint*. The more the intricate puzzle seemed to become clearer and clearer to me, the more our mutual positions began to diverge without any point of contact. We no longer spoke directly with Giorgio, but polemised at a distance.

After 30 years, when I decided to look again at the papers and documents of the investigation, I felt it was my duty to listen again to the world of Williams, looking for Patrick Head, Damon Hill and also Giorgio.

'Hello Franco,' he replied cordially, 'long time no speak.'

'I would like your opinion to be in the book about Ayrton,' I replied, 'are you willing to have a chat?'

'Of course, I appreciate your intellectual honesty,' replied Stirano. 'I didn't expect your call since we were in very different positions, but I am pleased that you intend to re-read the story without prejudice.'

I must admit that the engineer from Turin made himself available for an open discussion, in which not only divisions, but also several points of commonality emerged. The suffering over the lack of Magic had faded. As had the anger of those who sought a truth that was difficult to bring out. It is amazing how the passing of time has the power to make one re-read history on a less emotional, more rational basis. Let's be clear, neither of us changed our minds, but we spoke calmly: we were not in a courtroom and could review the facts with the knowledge of today's technology. Ayrton would not have died in 2024: the blade that pierced him would not have penetrated the helmet at the most vulnerable point, between the visor and the shell, because today's visors have protections made of zylon, an anti-shattering material.

'The interesting fact that I wanted to tell you,' Stirano resumes, 'is that Williams contacted the British Ministry of Defence to analyse the data on the column, the issue around which the whole process gravitated. Being British, it was normal for them to look in, also because we Italians were viewed with a bit of mistrust. I, on the other hand, got in touch with Alenia Spazio, where I had connections: they spoke Italian and in the process that was certainly an advantage, plus they were very well prepared. As consultants they did an extraordinary job.'

You were very critical of Mauro Forghieri's expertise on the steering column ...
We all have great respect for Mauro, but he wrote in his report that the column was 60–70 per cent cracked and we knew this was not the case. So we passed all the information on to Alenia, who came to other conclusions, after repeating a series of laboratory tests: 60 per cent of the column was still connected, 20 per cent had fatigue curves and for the remaining 20 per cent we could not say whether any cracks were present or not. The conclusions thus matched the report of Colonel Hallgas of the Air Force at Pratica di Mare, who spoke in court during the trial as a consultant for the prosecution.

What caused a lot of concern and controversy was that the central part of the column, made of a different material from the other two pieces, showed signs of rust as well as fatigue ...
That there were fatigue curves was never in doubt, but the effect on the structural strength of the column remained to be seen. We never disputed that there was fatigue; that was obvious. It could not be said otherwise.

Did you ever ask when the modification of the column with the diameter reduction was made?
I asked for a drawing, but I never exposed this problem. For me it was done in the workshop in Didcot, clearly before Imola.

Why did fatigue cracks arise?
Because the column did not have outlets with a minimum of connection, i.e. the grooves. From the point of view of mechanical quality, the first bushing that connected the pipes of the column was not properly engaged. And that is where, on one side, the fatigue cracks originated.

Williams at the time was considered the most technologically advanced Formula 1 team: how was it possible to use an unsuitable pipe for such a major modification?
I'll tell you what Patrick told me when I met him, before we did our analysis. Head told me: 'I look after the whole car, but the chassis is Newey's thing. What I can tell you is that I'm seeing this column now for the first time!'

I also had the same confirmation from Patrick Head: I asked him about this sensitive subject and he wrote to me that he was amazed to see certain changes made to the car that were not in line with Williams's quality standard.
You see, the versions coincide. But I did not give any weight to the timing, I always took it for granted.

'But at a certain point,' Stirano continues, 'we didn't even know where exactly the car had gone off the track. We had the car spinning at *Tamburello*, but we had to reconstruct Ayrton's accident moment by moment. We brought in luminaries on vehicle dynamics, Diego Minen and Michael Guttilla, who worked, thanks to the Adams system, on analysing the simulation of the car going off the road. The night before the hearing, we met at the Donatello hotel in Imola with all the experts. I had prepared a series of A4 sheets, which I would later give to Judge Costanzo, showing tenth of second by tenth of second the behaviour of the car. In reality the drawings were too small to be shown in the courtroom, so it would have been more useful to copy my sketches onto a large flipchart, so that the data could be readable for everyone: the judge, but also the lawyers and the consultants. I was dead tired after the day I had spent in Milan with Dominioni and Gandossi preparing for the hearing, so I appreciated that Alenia Suppo's industrial expert, who could draw well by hand, took the trouble to magnify my data sketches. Adrian Newey, who was following the scene from a corner, came out hissing a comment: 'It doesn't look too professional to me!' Of course the drawings

The test bench that Williams had built in Didcot to look for the causes of Senna's accident.

were not perfect, but the aim was to try to explain to everyone what had happened. I glared at him and he fell back into silence. I was impressed by Newey: you always get the feeling that he is brooding on something, but you never know what he is really thinking.'

From your reconstruction, it emerged that Senna would have started to lose the Williams on the second Tamburello *bump. So you wanted to direct the defence against the Imola circuit? Did you not know that Frank Williams and Federico Bendinelli, the Sagis administrator, had already agreed at the 1994 Monaco GP not to go to war with each other in court?*

We have never attacked the racetrack. Frank told me in a meeting: 'Bernie [Ecclestone, the promoter of the championship] advised me not to attack the racetrack.' Our way was to go for a technical defence. Engineer Saccenti, technical director of Gavio, a company expert in roads and asphalts, came up as a consultant, because in the meantime the track survey had also disappeared. The problem was not the track, but the newly changed F1 regulations and the abolition of active suspension.

Sir Frank Williams, the owner of the team, suffered for a long time from Ayrton's loss.

Those cars were going into aerodynamic stall every 50m at *Tamburello*. And, in fact, the question we asked in the trial years later was: how come the FIA, after the Senna drama, changed the cars and the tracks? There must have been a reason! At the beginning of 1994 they had banned active suspension, and some could no longer handle traditional suspension. If there had only been a quality problem on the Williams, why did the International Federation then change all the regulations? And let's not forget the statements of Max Mosley, the FIA president, who threatened to stop racing in Italy. The climate was very heavy for everyone.

In that hot climate, how was your relationship with the Senna family?
I never had any direct information. I remember that, at all the hearings, there was a lawyer to defend Senna's reputation. There was a lot of tension at Williams, because they all experienced the tragedy very badly: especially Frank and Patrick, but in my British travels I also saw the grief-stricken faces of the people in the team. There was a strong participation in the grief ...

Yet, certain feelings that you now describe did not emerge outside Didcot, and in the trial the defence seemed to find it very hard to prove certain theses ...
Don't be surprised, when you work on consultations it's the data you bring that counts, and it's normal for individual positions to stiffen and in some cases radicalise. I remember that Damon Hill, Ayrton's team-mate, was called to testify and Gandossi, who knew English, was not there. We went into the lawyers' room and I can tell you that Damon was terrified. Lawyer Dominioni asked him the questions he would later repeat in court, and I, who was translating, found the driver literally scared.

Speaking of testimonials, allow me the opportunity to clarify a doubt: how did the idea come about to have David Coulthard, the young Williams test driver, later chosen as Senna's replacement, say that the single-seater's steering columns are not fixed but can have a certain flexibility?
I confess, I asked for this first. I always thought a steering column didn't flex and was rock-steady stiff; until I went to Grove in 1997 to attend a meeting with lawyers. We walked out of the meeting room and there were F1 cars on display. I said to the lawyer, 'Come on, I'll show you a steering column.' And I approached the first car on display, which was not a Williams but a Ferrari. It was the 1990 F1-90 driven by Prost. Frank had obtained it as compensation from Maranello for the breach of contract of Alesi, who went racing in 1991 with the *Cavallino*, even though he had already signed a contract with Williams. I grabbed the column and was about to say, 'You see it's stiff!' At that point I realised that it was moving under my hand. The overhang between the steering wheel and the support, which – I quote from memory – was about 200mm, caused a fairly noticeable flex; I won't hide the fact that I made a fool of myself at the time. But the lawyers seized the ball, because they realised that the episode could be useful at the hearing.

It is one thing to hint at a certain flexibility, it is quite another to claim, as Coulthard did, that the column could move: the racing world was outraged by that testimony in court and, had it not been tragic, it would have made everyone laugh!

Well, David had a point, and in a hearing you do anything to throw water to your own mill. And then, if we refer to the last part of the trial, when they talked about the [apparent] movement of a button on the steering wheel [as seen on the in-car camera footage], it has to be said that the images were conditioned by the fact that the drivers at *Tamburello*, due to the effect of forces greater than 4G, bent their heads sideways and held onto the steering wheel exactly as I had done at the Williams Museum with the Ferrari. At a speed of 309km/h, which is the very speed you reach at *Tamburello*, lateral acceleration requires the neck muscles to be physically prepared.

In the in-car camera images, the famous yellow button on the steering wheel was seen to move and it had already been noticed after the pit exit at the *Tamburello* entrance. For some it was a clue that the column was breaking, but in fact the indication of the button movement was weak, and then a champion like Senna, if he had seen the column move, would have immediately lifted his foot. That seems clear, doesn't it? The in-car cameras of the time had lenses with a fish-eye effect, so they tended to distort the images. We were by then at the end of the hearing and Prosecutor Passerini had latched onto everything and was looking for clarifications to dismantle certain theses.

In short, there were episodes in the trial during which there were moments of high tension.

At one point Mauro Forghieri also expressed doubts as to whether Williams had really collaborated in extracting the data from the ECU. He laid down his cards and we had to defend ourselves with ours. The judge ordered an additional investigation into the ECU, and a simulation was ordered to see if it could be turned back on. I thought to myself: 'Wow! In Bologna they have Raychem connectors, which are aeronautical in nature. They are so cool!' And instead, a fortnight later, they asked me if I could get the connectors. I went to Williams to get them, but actually the technical consultants in Bologna already had all the information on the ECU, because back in 1994 we had already given them a report on how the car and the ECU itself worked. The fact is that they had not

IT'S INCREDIBLE HOW THE PASSAGE OF TIME HAS THE POWER TO MAKE US REREAD HISTORY ON A LESS EMOTIONAL, MORE RATIONAL BASIS.

read it. At Williams, I had to do a crash course because I hadn't read it either, so we started off on the same footing, but afterwards I had made myself knowledgeable on every detail.

The day before the hearing we had a preliminary meeting and I saw the control unit again, which was rather battered, since it had been mounted on the right side on the FW16, which was the one that hit the wall, so it wasn't in very good shape. All the connection pins were damaged, but in the night some of them had woken up. In my opinion, the ECU was not returned in the same condition as it had been delivered the day before.

'You see, the signals go in here and out there,' the prosecution consultant explained that there was an input and an output characterised by the connectors. When the testimony was over, it was my turn.

'I remember the ECU differently from the one I saw yesterday, but I don't make it a matter of principle.'

I merely said that the data did not come out from there [the connector]: instead, a slot was visible in the lid. It was used to pull out the card that contained the telemetry data. The card was also damaged and I had kept it in my pocket. I didn't take it out, because they had completely misdescribed the operation of the control unit and the subject was never spoken of again during the trial.

But that's when I realised the importance of a good lawyer. Landi, who represented the racetrack, asked me: 'I realise that the control unit was not working with the described input and output, but why didn't you try to operate it anyway?'

It was a question that left us silent, because it was obvious that an engineer wouldn't even think of doing it, knowing that it was broken, but in a court of law, proven evidence might have some effect. Let's be clear: that control unit would never have been able to work; if you just tried to pick it up you could hear the sound of the back-up battery slamming against the casing; however the lawyer, even if he got me pissed off, had asked the right question to put me on the spot.

When they are in court, lawyers are great at splitting hairs to prove themselves right.

The bodywork of the Williams, after the impact against the Tamburello wall, split open on the left side with a gash that reached almost to the other side. The failure started from the point where the carbon had been removed, to allow Ayrton not to rub his knuckles. Was there a connection?

I will answer you with a question. Why was it that after Senna's accident they started doing structural tests on bodywork? Simply because those chassis were not as strong as those that were made later. So surely the bodywork had weaknesses. I remember well that it was broken on the left side. But that was clearly a side effect: with a bump like that it could only break. It wasn't aluminium, which crumples, but carbon, which cracks at some point.

No need to say more.

CHAPTER 34

SENNA'S 'FIRST' FORMULA 1 CAR WAS REUTEMANN'S FERRARI

'ONE SHOULD always be in love. That is why one should never get married!'

Ayrton Senna may have read Oscar Wilde. Two myths who had been promised in marriage several times, but had never made it to the wedding were Ayrton Senna and Ferrari. They seemed to be made for each other, yet there had been four unsuccessful attempts, and nothing had come of it. So many words, so many – more or less – secret meetings at different times and with different people: Enzo Ferrari, Cesare Fiorio, Jean Todt and Luca di Montezemolo. All the big bosses of the *Cavallino* had tried, none had succeeded. Probably, the last contact with Luca di Montezemolo, four days before Ayrton's death, could have changed a written plan, but destiny decided to end this never consummated love in a different way.

In fact, for Ferrari, the Brazilian should have been considered the 'enemy' as, in a very thin period for F1 victories, Senna was a raider of successes, capable of taking the shine off the historic Maranello team. After winning the 1979 F1 World Championship with Jody Scheckter, Ferrari entered a period of famine of titles that would last until 2000, the year of Michael Schumacher's first laurel with the *Rossa*. Before the German, Ayrton could have been the champion capable of interrupting that negative cycle. However, even if he was an opponent, the *Cavallino* fans had always had great respect for Magic. Imola, or rather the Enzo and Dino Ferrari, was the home circuit for the Prancing Horse as it was for Senna, in a different way.

The seven pole positions obtained in a row from 1985 to 1991, with the addition of the one in 1994, meant something. But Ayrton was not seen as a usurper by the Italian fans at Imola: never booing, only applause. A phenomenon that is difficult to explain in the *'terra de' Mutor'* [Motorland], given that the 'hill of passion', or *Rivazza*, as well as *Tosa*, were completely swarming with red: that was the lair of the *Cavallino* ultras. Nonetheless, when Carlo Costa, the historic voice of the racetrack, certified Senna's umpteenth pole position on the waving of the chequered flag at the end of qualifying, a standing ovation, followed by thunderous applause, broke out in the stands. The fans, evidently, were witnesses to this love that sooner or later had to result in a marriage.

But when did this deep feeling for Ferrari originate? To find an answer we have to go back in time, rewinding the thread back to 1977, when Ayrton was little more than a young boy who had already made his mark in the Brazilian karting world with his first South American title.

Tino Gallone, the manager of the São Paulo kart track, had accompanied Senna to Interlagos to let him sniff the air of the Brazilian GP. Pietro Corradini, who in addition to being a pillar among Ferrari mechanics, was also a skilled karting driver, knew Gallone. The mechanic from Modena, who recently passed away, used to go karting in his free time on Tino's track, especially during the F1 winter tests in São Paulo. They had become friends and, for the occasion, Corradini had given him a couple of passes for the GP.

'The first time I saw Ayrton,' recalls Corradini, 'was in 1977. Tino came into the pits at Interlagos with a shy, quiet boy. I remember it was Thursday and I was checking the set-up of one of the 312T2s. I needed a ballast in the car to simulate the driver's weight before doing the checks, so I invited the young man into the cockpit. He understood, but he didn't dare get into the car. With an intimidated look he asked Tino in Portuguese: "Are you serious?" I had to insist: "If you are as fast in the kart as you are hopping into this car, we're not doing well …" Gallone hadn't yet begun to translate my reprimand: Ayrton didn't hesitate a second time and sneaked into the red car like a cat!'

Senna's 'first' Formula 1 car was Reutemann's Ferrari

Anyone thinking that Senna's 'first contact' with a Formula 1 car was in the Donington test with Keke Rosberg's Williams on 19 July 1983 is sadly mistaken, because it was actually with Carlos Reutemann's Ferrari 312T2, which finished on the front row in the 1977 Brazilian GP and went on to win the race. 'We used to prepare the cars before shipping,' Corradini explains, 'but then, once at the track, we would check if anything had moved during the journey, so we would put the single-seaters back on the scales. I told Senna to keep his foot on the brake and hold the steering wheel straight until we had finished all the checks. At the second check he pointed out to me that the steering wheel wasn't perfectly straight: that guy had a nose ...'

Between Corradini and Senna it was the beginning of a friendship that would be renewed as he travelled the world: 'I had seen him karting at Parma,' continues Corradini, 'and he was really very fast: he drove his Dap with just one hand, because he always put the other in front of the carburettor to adjust the mixing screw. He was already a perfectionist. Later, when he was racing in Formula Ford, he also did side races at the GPs and won everything: he had something more than the others. He used to visit me in the pits without even taking off his overalls, but my bosses, Marco Piccinini and Antonio Tomaini, didn't like seeing an intruder hanging around the garage: "The guy is my friend, I vouch for him. He's a good guy and, what's more, he is very fast."

'Then I said to Marco: "When he gets to F1 he will be world champion."

'Obviously my line sounded like bluster, but when he arrived at Toleman I reminded Piccinini that it was the "intruder" who had been sneaking into the pits. I have to say that Ayrton always drove very fast, but at Toleman he had Pirelli tyres, highly snubbed by the top teams, but with the right compound they could be very competitive and they helped him to show off.'

Pietro, karting was a common denominator that bound you together. There was also a revealing episode of your closeness ...
In 1986 I was supposed to participate in the World Karting Championship at Pomposa, as Fabrizio Giovanardi's team-mate. Ayrton proposed me to race with the Brazilian team, since they didn't have a representative in the 125 class and the yellow-green Federation would have supported me,

because Senna would have liked to see me race in their colours. Nothing came of it because of the opposition of our Federation.

The simple acquaintance, as it turned out, had transformed into a strong friendship. Pietro had become part of Senna's 'magic circle', a small group of people who could rely on Ayrton over time, even years later, when the Brazilian became the acclaimed champion and Corradini was no longer in the Ferrari F1 team.

He passed by Maranello with Gerhard Berger before McLaren's private tests in early 1991. Brenda Vernor, Enzo Ferrari's historic secretary, called me and said, 'Two persons are waiting for you over here. Will you come and say hello to them?' She did not add anything else. In normal times I wouldn't have moved, but at that time I was rather unmotivated at the Experience Department and I was curious to know who these people looking for me could be. She was very firm: '*Dai movet* – move!' she replied in an Emilian accent, with an incredible English undertone. I ended up standing in front of Ayrton and Gerhard: 'Tomorrow we will be testing at Imola,' Senna said. 'If you come to see us, you will be our guest.' As I was descending the stairs of the building I passed Adriano Pelloni. He was the track 'farmer' for me, a sort of Fiorano handyman: 'Pietro, I've been told Senna and Berger are here, what on earth have they come here for?'

I replied: 'They invited me to Imola tomorrow.'

And Pelloni said: 'Then I'll join in too, just don't play tricks on me!'

Adriano came with me, but when we got to the pits they wouldn't let us into the McLaren garage. It took Senna's personal order, impossible otherwise. I like to mention the following episode, because it is emblematic of Ayrton's impressive memory: Pelloni only met him that one time and, before we left, he presented Senna with a Ferrari key ring. Some time later, in an interview with the *Gazzetta dello Sport*, the Brazilian replied to a question about the Prancing Horse: 'Yes, I know some people in Maranello: one of them gave me a Ferrari key ring that I keep at home. It's the only *Cavallino* gadget I own, and it was given to me by a mechanic whose name I don't want to mention, because I don't want him to get into trouble.' The following year Pelloni went to Imola alone and Ayrton recognised him and welcomed him with: 'So how are we doing with the track work at Fiorano?' Senna had an extraordinary photographic memory.

And what did Senna mean to you as a driver?
I remember that in Detroit, in 1984, he crashed in the Toleman against the pit wall during qualifying, right in front of me, as I was displaying the board to my drivers. He had the third-fastest time with TG184-Hart and he was not satisfied. Never. When he was on track he was pulling to the limit: in this, he was very similar to another driver I loved: Gilles Villeneuve.

Pietro, it seems to me a bold parallel between two very different champions, who both had the ability to become myths ...
It is not true, as variously claimed, that Gilles did not drive with enough thought. He simply had an objective: to go fast, always. And this did not please Mauro Forghieri. But the public watching the GPs does not want to see 'taxi drivers', they love drivers who make their wheels smoke under braking. And Ayrton was always looking for the limit, he was never satisfied. Gilles and Ayrton are the names that stand the test of time: the people understood their urge of always trying to push to the limit. As opposed to Niki Lauda, who used to manage the car in order to win.

Did Senna invite you to Imola again, for that last San Marino GP?
Yes, but I must recount you an episode. That Friday I took the motorbike out to go to Imola. I just lingered too long and in the end I didn't go. I told myself: 'I'm going tomorrow.' On Saturday I got on the bike and stopped for breakfast at a bar. I was ready to go, but then I stopped by at the workshop in Fiorano, with the clear intention of staying for just a few minutes. Instead, yet again, I didn't go. On Sunday morning the same thing happened once more, so eventually I didn't go. It's as if my motorbike didn't want to go there. And on the afternoon of the GP I understood why ...

We found out, thanks to Pietro Corradini, how Ayrton's passion for Ferrari had started and about his desire to join the Maranello team sooner or later. That subject began to surface in conversations as early as 1985, when the Brazilian still considered the *Rossa* as a dream. The first concrete contact was in 1986. 'After the Belgian GP at the end of May,' says Angelo Orsi, the photographer who was a great friend of Magic's, 'Enzo Ferrari had expressed his wish to meet Senna at Maranello, but no agreement was signed, because it was too early for Ayrton, who wanted to stay at Lotus.'

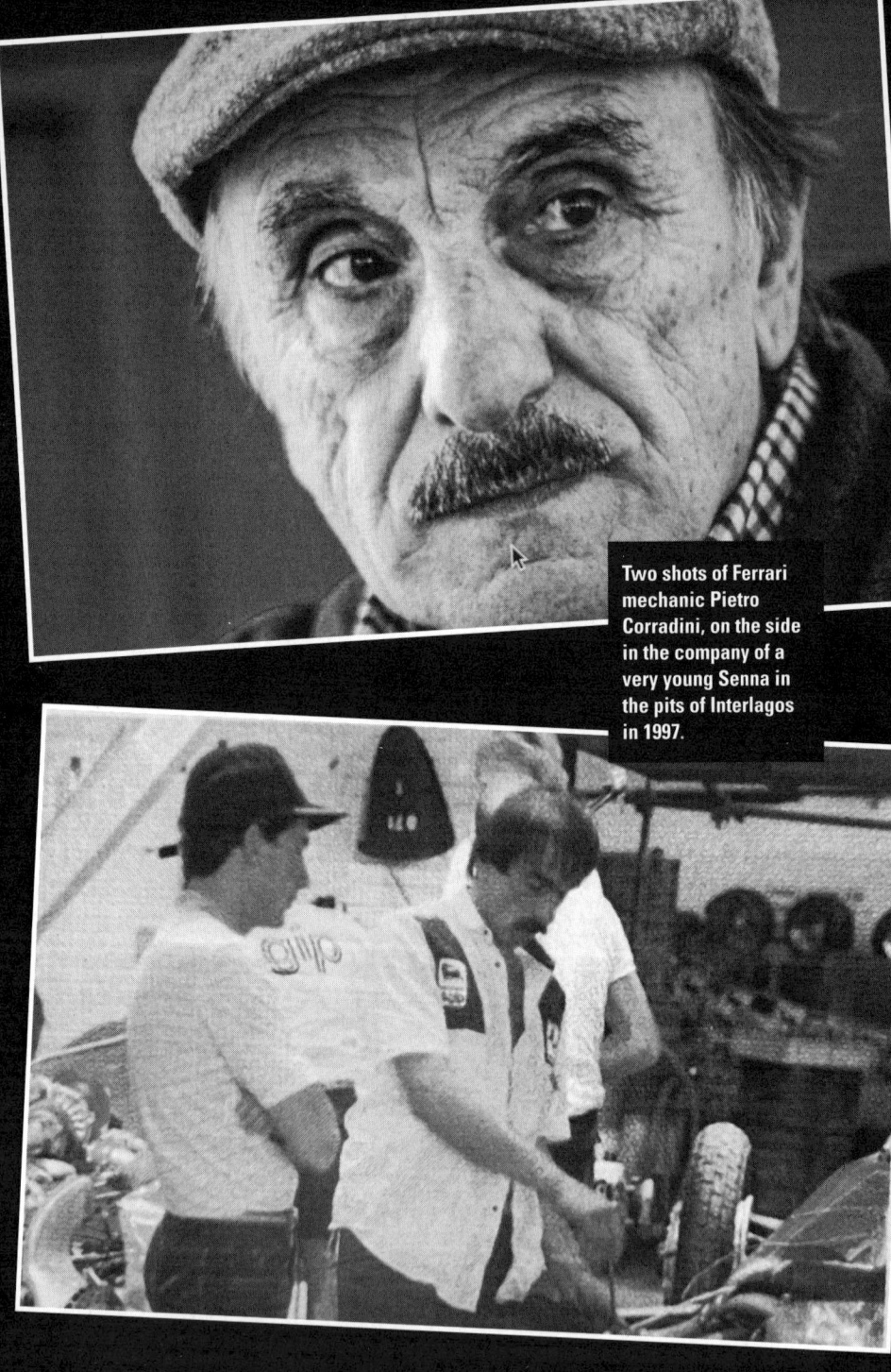

Two shots of Ferrari mechanic Pietro Corradini, on the side in the company of a very young Senna in the pits of Interlagos in 1997.

Piero Ferrari, vice president of the *Cavallino*: in 1986 with his father Enzo and Piccinini he had invited Ayrton to Maranello.

The Brazilian's performance had not only aroused Enzo's interest: Ron Dennis had also explored the possibility of bringing the emerging talent to McLaren. The coup was unsuccessful, but the Woking boss was patient, well aware that Lotus, in order to keep the 'prized piece' of the F1 market, would have sold out financially, taking a step too far for a team in a precarious financial position.

Marco Piccinini, the *Cavallino* sporting director, was the channel through which Senna received Ferrari's invitation. But Mauro Forghieri, the technical genius of the *Rossa*, an influential figure and much listened to by the *Commendatore* Enzo Ferrari, had also favoured this meeting. Ayrton spoke excellent Italian, because of his time in the country during the karting period, so it is likely that there were no problems of mutual understanding in what could be described as a meeting that has always remained a mystery.

To find out more, I disturbed Piero Ferrari, vice president of the Maranello brand, while he was on a boat on holiday. The boat was in a stretch of sea with no telephone line, but as soon as he found wi-fi he called me back.

Piero was the third man in that meeting at Maranello: he was introduced to Ayrton by the omnipresent Angelo Orsi, during pre-season testing at Imola. The acquaintance was superficial: a handshake and a few pleasantries, but the esteem was enormous.

'I can't remember the exact day Senna came to Maranello. Apart from my father, only Piccinini and I were present. The funny thing is that, just a few days ago, I met a Ferrari test driver, now retired, who reminded me that he was the one in charge of accompanying Ayrton to the airport.'

I wasn't clear about whether it was a pleasure meeting, to sniff out one of the new generation of drivers, or whether the aim was to close a contract to snatch him away from Lotus. Ferrari's driver duo of the moment was Michele Alboreto and Stefan Johansson, but the F1/86 they were driving was a single-seater with many problems, very bad in qualifying (it struggled to get into the top ten!), slightly better in the race. The team finished fourth in the Constructors' Championship that year, with five podiums: four third places for Johansson and a second place for Alboreto in Austria. Too little for the *Cavallino*'s ambitions, especially as Ferrari did not win a Grand Prix during the season for the first time since 1980. It was obvious that Senna's signing could have been a formidable way to re-motivate a team that, the year before, had been fighting for the World Championship with Alboreto until three races from the end. The Milanese driver's place in the team was not in question, but the Swede's was contestable …

'It was not a social meeting,' says Piero Ferrari. 'We wanted to talk about a possible contract. Ayrton initially seemed very determined and motivated. Among other things, he did not set any particular conditions, simply, he would have come to Ferrari only if he could bring along Gérard Ducarouge, the technical director who was following him at Lotus and whom he trusted completely. He had mentioned also other names, but he would have settled for the French engineer.'

Did he make unreasonable financial demands?
It wasn't a question of money, but I can't remember the details. On the salary we could easily have come to an agreement.

The feeling is that Enzo Ferrari was willing to take Senna right away, while the Brazilian probably went to the *sancta sanctorum* of F1 convinced that he would not find a concrete offer waiting for him. The *Commendatore*'s call had to be honoured, but the driver still had a one-year contract to go with Lotus and nothing came of it. 'I think that was the key,' confirms Piero. 'He came in determined and left doubtful.'

The Maranello meeting played into his hands because Peter Warr had to review his salary, also putting on the table the supply of the Honda V6 Turbo engine, indisputably a more powerful unit, which would take the place of the customary Renault.

What were King Enzo's thoughts after meeting him in person?
He liked him. Very much. As a driver he was absolutely not in question, but my father liked to come to an agreement quickly, if there was a contract to be signed. If he decided to open a negotiation it was because he intended to close it, while Ayrton was not ready to sign a commitment. And my father didn't like that. He relived a bit the same thing that had previously happened with Jackie Stewart. When the Scot said to him: 'I'll let you know,' after shaking his hand, he had immediately gone cold in the negotiation.

Was Senna, for Enzo Ferrari, the déjà vu *of Jackie Stewart in 1967?*
Probably so: Enzo, who was already 88 years old, had not lost his good nose. Seeing the Brazilian going out of his office, the old man understood that nothing would happen and, quickly, during the British GP at Brands Hatch in mid-July, Ayrton confirmed to Marco Piccinini that he would remain at Lotus. The first attempt had failed …

In driving, he was an ace. I also remember that, after that meeting in Maranello until the day he died, Senna would send me Christmas greetings; a gesture I appreciated from a very polite guy. He was very aggressive on the track and with his adversaries, but that was part of the competition, while outside the cockpit and in private he was a fantastic person, who had earned enormous attention around the world and especially in his own country, Brazil. He had become so famous that … he ran away from people a bit. Personally, I liked him very much.

My father, on the other hand, was a little afraid of the difficulty of bringing a driver into the team who was already a winner and had a lot of experience. He preferred young people to champions already made, and for that reason alone he was a little doubtful. He was of the opinion that it would be more difficult to integrate him, because Senna already had his ways. Those were Forghieri's last years with us, and I remember

Mauro pushing, because he liked Ayrton. Everything became just terribly complicated with my father: Mauro would get straight into a discussion that sometimes would turn extremely heated and then dad would get in the way.

Two men with very strong characters, capable of creating sparks even with words…
Of course. And I can say that several times, in front of my father, I defended Mauro. Dad could be very aggressive, but he did his job well. Everyone played their part, but Enzo always had the last word.

Corradini, in our long chat at the *Belle Epoque* team headquarters in Corlo di Formigine, where he still 'played with cars' from time to time, confided to me: 'In 1987 we were in Brazil and Ayrton was racing for Lotus-Honda. Piero Ferrari had come to see us in the pit and I asked him about Senna: "When are we going to get him to Maranello?" His reply was lapidary: "He's not a suitable driver for Ferrari." I was very disappointed and inwardly I thought: last year he killed us in qualifying and we don't consider him. Well, inexplicable …'

Explicable, Pietro. Explicable …

Senna's 'first' Formula 1 car was Reutemann's Ferrari

YOU SHOULD ALWAYS BE IN LOVE. THAT'S WHY YOU SHOULD NEVER GET MARRIED!

CHAPTER 35

MONTEZEMOLO: AYRTON WANTED TO LEAVE WILLIAMS TO COME TO MARANELLO

'NO TWO without three,' goes an old, popular saying.

Senna had a Ferrari contract in his pocket, waiting to be signed, for the 1991 World Championship, but he had to come to terms with the fact that it was only waste paper. Cesare Fiorio, as already illustrated, had 'burnt himself' to bring him to Maranello and, for the second time, the door of the Prancing Horse had closed for him. Yet the lure of the red car was intact: in Ayrton's soul still remained that seed of love for Ferrari, sown in 1977 by Pietro Corradini in the pits at Interlagos.

In the meantime, the *Scuderia* was again in a restructuring phase: president Luca di Montezemolo had to rebuild Ferrari's sports team management and bet on Jean Todt, the Frenchman who, from co-driver in rallies, had become Peugeot's leader. He had led the Lion team to win two world titles in 1985 and 1986 with the 205 Turbo 16 Group B, driven by Timo Salonen and Juha Kankkunen. Then, he had made a name for himself in the Paris–Dakar, again with Peugeot, first with the 205 and then with the 405 Grand Raid, achieving four victories and, finally, with the 905 he had won the 24 Hours of Le Mans in 1992 and 1993. In short, he was an extraordinary racer, who knew nothing about F1, but was to bring prestige back to the *Cavallino*, because he won wherever he decided to participate.

'I arrived at Ferrari on 1 July 1993,' recalls Jean Todt, 'and I contacted Senna to see him and understand if he would like to drive a Ferrari from 1995 onwards. We decided to meet each other and, for us, the most convenient meeting was during the Italian GP weekend, i.e. in September. We arranged to gather together at Villa d'Este, where we at Ferrari were staying, and Ayrton arrived at around 10pm. I welcomed him in my room and we spent two hours talking. The surprise was that the Brazilian said he would be available for the following season, i.e. 1994, and I told him that I saw it as difficult, because for that season I already had two drivers under contract, namely Gerhard Berger and Jean Alesi.'

Senna was aware that his adventure at McLaren was at an end. In 1992 Nigel Mansell had won the World Championship with the Williams FW14B, equipped with active suspension, and in 1993 it was the turn of the 'enemy' Alain Prost to climb into the FW15C to win his fourth world title. Ayrton no longer had an official engine: Honda had withdrawn, and the Japanese V12 had been replaced by a Ford HB customer engine, much less powerful and underperforming. The Brazilian had managed to win five races, still giving Prost a hard time, in a game in which he was, however, destined to succumb. The relationship with Ron Dennis had also frayed with a $1 million contract being renewed race after race. Senna's hope was to snag a Williams for 1994, but the alternative was certainly Ferrari, although the team was immature and emerging from a three-year winless period.

Todt had been taken aback by Senna's availability for 1994, and the revolving door at Maranello was closing even before it had actually opened. 'Senna intervened and told me: "Contracts can be changed …". And I answered him that in my way of running things, contracts were made to be respected. The discussion went on for a couple of hours: it was a clear, sincere and very open talk. Ayrton asked me for time to think it over and afterwards he called me back from his home in Sintra, Portugal, telling me that he could not consider being available at Ferrari from 1995, and from 1994 he would go to Williams. I could only take note of the situation and the matter ended there …'

What Jean Todt, Ferrari's new team principal, had in mind was to create a big team at Maranello in 1995: Ayrton Senna as lead driver and

Adrian Newey as technical director. But the two shots didn't go his way: 'I didn't have a car for Ayrton in 1994, whereas, regarding Newey, I had contacts with him at the time, when we intended to bring the whole technical staff back to Maranello. I remember I also met his wife, but Newey replied negatively for personal and family reasons, and that was the end of it. I had to change my strategy. I looked for Ross Brawn, to offer him the role of technical director, which he then took on in 1997, and I contacted Rory Byrne as chief designer. Neither was aware of the negotiations with the other. Both agreed to come to Ferrari in 1997, a year after Michael Schumacher arrived. When both of them signed the contract, I suggested that they talk to each other, as they were working together at Benetton. Ross smiled and replied: "Yes, we will go and have a beer together."

Who was Ayrton Senna to Jean Todt?
I met him two or three times when we were free to talk, and I must say that I was fascinated by his voice and his slow way of speaking. For me he was a great character, a driver of enormous value who impressed me a lot. He had already caught my attention in 1984, at the wet Monaco GP, when with the Toleman he had made an extraordinary comeback, finishing behind Alain Prost, who was leading the race; he probably would have won, but the race was interrupted by a red flag due to rain. Senna, besides being a great driver, was also very charismatic. He was a person who knew how to have fun: Berger told me that sometimes Ayrton was the victim of his pranks. Once Gerhard opened his briefcase while they were in a helicopter. The Brazilian saw his keys, documents and passport fly away, but he played along. I can say that he was one of the few drivers who contributed to the myth of Formula 1.

From what you've told me, it seems clear that Senna could have taken the place at Ferrari, which was later occupied by Michael Schumacher, starting an extraordinary cycle of world success. In the short list of drivers who created the F1 myth, would you put Ayrton ahead of or behind King Schumi?
This question has no answer. The comparison makes no sense: Michael arrived in F1 when Senna was at his peak, but Michael had a slightly better car than Ayrton and the German had been ahead of him. We know that, at this level, it is the car that makes the difference, so I cannot say who was better. They both wrote F1 history, but the one who had the better car won, that's all I can say.

Between two drivers from the same team you can venture a guess as to who is the stronger, because, with an identical car, the best will more often be ahead of the other, but you can't go any further. Michael had come to us after dominating with Benetton for two years, and with Ferrari he won three GPs in his first year, but then he had to wait a long time before he had a winning car. In 2005 we gave him a bad single-seater and he won practically nothing, except a very controversial race in the USA with very few participants. This has also been seen at Ferrari with Vettel and Alonso: with a good single-seater the results come, otherwise not, even if there are good drivers.

A fourth (and final) contact between Ferrari and the restless Brazilian champion deserves to be recounted. This time Luca di Montezemolo himself came into the picture: 'I met Ayrton at my house, in Pianoro, on the Wednesday before the 1994 San Marino GP. Senna had come alone and had stayed for dinner. We ate early: at 19:30. It's less than an hour's drive from my house to Imola, so we talked quietly, touching on three things: first, Ayrton complimented Ferrari for the battle we were waging against the excessive presence of electronics on the single-seaters. At that time we were still talking about traction control, after the abolition of active suspension. Senna felt that the aids took away from the more skilful drivers: 'It's like a plane landing on autopilot,' he argued. 'You have to give some value back to the driver, because electronics are too invasive and tend to equalise performance.' The second topic was Ferrari: he confided to me that ever since he had been a child the red car had been a myth for him, and we also talked about Brazilian drivers, like Carlos Pace for example, who had driven for Ferrari in the past. But the real reason for our meeting was the third topic: Ayrton had come to tell me, very clearly, that he wanted to come to Ferrari and race for us. His idea was to end his career with the *Cavallino*: and not just with a one-year contract, but with a long agreement, because he felt super-competitive and anything but on a downward trajectory. He told me that he had a contract in place with Williams, but it would be up to him to find a way out of that bond, which had clauses that we didn't enter into.

After two races had gone wrong with Williams, although he had started from pole position, Senna was ready to change teams the following year. It's a sensational revelation…

Portrait of Senna and Luca di Montezemolo.

The Brazilian driver with Jean Todt: Ferrari tried four times to hire Ayrton, but the Maranello one remained move a dream.

He asked me what programmes I was preparing and, above all, Senna wanted to know how the team would be organised. I really appreciated the fact that he realised how Ferrari wanted to build a team to win, so much so that he was willing to come to Maranello as early as 1995: 'Freeing myself from my contract with Williams,' Senna said, 'is my problem, but I need to know if you are willing to take me on board.' I reassured him immediately. We agreed that we would meet again secretly in the summer, also because we usually made our driver pairings official at Monza. I told him very frankly that we didn't want to end up in legal battles with Frank and, therefore, he would have to be the one to get out of the contract with Williams. I remember he told me that he had arrived in Bologna directly from Portugal and that we could also meet at his house, a place close to where Umberto Agnelli often went to play golf.

Luca, had you had any other previous meetings with Senna?
There are photos in which we were dressed in dinner jackets on a sofa, I think at an FIA award ceremony: we had already spoken in a formal way before. Ayrton, of course, I knew him and I remember an occasion at Monte Carlo when, with lawyer Agnelli, we spoke to him before the tests. He closed with a recurring line: '... It's only a matter of time, sooner or later I will come to race for Ferrari.'

The refrain was not a new one; Senna was very unhappy with Williams, not only with the car but also with the environment, and was thinking of turning his career around ...
No comment. In my head, I considered that the reorganisation of the team would come to an end and we would be able to afford a top driver to try and win again. With Ayrton we had come to the point where we were talking to each other directly, without interlocutors. If he had come earlier it would have been premature, because we wouldn't have been able to give him a competitive organisation: not even a super hero would have been able to fight with a non-winning car. The pieces were falling into place and I was very happy that the situation could finally be resolved.

The Imola tragedy took the Brazilian away and Ferrari then sought out Michael Schumacher, who arrived in Maranello in 1996: 'I remember that I asked Niki Lauda to do the first approach with Willy Weber,' [Schumi's manager] concludes Montezemolo. 'I didn't want Ferrari to appear, let alone myself, while with Ayrton I had sought a personal meeting, because it was time to get a driver who would make a difference.'

Did Ayrton set conditions or make specific demands of people he would want by his side?
No, zero. He wanted the certainty from me that, if he got rid of Williams, he would find a Ferrari waiting for him.

The Red, however, remained just a dream. Four times the chink that had opened, closed. The last time, unfortunately, for good.

CHAPTER 36

AFTER THE HELMET AND THE FW16-02 WERE DEMOLISHED, NO SIGNS OF THE TRAGEDY REMAIN

AYRTON'S MEMORIAL stone, in the *Acque Minerali* Park in Imola, has been Senna's 'home' since 26 April 1997, more so than the Morumbi cemetery in São Paulo, where the Brazilian champion rests. The visits to the statue happen daily. Continuously. Never interrupted, despite 30 years having passed, since 1 May 1994.

Symbolically, it is the gathering point where Magic's fans converge to indulge in a silent moment of reflection. More so than the *Tamburello* corner which, periodically, is scattered with bouquets, flags, photographs, drawings and messages. The spot where the tragedy took place still gives many a chill. The drama of 'the best' who left us in such a cruel way is unbelievable, it awakens strong feelings and floods of tears.

The pilgrimage towards the 'bronze' Ayrton – a 2m-tall statue by Stefano Pierotti, the Tuscan sculptor who worked at the Del Chiaro art foundry in Pietrasanta – softens many emotional contrasts. At each occasion, in the busy calendar of races that the Enzo and Dino Ferrari offers every year, there is always a sort of transhumance from the track paddock to the *Acque Minerali* Park. In small groups, more often in solitude, people take a moment of silent remembrance of the champion. And more than just a few foreign tourists leave the Adriatic motorway, while on holiday on the Romagna Riviera, making a brief diversion to Imola, to take a look at the Enzo and Dino Ferrari circuit from outside the fences, but above all, to pay their respects to Senna.

Almost everyone is asking two questions that resonate most frequently: 'What happened to Ayrton's helmet and where did the wreckage of the Williams FW16-02 end up?'

Once the media hype was over, the Senna case died down and nothing more was heard of them. I can assure you that there is no trace of the symbols of the tragedy, not any longer. Both the single-seater and the helmet have been demolished.

Patrick Head wrote to me specifying that about a year after the car had been returned from seizure by the Italian judicial authorities, it was sent for demolition. According to the team, now based in Grove, there is nothing left of Senna's chassis and Adrian Newey confirmed the same in his autobiography, believing strongly that it had been the correct course of action to have it crushed.

The same can be said of the yellow and green Bell helmet that had been worn by Magic at the start of the 1994 San Marino GP. On 10 April 2002, the Traffic Police of Bologna ordered the return of the helmet to Martine Kindt-Cohen, the Belgian lady acting as legal representative of the helmet manufacturer. After consultation with representatives of the Senna family, and those of Williams, it was jointly decided to demolish the helmet. It never left Italy again: it was crushed and disposed of in the landfill in Via del Frullo in Castenaso, thus closing an issue that had remained open for years.

I believe it is a good thing that there is nothing left from the tragedy of 1 May. Demolishing those relics somehow makes it possible to overcome the grief for the loss of a symbol of world motoring. A choice of human *pietas* which can only be shared.

It did not take a wrecked car, or a helmet violated by the suspension arm, for Senna to be remembered. His myth, his legend, is eternal in the memory of the fans. And that is just enough …

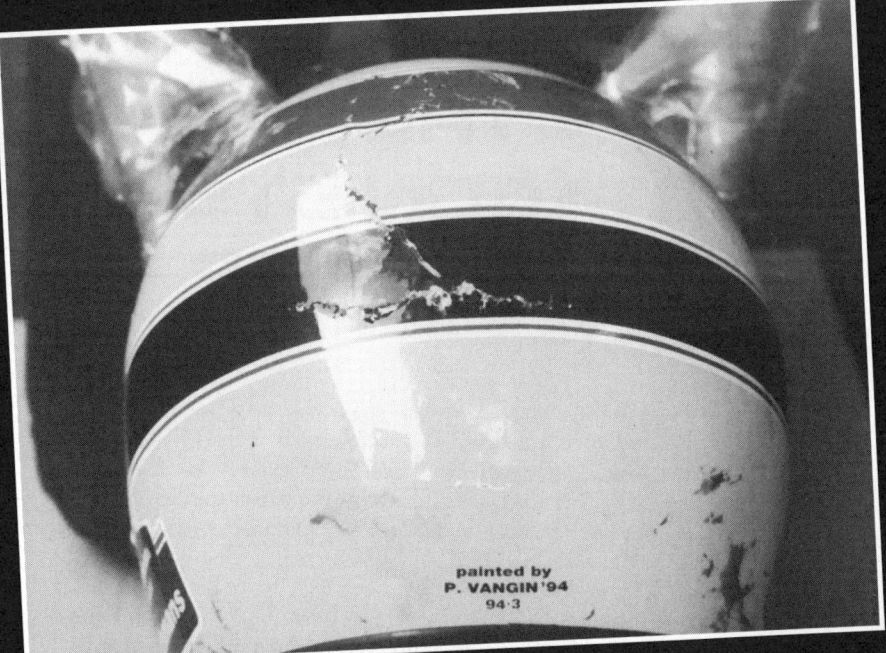

The back of Ayrton's helmet demolished in 2002 at the end of the long legal case.

Senna's gravestone at Morumbi Cemetery in São Paulo.

APPENDIX

THE PROTAGONISTS IN MAGIC'S STORY

Massimiliano Angelelli: manager, former driver. Born in Bologna in 1966, after winning the Italian F3, in 1992 he specialised first in GT and then in endurance racing: he won two 24 Hours of Daytona and was Grand-Am champion in 2005. After his success with Dallara-Pontiac at the Armed Forces 250, he joined the staff at Varano as endurance race manager. In 1994 he drove the safety car at the San Marino GP.

Giorgio Ascanelli: engineer. Born in Ferrara in 1959. He was Ayrton Senna's favourite track engineer. He worked in F1 for Ferrari, McLaren, Benetton and, in 2007, he became technical manager of Maserati Corse, taking care of the MC12 dominating in GT. He returned to F1 with Toro Rosso, before becoming technical director of Brembo. Now he has chosen retirement.

Federico Bendinelli: lawyer. Florentine by birth, but Bolognese by adoption, born in 1942. He is the president of the Automobile Club of Italy Bologna, but from 1978 to 2006 he was at the helm of Sagis, the company that managed the Imola racetrack, in the role of president and managing director, then he was also in charge of Monza. He was a member of the F1 Commission of the FIA. He has played a role in politics as provincial secretary of Forza Italia.

Carlo Cavicchi: journalist and writer. Born in Bologna in 1947. He was editor of *Autosprint* from 1984 to 1999, before starting the weekly *SportAutoMoto*. In 2008, he joined *Quattroruote*, which he directed from 2010 to 2014, before going on to join *Accademia Editoriale Domus*. An acclaimed rally driver, he has written many successful books. He is responsible for communication at Isotta Fraschini.

Érik Comas: former F1 driver. Frenchman from Romans-sur-Isère, born in 1963. He won all the preparatory series for the Circus. In GP he ran 59 races with Ligier and Larrousse from 1991 to 1994. He was saved by Senna after a crash at Spa in 1992. In 1998 and 1999 he won the Super GT with the Nissan GTR and became Italian and European champion in historic rallies with Stratos.

Pietro Corradini: F1 mechanic. Emilian from Formigine, born in 1947. His life was linked to Ferrari, where he was chief mechanic to many of the Prancing

Horse champions, starting with Gilles Villeneuve. Once retired, he became technical manager of the *Belle Epoque* team. A friend of Senna, he was the first one to put the young Brazilian in the cockpit of an F1 car, and it was a red one.

Piero Ferrari: Ferrari vice president. Born in Castelvetro di Modena in 1945, he is the son of the *Cavallino* founder. In 1980 he was executive director of the sports team management. In 1998 he founded the HPE, a research centre of international value, and was president of CSAI. He chairs Piaggio Aero Industries and, in the field of boats, also oversees the Ferretti shipyards.

Andrea Ficarelli: manager and journalist. From Reggio Emilia, 1958. He was a journalist for *Autosprint* before becoming PR and marketing consultant for Indy Lights. In F1 he was PR manager for Benetton and Toyota from 2000 to 2006. Since 2018 he has been the director of Motorsport Project and is the organiser and promoter of the Gulf 12 Hours of Abu Dhabi through Driving Force Events Limited. He was the first one to believe in Senna: but he was just his friend, not his manager.

Cesare Fiorio: manager. From Turin, 1939. He graduated in political science. In 1963 he founded Lancia's HF Reparto Corse. In roles at DS Lancia and Fiat, and then as head of sporting activities at Fiat Auto, he won 18 world rally titles and three brand titles in endurance. He was team principal at Ferrari from 1989 to 1991, winning nine out of 36 GPs. He went from Ligier, Forti, Prost, to Minardi and helped launch Alonso. Later he was a TV commentator for RAI and Sky.

Giovanni Gordini: physician. Bolognese, born in 1954. A great rally fan, after specialising in anaesthesia and resuscitation at the University of Bologna, he specialised in clinical pharmacology in Milan. He has been an anaesthetist and resuscitator since 1981. In 2000, he became director of UOC Resuscitation-118 and, since 2007, he has been director of the AUSL Bologna Emergency Department. He was on the 118 helicopter that transported Senna to the *Ospedale Maggiore*.

Gian Carlo Minardi: Minardi owner. Born in Faenza, in 1947. After some experience as a driver, he founded the Passatore racing team in 1972, which turned into the Everest team before becoming, in 1980, the Minardi team that raced first in F2 and then in F1, in 1985. He led the team for 340 GPs, until 1997. A great friend of Senna, he collaborates with ACI Sport, is supervisor of the Federal School and chairs Formula Imola, the company that manages the Enzo and Dino Ferrari.

Luca di Montezemolo: manager and entrepreneur. Born in Bologna in 1947, he was president of Ferrari from 1991 to 2014, after having been the team's sports director from 1973 to 1975. More recently he was chairman of Alitalia, founder and CEO of NTV, and currently vice chairman of Unicredit. From 2004 to 2010 he was head of Fiat and then Maserati. He is on the board of Telethon.

Adrian Newey: F1 designer. British, from Stratford-upon-Avon, born in 1958. He is considered the most brilliant designer in the world of GPs: he has won world championships with Williams, McLaren and Red Bull. He was the project manager of the Williams FW16 and, since 2006, he has been the technical manager of Red Bull. He is also a proven amateur gentleman driver, who occasionally gets involved in racing.

Angelo Orsi: photographer. Bolognese, 1948. He started by following football and basketball for the Villani agency. He attended his first F1 GP in 1974, at Paul Ricard, and then became a Circus personality. In 1985 he was hired at *Autosprint*, where he remained until 2016, before retiring. He was Ayrton Senna's true friend and confidant.

Maurizio Passerini: magistrate. From Bologna, 1957. He entered the judiciary in February 1984 and was a magistrate in Sardinia, while from 1988 he was a criminal judge at the Court of Brescia and, in 1991, the public prosecutor of the Bologna Magistrates' Court, in charge of the Senna case. In 1996, he became PP of the Bologna Court Prosecutor's Office. In 2001, he then became a judge at the Court of Bologna and, since 2009, a councillor at the Court of Appeals of Bologna.

Riccardo Patrese: former F1 driver. Born in Padua in 1954, he was world karting champion, Italian and European F3 champion and raced in F1 from 1977 to 1993, racing 256 GPs and winning six. After retiring, he offered to give Senna a hand in tuning the FW16 in 1994, but then refused to take Ayrton's place after his death. He now follows his son Lorenzo, who is starting out in the GT championships.

Giorgio Piola: F1 technical designer. Ligurian from Santa Margherita, born in 1948. A journalist with an artist's hand, he was awarded a commemorative coin after the 1,000th GP he took part in, starting with the 1969 Monaco GP. He works for the Motorsport.com network after having worked for *Autosprint*, *Gazzetta dello Sport* and, on television, with RAI and Sky. In 1994, he also supplied steering wheels to Ayrton's Williams.

Jo Ramirez: sports executive. Mexican, from Mexico City, born 1941. He left home in the 1960s to follow his racing driver friend Ricardo Rodriguez. He worked at Ferrari for two years and then moved on to Maserati and Lamborghini, as a mechanic. He followed Ford GT40s before going to Dan Gurney and then John Wyer. He joined Tyrrell in F1, and from 1983 he became McLaren coordinator and team manager, where he managed the Senna–Prost rivalry.

Alberto Sabbatini: journalist and writer. Roman but Bolognese by adoption, born in 1958, he worked first at *Corriere della Sera* and then at *Gazzetta dello Sport* as F1 correspondent. He was editor of *Rombo*, *Auto* and, for 11 years, of *Autosprint*. He wrote the book *Senna, the Magic of Perfection* and distinguished himself as an amateur gentleman driver in GT and Turismo races.

Domenico Salcito: doctor. Apulian from Torremaggiore (Foggia), born in 1944. Graduated in medicine and surgery at the University of Bologna in 1970, he specialised in general, thoracic and vascular surgery. Co-manager with Dr Giuseppe Piana of the medical service of the Enzo and Dino Ferrari Racetrack in Imola, with track management duties from 1975 to 1994. He then became sole manager from 1995 to 2000 and from 2004 to 2006. He held the same position at Adria from 2007 to 2011.

Stefano Stefanini: deputy commissioner of the Traffic Police. Born in Bologna in 1964. After completing his studies, he entered the police force and started in the Traffic Police at a very young age. He was assigned to follow the investigation into the Senna case by Public Prosecutor Passerini.

Giorgio Stirano: engineer. Born in Turin, 1950. Journalist for *Tuttosport* in 1970, he graduated as an engineer at Turin Polytechnic in 1975, and in 1980 he entered F1 with Osella, before creating Alba Engineering and winning the FIA C2 World Cup in Group C. He worked with Alfa Romeo in F1 in 1984, and then took care of the F. Europa Boxer and the development of the *Turismo* cars. He was part of the Williams defence in the Senna case and is now active as a consultant in the automotive world.

Gabriele Tarquini: driver. Born in Giulianova, in 1962. Karting world champion in 1984. In F1 he raced 38 GPs with Osella, Coloni, AGS, Fondmetal and Tyrrell. In 1994 he won the BTCC with the Alfa 155, while in 1996 he was in the DTM, again with Alfa. He then switched to Honda, but it was with Alfa Romeo that he won the European Touring Car title in 2003. Since 2005 he has been with Seat and, in 2009, he was WTCC champion, which made him the oldest driver to win an FIA title. He has had experience with Honda and Lada. With the Hyundai TCR he won his fourth championship at the age of 56.

Jean Todt: manager. A Frenchman from Pierrefort, born in 1946, he started as a navigator in rallies and went on to become director of Peugeot Talbot Sport from 1982 to 1993, before moving to Ferrari as general manager, winning five world titles with Michael Schumacher. From 2004 to 2009, he was director and administrator of the *Cavallino*. He then became president of the FIA for three terms. He is UN special envoy for road safety.

Giancarlo Tomassetti: TV director. Born in Ascoli Piceno, in 1945. After obtaining a high school diploma in radiophony and television and attending a course in cinematography, both at Luiss University, he has been an RAI employee since 1975. Specialising in live coverage of sporting events, he supervised the filming of the San Marino GP at Imola in 1994. Now retired, he has written books and taught at the School of Journalism.

ACKNOWLEDGEMENTS

THIS BOOK came about thanks to the insistence of Carlo Cavicchi, who spurred me on to write it for five years, and thanks to the insight of Roberto Mugavero, an enlightened publisher.

I would like to thank Elisa Azzimondi, an extraordinary editor and Emiliano Tozzi, curator of the *Flat Out* series, as well as Martina and Guido Mugavero, the irreplaceable ganglia of a system that made me feel at home.

How can we fail to mention Mike Zoi – owner of LAT Images – who made the splendid pictures from his archive available to me. I am grateful to Nicola Acciarri, Matteo Nugnes and Luigi Massari, precious travelling companions in this editorial adventure, and to my colleagues at Motorsport.com for the scraps of time they took away from the working group.

1982, Kalmar (Sweden). For the last time, Senna attempts to win the title in a single event in the karting world championship, after two second places obtained in 1979 and 1980.

Ayrton with his mother Neyde Senna.

Ford's Van Diemen with which Senna won by a landslide between '81 and '82

On 18 July 1983, Senna drove an F1 car for the first time in his life, taking the Williams FW08C onto the track for a test at Donington.

25 October 1983. Senna is at Silverstone in a McLaren MP4/1C. The test organised by Marlboro will see the Brazilian alternate driving with the British Martin Brundle (photo below) and the German Stefan Bellof. His is the best lap of the day, with a time of 1'13"9.

9 November 1983, Silverstone circuit. Senna in a Toleman TG 183B, the car with which he will initially start his first F1 season.

Ayrton in Toleman suit.

Monaco '84. The world suddenly knows Ayrton Senna.

Monaco Grand Prix 1984 Awards Ceremony. This second place will still be Ayrton's first podium in F1, despite a halved score due to the early end of the race.

British Grand Prix. After Monaco comes the second podium in F1 in Ayrton's career, third behind a smiling Lauda with McLaren and Derek Warwick with Renault.

Senna at Estoril, driving the Toleman which, in this race only, has an unusual red and white livery in honour of the German sponsor Magirus.

Portuguese Grand Prix. Senna ahead of Ferrari driver Alboreto.

Estoril, epilogue of the 1984 World Championship, Lauda in first place, his team-mate Prost in second, Senna in third. Behind them, from left: the chief designer of Woking's single-seaters John Barnard and Ron Dennis, the then owner of McLaren.

Ayrton's first season in F1 was also marked by a few accidents. Here we are at the start of the European Grand Prix, on the then new Nürburgring circuit.

Estoril Circuit, 1985

Senna thus achieved his first victory in F1 at the Portuguese Grand Prix, beating second-placed Ferrari driver Alboreto by more than a minute. Tambay, driving for Renault and third, was even lapped.

Portrait of the first victory.

Senna and the Lotus 97T. His first single-seater with the team founded by Colin Chapman.

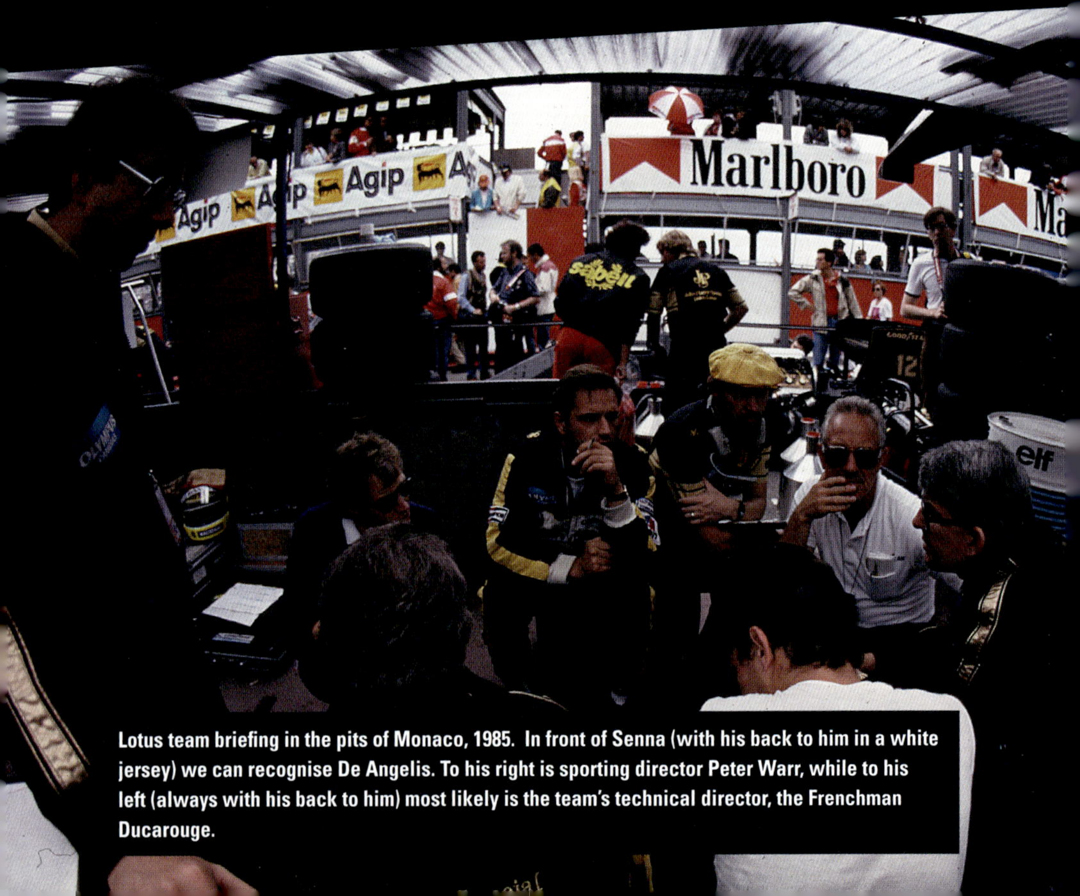

Lotus team briefing in the pits of Monaco, 1985. In front of Senna (with his back to him in a white jersey) we can recognise De Angelis. To his right is sporting director Peter Warr, while to his left (always with his back to him) most likely is the team's technical director, the Frenchman Ducarouge.

Spa, 15 September. Senna beats Prost at the start, starting from pole. Only the ninth lap will not see Ayrton in the lead in the Belgian race of that year.

United by a tragic fate: Senna and De Angelis.

On the podium at Spa, Senna celebrates his second victory. Next to him is the second-placed driver, Mansell with Williams.

Jerez '86. Senna beats Englishman Nigel Mansell of Williams by just 14 thousandths of a second. On the podium: Senna first, Mansell second (to his right) and third the reigning world champion Alain Prost.

Estoril. From left: Senna, Prost, Mansell and Piquet.

1987. Senna returns to winning ways with Lotus, now in the yellow livery desired by Camel.

In the photo below: 31 May, the first victory at the Monaco Grand Prix. Behind him, the family of Prince Rainier and, at his side, the sporting director Peter Warr.

Senna wins on the Detroit street circuit, his sixth and final victory with the Lotus team, driving the Honda-powered 99T.
Below, on the podium with his compatriot Piquet to his right and Prost on the left.

Ayrton in his McLaren MP4/4.

Santerno Circuit. Senna takes his first win with McLaren with just two and a half seconds of advantage over his team-mate Prost. Piquet third with Lotus.

Two weeks later, the Monaco circuit was the theatre chosen by the Brazilian to execute the 'perfect pole'.. He beat his team-mate Prost by 1.427 seconds.

Senna's McLaren into the Portier Curve at the Monaco Grand Prix.

Senna in the McLaren MP4/4, a perfect combination.

Senna arrives at the Monaco circuit on his scooter.

Japan 1988. After a terrible start, Senna staged a great comeback.

Suzuka. Senna is world champion, ahead of the Japanese Honda.

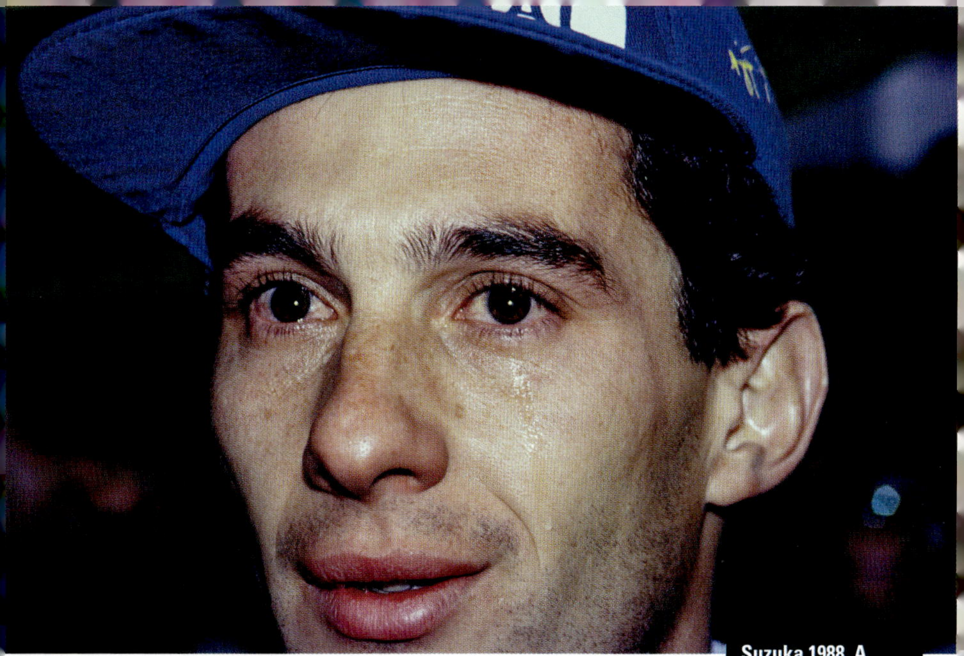

Suzuka 1988. A new era: Ayrton is world champion.

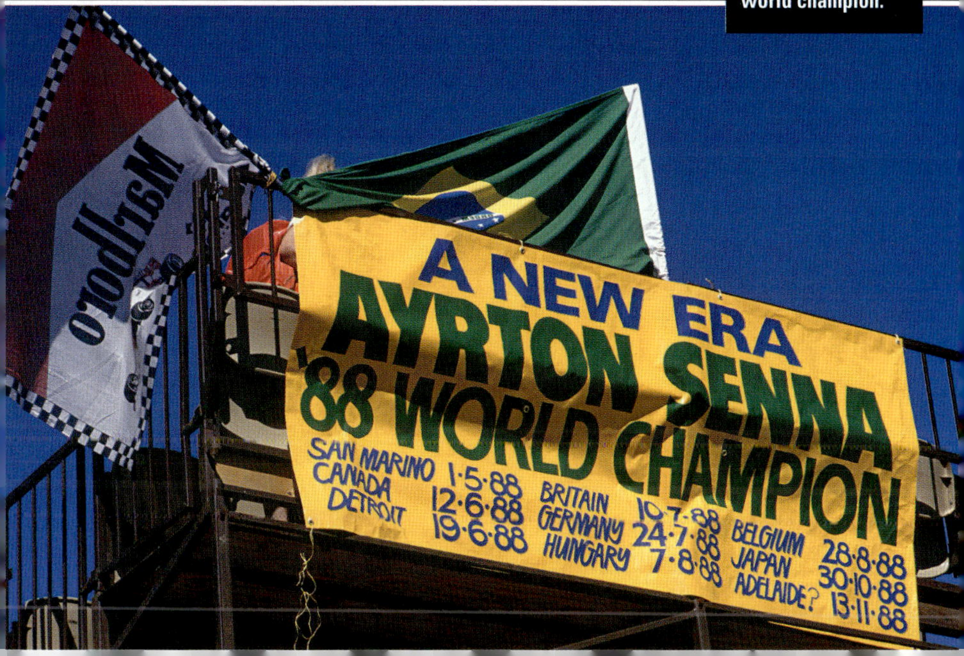
Marlboro
A NEW ERA
AYRTON SENNA
'88 WORLD CHAMPION
SAN MARINO 1·5·88
CANADA 12·6·88
DETROIT 19·6·88
BRITAIN 10·7·88
GERMANY 24·7·88
HUNGARY 7·8·88
BELGIUM 28·8·88
JAPAN 30·10·88
ADELAIDE? 13·11·88

1988. Prost with 11, Senna with 12.

Italian GP 1989. In the garage, the Honda staff led by Osamu Goto (second from left) celebrate with Senna the 50 victories of a Honda engine in F1.

Estoril 1989. Nigel Mansell with his Ferrari 640, hits the Brazilian driver's McLaren MP4/5.

Suzuka 1989. The rivalry between Senna and Prost reaches one of its most violent peaks.

As Prost abandons his McLaren, Senna is pushed back onto the track by the Japanese stewards stationed at the 'Casio Triangle'.

The 1990 World Championship opens with Senna's victory on the Phoenix circuit at the US GP. Challenging him for the win is a young Jean Alesi in his first 'full' season in F1, with the Tyrrell 018.

Senna at the next GP in Brazil. The torn nose of his McLaren is evidence of the collision with the Tyrrell of the Japanese Nakajima.

Autodromo Enzo e Dino Ferrari, 1990. Ayrton Senna and Michele Alboreto with some little fans.

Mexican GP. Senna's right rear explodes after leading the race for 60 of the 69 scheduled laps.

Senna's McLaren, with its front end destroyed after the impact with Prost's Ferrari. With both retiring at the first corner, Senna is world champion for the second time in his career.

The 1991 season started in the best possible way for Senna, with four victories in the first four Grands Prix.

1991. Ayrton takes his fourth victory in Monaco (third in a row).

Mexican GP 1991. Senna's McLaren overturned in practice on the outside of the 'Peraltada' curve. Ayrton emerged unharmed from the accident and raced regularly, taking third place.

Silverstone 1991. Mansell brings Senna back to the pits as the winner of the race after he ran out of fuel with one lap to go. He will finish in fourth place.

Hot discs for the '92 McLaren MP4/7. Woking's last single-seater, powered by the Japanese Honda.

With the victories in Hungary and Belgium (photo) Ayrton gains over 20 points on his English rival and conquers his third and final laurel on the Japanese circuit of Suzuka.

Monaco '92. On the Principality circuit, Mansell fails to get the better of Senna. Monaco is his for the fifth time.

11 April 1993. Senna, driving a Ford-powered McLaren MP4/8, delivers the masterpiece performance of his career as a driver.

Senna on the podium of the European Grand Prix. Behind him, Damon Hill and Alain Prost, Williams drivers.

23 May 1993, the victories in Monaco officially become six, surpassing the record of five successes held by Graham Hill.

Adelaide, 1993. Senna's last race for McLaren, his last victory in 161 Grands Prix contested, bringing his total to 41, the last time Ayrton and Jo Ramirez would work together.

The 1993 Australian Grand Prix also effectively marked the end of the epic rivalry between Senna and Prost, who, already at the Portuguese Grand Prix (with the title won), announced his retirement from racing at the end of the championship.

A smile outside the paddock of the Interlagos circuit between Senna and Adriane Galisteu, his latest historic girlfriend.

Ayrton and the rain. On Saturday at Interlagos, he would then get what would prove to be his last pole ahead of the 'Torcida' from São Paulo. Senna would retire on lap 55 due to a spin. Ayrton's last Brazilian GP.

Senna and Schumacher compared. The two consecutive victories at the start of the season, obtained by the German with Benetton Ford, immediately put the Brazilian driver in serious difficulty.

Pacific Grand Prix, 1994.

Senna takes pole in the 1994 Pacific GP and the race ends at the first corner after a collision with the Ferrari of Nicola Larini, who was driving the Red to replace an injured Alesi. Ayrton was not one to look in his mirrors too much …

Imola '94. Senna talking to his compatriot Barrichello, after the frightening accident he was involved in on Friday with his Jordan at the *Variante Bassa*.

Senna with Berger in the Santerno paddock. The friendship between the two drivers will have few equals.

A few minutes to the start of the 14th edition of the San Marino Grand Prix. Strangely, after the formation lap of the grid, Senna remains inside the cockpit of his Williams. Something completely unusual for him.

The helmet visor was perforated by the suspension uniball which, after the impact of the wheel on the *Tamburello* wall, transformed into a blade that slipped between the rubber gasket and the shell, killing the pilot.

Monaco GP 1994. The last farewell to Ayrton on the track, from his colleagues, before the start of the race.